Decolonizing
the Westernized University

Decolonizing the Westernized University

Interventions in Philosophy of Education from Within and Without

Edited by
Ramón Grosfoguel,
Roberto Hernández,
and Ernesto Rosen Velásquez

LEXINGTON BOOKS
Lanham • Boulder • New York • London

Published by Lexington Books
An imprint of The Rowman & Littlefield Publishing Group, Inc.
4501 Forbes Boulevard, Suite 200, Lanham, Maryland 20706
www.rowman.com

Unit A, Whitacre Mews, 26-34 Stannary Street, London SE11 4AB

British Library Cataloguing in Publication Information Available

Library of Congress Cataloging-in-Publication Data Available

ISBN 978-1-4985-0375-4 (cloth : alk. paper)
ISBN 978-1-4985-0377-8 (pbk. : alk. paper)
ISBN 978-1-4985-0376-1 (electronic)

∞™ The paper used in this publication meets the minimum requirements of American National Standard for Information Sciences Permanence of Paper for Printed Library Materials, ANSI/NISO Z39.48-1992.

Printed in the United States of America

For Bob "Poncho" Rosen

Contents

Introduction

Ernesto Rosen Velásquez

There is a lot of blood under these universities. Yet education is often broached in a way that forgets about the soil upon which these buildings rest. It is assumed institutions of higher education are a means to upward socioeconomic mobility and in turn a way of addressing poverty which is tied to certain racialized/sexualized bodies. The topic is registered as poor people's problem. But if we, in the United States and in the rest of the world, are and have been in an education crisis, then it seems we scholar/activists, community organizations, social movements, artists, and youth still have our work cut out for us, theoretically and in terms of praxis. As a way of rolling up our sleeves and getting our hands dirty, this edited collection aims, in part, to flesh out the various dimensions of the education crisis as it unfolds on the US terrain, Europe, and Latin America. This is no small order because the various candidates that could serve as a basic unit of analysis—elementary, high schools, and universities—each have their complex political dynamics, historical formations, and internal heterogeneity; they can be public, private, Catholic, for profit, non-profit, or some combination of these. Furthermore, the education crisis is technically not an American or European problem in the geographic sense. It is a global problem that plays itself out differentially across space and time. Thus in order to provide a sharper understanding of the education crisis and the responses to it the book focuses on the westernized university at multiple sites around the world. Specifically, this book addresses the following questions: (1) What is the westernized university? (2) How did it emerge in various locales around the world? (3) What is westernized about it? (4) What have been and are the aims of the westernized university? (5) What is the future of the westernized university? (6) What should be the aims of higher education in the US and/or in other regions on the planet? (7) How can we who work in, through and outside these sites of knowledge production—with local or global social movements—participate in the slow careful process of decolonizing the westernized university from within and without? (8) How have others responded to the crisis in higher education?

This collection is distinct from other works in philosophy of education such as Steven M. Cahn's anthology, *Classic and Contemporary Readings in the Philosophy of Education*.[1] Although a useful source for locating selections of primary texts in one condensed place, this anthology's organization of materials assumes a Eurocentric history of the philosophy of education that begins in ancient Greece and moves along a linear developmental track to the medieval, modern, then contemporary period. This narrative is so normalized that it is not questioned. It forms the unspoken background from which this and other earlier anthologies like this are framed, such as Fredrick C. Gruber's anthology *Historical and Contemporary Philosophies of Education*.[2] The problem with this internalized historical narrative is it informs a methodology that either excludes whole continents and islands with histories where thinking on these matters occur such as Latin America, Africa, and the Caribbean, or it integrates one token figure in a ghettoized fashion that is tacked on at the end of a book as a diversity afterthought, unconnected to the wider conversation and history of philosophy. Thus, the title of Cahn's anthology when it is decoded should really be called *Classic and Contemporary Readings in Western European Philosophy of Education*. A similar logic is by extension reproduced in the other aforementioned anthology and in Randal Curren's edition of *A Companion to the Philosophy of Education*.[3] This does not imply we cannot learn anything from that philosophical tradition. What it does imply is thinking happens elsewhere and that the field should not be dominated and framed by the interests, concerns, and social historical experience of a small sector of society that is white, heterosexual, male, and upper-middle class. Plus, it is not simply that thinking on education matters happens in these other places but others are responding to the westernized university and are in the slow process of decolonizing it from within and without. This edited collection is an intervention in the philosophy of education discourse which tends to assume the university is a neutral space, a tendency normalized by the fact that these education spaces are often referred to as simply "universities" and less frequently as "westernized" or "historically white male universities." This work hopes to, in part, respond to a few methodological obstacles in the field of philosophy of education.

One methodological obstacle to understanding the education crisis in the United States is not historicizing it. By not situating it within colonial historiography, what becomes invisible are the intermingled causal roles race, ethnicity, sexuality, gender, class, and religion have and continue to play in the creation and perpetuation of the problem. Frequently the education crisis and the proposed solutions seem to get articulated in a way that naturalize school. The formal institution of the school, of youth mandatorily going to a space to learn from a teacher according to a pre-established curriculum that proceeds along increasing levels of difficulty on the basis of a notion of childhood development, is so normalized it becomes easy to forget that formal school was one among an array of institutions Spaniards brought with them and imposed on Muslims and

Jews living in the Islamic territory of Andalusia in southern Spain in 1492 and exported and imposed across the Atlantic in the Amerindian region of the Americas in the same year. Formal schools were also one among an array of institutions seventeenth-century English settlers brought with them when they emigrated from Europe—without passports—and transplanted in the "New World" and imposed on Native American Indians in the early US colonies. In the time of pre-settler US colonialism the education of Indian children did not take place in the formal setting of what we call "schools"; rather it was integrated into the life-world of the tribe—the story-telling of elders, working with adults, participation in ceremonies, puberty rites, and customs of the clan and tribe educated them for tribal life. Before Europeans arrived Native American children were being educated without schools. Having US colonial history in one's consciousness helps to begin to consider the birth of the school, its life over time, and perhaps consider its death.

Another methodological obstacle to understanding the education crisis is it is broached in a way that is related to food, energy, climate, and the economy but tends to do so in a Eurocentric way. In other words, teachers/students learn to master Western European theories via the written alphabetic text on these matters. These theories are studied within their respective disciplines such as economics and environmental studies, each of which are discreet areas of knowledge that correspond to a compartmentalized domain of reality those disciplines study as units of analysis. After learning these conceptual tools, one proceeds to apply them to solve discreet problems outside the university community in an innovative way that is guided by the *telos* of development with its concomitant sense of economic growth that ultimately assimilates people and projects into the world economy. For instance, the education crisis gets articulated in a way that invokes the usual suspects: what the aims of education should be, the curriculum, and pedagogy. These topics, while important to some extent, often are librocentric and accord centrality to professors and students while ignoring the materiality of a school: the land it is on, property tax, the bricks, the chairs, the electricity in classrooms, the water, sewerage systems, heat, the food, toilets, the janitors, cooks, workers, and a whole host of interconnected elements that allow a school to operate on a daily basis as an institution that is simultaneously somewhat self-operating while also linked to the wider political economy: energy, electric, and phone companies, and food manufacturing industries. The Zapatista's supported school—the Universidad de la Tierra (University of the Earth)—in Chiapas not only offers living proof that another world is possible but also invites scholars/activists to open up their imaginations in creative ways that marginalize the economy and gives priority to those at the bottom of society. The materiality of school becomes visible when you see Mayan students and others build a university from the ground up—from the bricks and chairs one sits in to the curriculum. We hope this edited collection provides a space for scholar/activists to push the philosophy of education discussion toward these other futures.

The materiality of schools acquires salience when these multiple and intersecting crises are understood in the context of some contemporary critical philosophy of race discourses that increasingly focus on themes of implicit bias and unconscious habits of racial privilege. Some of these authors suggest that reducing racism and sexism is to a certain extent not so much simply a cognitive matter that we can talk ourselves out of but instead involves cultivating new habits of perception and doing other things. To take steps toward the latter requires something more indirect and different than conscious argumentation; it requires a change in the environment, which is not merely a container of habits but is also something we inhabit. To think of racial and gendered privileges, racism, and sexism as environmentally constituted habits opens up a conceptual space for seriously considering the material construction of education spaces where learning is supposed to happen and how we—scholars, activists, artists, students, organizations, and social movements—can creatively begin to construct learning spaces in ways that are not simply anti-racist and anti-sexist but also anti-capitalist, anti-Eurocentric, anti-imperial, and anti-colonial. This seems to be one of the significant contemporary challenges when thinking about the education crisis in the United States and the world, with all of their particularities, histories, different peoples, ideologies, geographies, artistic and religious practices, and ways of life. How can we create learning spaces in ways that are historically rooted in local histories and conscious of global designs while oriented by a negative decolonial ethics—that is sensitive to the aforementioned multiple intersecting axes of oppression—and a positive decolonial ethics—guided by notions such as *pachamama* (Mother Earth), *buen vivir* (collective well-being), and other Afro-indigenous horizons from around the world where there are other centers of meaning, some of which seem to move beyond the white political and ethical fields? Although alternative sites of knowledge production in the United States, Europe, Latin America, and Africa each face their own challenges, these sites are living examples that suggest another world is possible and they are not waiting for Superman.

In chapter 1 Boaventura de Sousa Santos shifts the geography of reason in the philosophy of education by posing a series of twelve questions that thinkers in this field do not tend to confront, not so much because the questions are dismissed—this assumes the recognition of the questions de Sousa Santos makes visible and then looking the other way—but because of the methodological obstacles mentioned earlier that do not allow for the emergence of certain questions. Part of the education crisis involves confronting colonial methodologies that systematically block the asking of certain questions, a kind of methodological silencing that chokes the neck of bodies in a way that does not allow them to speak from their subaltern epistemic locations. The opening chapter by de Sousa Santos offers a method and framework for removing the choke hold so these bodies, in different locations across the planet, can breathe. After coughing, reopening the windpipes, and taking a deep breath, de Sousa Santos speaks and makes visible a series of what he calls "strong questions" that either lack visibility in the field of philosophy of education or have weak answers in the humanities and social sciences. He envisions a future in which stronger answers can be provided and the westernized university can rebuild its humanistic aims in a new "internationalist, solidary, and intercultural way."

Kwame Nimako directs his attention on the westernized university in the Netherlands in chapter 2. He traces two parallel processes of knowledge production: a "frontier social science" tradition and a black social movement, a tradition of agency that creates their own centers of meaning separate from but parallel to the mainstream Dutch universities. The former continually constructs problem people in order to manage these populations in ways that divert attention away from the structures of domination and colonial history that produce racialized populations as objects of knowledge—problem people—as opposed to knowledge-producing subjects—people who face problems. The latter operate in the shadows of what Nimako calls "Fortress Europe" and work to combat racism, demystify official white-washed narratives of the Dutch legacy of slavery, and approach knowledge production by viewing racialized folks on the margins as knowledge producing subjects.

In chapter 3 Ramón Grosfoguel identifies the conceptual parochialism and epistemic racism/sexism undergirding the westernized university in the United States and the world system. As ethnic studies navigate around a universalist disciplinary colonization that hides its cultural particularity by normalizing the way fields of knowledge are identified and bobs and weaves through the identity politics that traps knowledge production in essentialized identities that make the link between social and epistemic locations too tight, he argues for a transmodern decolonial studies as a way to move beyond the highlighted limits.

In chapter 4 Nelson Maldonado-Torres underscores one of the most devastating dimensions of the education crisis: when the value of knowledge is defined within the parameters of liberal humanities and neoliberalism, ethnic studies and other epistemologies are deemed unprofitable, useless, illegal, dangerous, dispensable or supplementary, cosmetic, and optional. He discusses several examples which offer ways of rethinking westernized universities through the lens of neoapartheid and racial neoliberalism instead of only in economic reductionist terms.

In chapter 5 Ernesto Rosen Velásquez builds on Burman's distinction between nonautonomous indigenous universities and autonomous indigenous universities by philosophically reflecting on the strengths and challenges faced by both kinds of universities. He focuses on Universidad de la Tierra in San Cristobal de las Casas Chiapas, Mexico. He offers a way of reconceiving dropouts in a way different from their invocation in US minority education discourses.

Anders Burman, in chapter 6, discusses the coloniality of reality in Bolivia and the tensions between two senses of decolonization; one as an indigenous alternative to modernity presented to its international audience and the other as modernization, progress, and extractivism used internally in state politics and government discourse. Burman argues not only for epistemic disobedience but also for ontological disobedience in which historically subalternized beings and ontologically informed lifeworlds—"*damnés* realities"—are being unfolded and making themselves present through concrete and situated practices and conversations, by no means in isolation from a dominant world, but in spite of it, in defiance of it, in the face of it.

Robert Aman, in chapter 7, argues that the decolonization of the modern university requires a move away from its almost exclusive reliance on Eurocentric modes of reasoning. He discusses the pitfalls of the concept of interculturality and considers the potentials the notion of *interculturalidad* has for this delinking which takes into account colonial difference. Aman argues it is only by such commitment to epistemic disobedience that it is possible to radically reform the westernized university's insistence on relying on provincial epistemological traditions claiming universality for themselves to creating a space open to a horizontal dialogue between epistemes from different traditions.

In chapter 8, Tendayi Sithole interrogates the humanities from the perspective of those who are relegated outside humanity. He shows how through this decolonial intervention the ontological distinction between the *humanitas* (the human) and the *anthropos* (the non-human) is made clear and the manner in which this difference is reproduced in the humanities. The author argues that these two do not coexist in that the *humanitas* are inscribed while the *anthropos* are erased. Decoloniality is mobilized in order to unmask modernity by authorizing the critique from those who are dehumanized and to make a case that the humanities need to face up to its limits.

In chapter 9, Nassim Noroozi elaborates on how a pedagogy that is committed to provoking thinking about modified presences and different experiences of pasts and futures can be a decolonial engagement. She argues that this endeavor—what she calls pedagogy of time—aims to disrupt what regulates students' and readers' economies of knowledge without appointing conclusive endpoints for this disruption. Pedagogy of time does not aim for oversimplified and hurried theoretical reflections. As such, it is committed to critically confront politics of speed in thinking. She maintains that this critical confrontation with politics of speed is an important commitment for decolonial endeavors in education: this is especially true in times when decolonial pedagogies have been examined and critiqued for having been too often "fixated on a simplistic decolonization of Western knowledge and practices" and too often favoring resorts to a quick re-claiming the indigenous practices as superior to Western ones as opposed to "fostering analytical arguments," and when there is a call by indigenous pedagogues to encourage openness to further inquiry in and through complex and contested knowledge terrains. Hence, decolonial educational philosophies can benefit from a pedagogy that aims for a different regulation of economies of knowledge in the classroom: one that confronts politics of speed by refraining from rushing to simplistic conclusions when analyzing present times.

Camilo Pérez-Bustillo, in chapter 10, explores conceptual aspects of the need to decolonize the epistemology, history, theory, and praxis of human rights "from below," with emphasis on issues related to migrant rights and the rights of indigenous peoples and on the contexts of Mexico, Colombia, and Latin America. This chapter emphasizes the challenges to teaching, research, and advocacy regarding human rights in universities in both the Global North and Global South given the tendency to assume a Western origin for, and the supposed universality of, dominant paradigms as to such rights. Attention is also focused on the intertwined trajectories of human rights, hegemony, and utopia in these contexts.

In chapter 11, Andrea Pitts analyzes the 2010 banning of the Mexican American Studies program in Arizona's Tucson Unified School District. Three interrelated sets of norms surfaced throughout the legal documents that supported the ban: nativism, individualism, and the Latino-threat narrative. It is argued that each set of norms bears implicit second-personal vocatives that support anti-Latina/o racism. It is proposed that even in fact-stating cases of third-personal address, an implicit "you" or "you all" is invoked by the speaker, and that such hails bear normative weight. These indirect hails describe a form of "racial interpellation" and, as such, they point to the function of political discourse in the perpetuation of anti-Latina/o racism and white supremacy in the United States. Decolonization efforts can be difficult and frightening. In certain atmospheres when the bodies of racialized subjects simply show up on the scene they already are perceived with the aura of a threat. When they begin to speak ethically they are targeted as being violent. As folks constructed as problem people make assertions on behalf of life and dignity, they are perceived, with each assertion and bodily movement, as increasingly violent, threatening.

Amy Reed-Sandoval, in chapter 12, offers a historical-philosophical contextualization of the recent disappearance of the forty-three students in Ayotzinapa. She argues that the violence and trauma unleashed on the students, families, and others in Ayotzinapa are an attack on Latin American philosophy itself.

In the final chapter, Luis Rubén Díaz Cepeda thinks through the challenges with building coalitions across difference. He argues that Dussel's analectical method has potential for preventing various social movements around Ayotzinapa from fragmenting.

The hope is that each chapter contributes toward illuminating the various intersecting aspects of the westernized university that is differentially spread out across space and time. This book attempts to meet people where they are at—whether positioned inside these sites or outside of them. You are invited to think through and work with and alongside social movements that offer other conceptual constellations and praxis as they struggle to continually create the conditions of possibility for genuine educational options—alternatives to modernity—instead of a diversity of choices within the same underlying logic—alternative modernities.

I wish to thank John Inglis for his support. I also thank Marilyn Marx for her editorial assistance and Diane Witt for her help with the index. I thank Jana Hodges-Kluck for moving the project forward and to the editors at Lexington for bringing it to its fruition.

NOTES

1. Cahn Steven, *Classic and Contemporary Readings in Philosophy of Education*. New York: Oxford University Press, 2012.
2. Gruber Fredrick, *Historical and Contemporary Philosophies of Education*. Syracuse: Crowell, 1976.
3. Curren Randall, *A Companion to Philosophy of Education*. Indianapolis: Wiley, John & Sons Inc., 2005.

Part I

The Underside of Philosophy of Education

ONE

The University at a Crossroads

Boaventura de Sousa Santos

When we consider the European university, or indeed the university worldwide, the present is a moment in which it is as important to look back as to look forward.[1] In the case of Europe, we are now in the middle of the Bologna Process—named after the Bologna Declaration organized by the European Union education ministers in 1999 aimed at reforming higher education in Europe and creating the European Higher Education Area (EHEA).[2] It is a period prone to intense fluctuations between positive and negative evaluations, between a sense that it is either too late or too early to achieve the intended results. In my view, such intense fluctuations in analysis and evaluation are a sign that everything remains open, that failure and success loom equally on the horizon, and that it is up to us to make one or the other happen. The great philosopher Ernst Bloch wrote that by each hope there is always a coffin: Heil and Unheil. Though it is our main objective to focus on the European university, it would be foolish not to think that the challenges facing the European university today are to be found in all continents, however different the reasons, the arguments, or the proposed solutions may be.

In general we can assert that the university is undergoing—as much as the rest of contemporary societies—a period of paradigmatic transition. This transition can be characterized in the following way: we face modern problems for which there are no modern solutions. Very succinctly, our modern problems are the fulfillment of the ideals of the French Revolution: *liberté, egalité, fraternité*. In the past two hundred years we have not been able to fulfill such objectives in Europe, let alone elsewhere. The solutions designed to fulfill them—I mean, scientific and technological progress; formal and instrumental rationality; the modern bu-

3

reaucratic state; the recognition of class, race and gender divisions and discriminations; the institutionalization of social conflict raised by them through democratic processes, development of national cultures and national identities, secularism and laicism; and so on and so forth—have not been able to deliver the objectives so strenuously struggled for. The modern university, particularly from mid-nineteenth century onward, has been a key component of such solutions. It was actually in light of them that institutional autonomy, academic freedom, and social responsibility were originally designed. The generalized crisis of modern solutions has thereby brought with it the crisis of the university. After the Second World War, the early 1970s was a period of intense reformist impulses worldwide. In most cases, the student movements of the late 1960s and early 1970s were the motive behind them. In the past forty years, however, for different but convergent reasons, in various parts of the world the university has become, rather than a solution for societal problems, an additional problem.

As far as the university is concerned, the problem may be formulated in this way: the university is being confronted with strong questions for which it has so far provided only weak answers. Strong questions are those questions that go to the roots of the historical identity and vocation of the university in order to question not so much the details of the future of the university but rather whether the university, as we know it, has indeed a future. They are, therefore, questions that arouse a particular kind of perplexity. Weak answers take the future of the university for granted. The reforms they call for end up being an invitation to immobilism. They fail to abate the perplexity caused by the strong questions and may, in fact, even increase it. Indeed, they assume that the perplexity is pointless.

As proposed and further investigated below, I submit that we must take up the strong questions and transform the perplexity they cause into a positive energy both to deepen and to reorient the reformist movement. The perplexity results from the fact that we are before an open field of contradictions in which there is an unfinished and unregulated competition among different possibilities. Such possibilities open space for political and institutional innovation by showing the magnitude of what is at stake.

STRONG QUESTIONS

Let me provide some samples of the strong questions facing the university at the beginning of the twenty-first century. Without claiming to be exhaustive, I select twelve such questions.

The first strong question is this: Given the fact that the university was part and parcel of the building of the modern nation-state—by training its elites and bureaucracy, and by providing the knowledge and ideology underlying the national project—how is the mission of the university to be refounded in a globalized world, a world in which state sovereignty is increasingly a shared sovereignty or simply a choice among different kinds of interdependence, and in which the very idea of a national project has become an obstacle to dominant conceptions of global development? Is the global university a possible answer? If so, how many such global universities are viable? What happens to the large number of the remaining ones? If global elites are to be trained in global universities, where can be found in society the allies and the social base for the nonglobal universities? Which kinds of relationships between global and nonglobal universities will there be? Will the focus on ranking contribute to the cohesion of the European higher education area or, on the contrary, to its segmentation through unfair competition and the rise of commercial internationalism?

A second strong question may be formulated as follows: The idea of a knowledge society implies that knowledge is everywhere; what is the impact of this idea on a modern university which was created on the premise that it was an island of knowledge in a society of ignorance? What is the place or the specificity of the university as a center of knowledge production and diffusion in a society with many other centers of production and diffusion of knowledge? Will academic review and refereeing practices continue to significantly determine scholarship evaluations and recruitment and promotional opportunities in universities worldwide? Will they go on doing that in such a way that it promotes narrowly defined, monoculturally generated conceptions of good scholarship, methodological rigor, and theoretical soundness, as it happens, in general, today? Or, on the contrary, will the new technologies of production and dissemination of knowledge (internet/ebook/ejournal/elibraries, etc.) undermine the traditional, elitist practices of gatekeeping in scientific and academic journal and book publishing, making it possible to pursue new, creative, and more egalitarian, culturally sensitive, and paradigmatically open-minded practices of peer reviewing?

Third strong question: At its best, the modern university has been a locus of free and independent thinking and of celebration of diversity, even when subjected to the narrow boundaries of the disciplines, whether in the sciences or the humanities. Bearing in mind that for the past thirty years the tendency to transform the truth value of knowledge into the "market truth" value of knowledge has become increasingly strong, could there be any future for nonconformist, critical, heterodox, nonmarketable knowledge, and for professors, researchers, and students pursuing it? If yes, what will be its impact upon the criteria of excellence and interuniversity competitiveness? If not, can we still call university an institution that produces only competent conformists and never competent rebels, and that only regards knowledge as a commodity and never as a public good?

Fourth strong question: The modern university has been from the beginning a transnational institution at the service of national societies. At its best, the modern university is an early model for international flows of ideas, teachers, students, and books. We live in a globalized world but not in a homogeneously globalized world. Not only are there different logics moving globalized flows but also different power relations behind the distribution of the costs and benefits of globalization. There is transnational greed as there is transnational solidarity. Which side will the university be on? Will it become a transnational corporation or a transnational cooperative or nonprofit organization? Is there a contradiction between our emphasis on cultural and social development and the emphasis of some European politicians and powerful thinktanks on economic development and the university's contribution to the global competitiveness of European businesses? Why have some major reform efforts outside Europe chosen the slogan: "Neither Bologna nor Harvard"?

Fifth strong question: In the long run, the idea of Europe is only sustainable as the Europe of ideas. Now, the university has historically been one of the main pillars of the Europe of ideas, however questionable such ideas may have been. This has been possible by granting to the university a degree of institutional autonomy unimaginable in any other state institution. The dark side of this autonomy has been social isolationism, lack of transparency, organizational inefficiency, and social prestige disconnected from scholarly achievement. In its original design, the Bologna Process was to put an end to this dark side without significantly affecting the university's autonomy. Is this design being carried out without perverse results? Is the Bologna Process a break with the negative aspects of the traditional university, or is it a brilliant exercise in reshuffling inertias and recycling old vices? Is it possible to standardize procedures and criteria across such different university cultures without killing diversity and innovation? Is it possible to develop transparency, mobility, and reciprocal recognition while preserving institutional and cultural diversity? Why are bureaucrats taking control of the good ideas and noble ideals so easily?

Sixth strong question: Job prestige goes together with job qualification and scarcity. The modern university has been at the core of the social production of high-powered job qualifications. If rankings manage to fragment the European and the future global university system, which jobs and which qualifications will be generated by which universities? The world system is built on an integrated hierarchy of core, peripheral, and semiperipheral countries. The current financial and economic crisis has shown that the same hierarchy holds in Europe and, as such, social cohesion is showing its dark side: it exists on the condition that the structural hierarchy not be affected, that countries remain as core, peripheral or semiperipheral, without moving either up or down in the hierarchy. Not necessarily coincident with location in the hierarchy of the countries in which they are located, are we going to have peripheral, semiperipheral and central universities? Will the Bologna Process rigidify such hierarchies or make them more liquid? Depending on the geopolitical distribution of rankings, will hierarchy among universities contribute to accentuate or rather to attenuate the hierarchies among European countries?

Seventh strong question: As the university diversifies the degrees of qualification—first, second, and third cycle and postdoctoral degrees—social illiteracy increases in the lower degrees, thus justifying the greater value of higher degrees. This is in fact a spiral movement. Has it exhausted its development potential? How many more cycles are we going to have in the future? Are we creating endless illiteracy in the same process that we create endless knowledge? Will peripheral, and semiperipheral universities be charged with solving the illiteracy problem, while the core universities will have the monopoly of highly qualified knowledge?

Eighth strong question: Can the university retain its specificity and relative autonomy while being governed by market imperatives and employment demands? Given the highly problematic validity of cost/benefit analysis in the field of research and development, will the university be allowed to assume certain costs in the expectation of uncertain benefits, as it has always done in the past? What will happen to knowledge that has not and should not have market value? Regarding marketable knowledge, which impact on it is to be expected if such knowledge is going to be valued exclusively according to its market value? What is the future of social responsibility if extension is reduced to an expedient or burden to raise financial resources? What will happen to the imperative of making the university relevant to the needs of society, taking for granted that such needs are not reducible to market needs and may actually contradict them?

Ninth strong question: The university (or at least the public university) has historically been embedded in the three pillars of modern social regulation—the state, the market, and civil society; however, the balance of their presence in the structure and functioning of the university has varied in the course of time. Indeed, the modern European university started in Bologna as a civil society initiative. Later on, the state strengthened its presence, which became dominant from mid-nineteenth century onward, and in the colonies particularly after they became independent. In the last thirty years the market took the lead in structuring the university life. In a few decades the university went from producing knowledge and professionals for the market, to becoming itself a market, the market of tertiary education, and finally, at least according to powerful visionaries, to being run like a market organization, a business organization.

Since then, civil society concerns have been easily confused with market imperatives or subordinated to them, and the state has very often used its coercive power to impose market imperatives on the reluctant universities. Is the Bologna Process a creative response to neoliberal, one-dimensional demands or, on the contrary, a way of imposing them through a transnational European process that neutralizes national resistance?

Tenth strong question: The European universities and many other universities around the world that followed their model were instrumental in disseminating a Eurocentric view of the world, a view powerful enough (in both intellectual and military terms) to claim universal validity. This claim did not involve ignoring the cultural, social, and spiritual differences of the non-European world. On the contrary, it entailed knowing such differences, even though subjected to Eurocentric purposes, whether the romantic celebration of the Other or the colonial subjugation and destruction of the Other. In both cases, knowing the Other was at the service of showing the superiority and therefore the universality of European culture; a detailed, colonial, or imperial knowledge of the Other was required. My university, for instance, the University of Coimbra, founded in 1290, contributed immensely to the development of knowledge committed to the colonial enterprise. The quality and intensity of the homework done by the missionaries before embarking overseas are astounding, all the more astounding when we compare them with the homework done by World Bank and International Monetary Fund (IMF) executives when they go around evangelizing the world with the neoliberal orthodoxy in their heads and pockets. Of their knowledge claims it cannot be said what the great leader of the African Liberation movements, Amilcar Cabral, said about colonial knowledge: "The search for such knowledge, in spite of its unilateral, subjective and very often unfair character, does contribute to enriching the human and social sciences in general."[3]

The eleventh question is this: Is the university prepared to recognize that the understanding of the world by far exceeds the Western understanding of the world? Is the university prepared to refound the idea of universalism on a new, intercultural basis? We live in a world of norms in conflict and many of them are resulting in war and violence. Cultural differences, new and old collective identities, antagonistic political, religious and moral conceptions and convictions are today more visible than ever, both outside and inside Europe. There is no alternative to violence other than readiness to accept the incompleteness of all cultures and identities, including our own, arduous negotiation, and credible intercultural dialogue. If Europe—against its own past—is to become a beacon of peace, respect for diversity and intercultural dialogue, the university will certainly have a central role to play. Are the European universities being reformed having such role in mind as a strategic objective of their future?

The twelfth question, probably the strongest of them all, is the follow-ing: Modern universities have been both a product and a producer of specific models of development. When the Bologna Process started there were more certainties about the European project of development than there are today. The compound effect of multiple crises—the financial and economic crisis, the environmental and energetic crisis, the crisis of the European social model, the migration crisis, the security crisis— points to a civilizatory crisis or paradigmatic change. The question is: In such a tumultuous time, is the university's serenity possible? And, if possible, is it desirable? Is the Bologna Process equipping the university to enter the debate on models of development and civilizatory para-digms, or rather to serve as critically and as efficiently as possible the dominant model decided by the powers that be and evaluated by the new supervisors of the university output at their service? At the international level, given the conflict between local conceptions of autonomous devel-opment and the global development model imposed by the rules of the WTO, and given the fact that the European states are donor states, will the European university contribute to a dialogue among different models of development? Or will it rather provide intellectual legitimacy to uni-lateral impositions by the donor states, as in the colonial period?

THE PRESENT AS THE FUTURE'S PAST

In my view, one decade after the beginning of the Bologna Process, we have so far been providing only weak answers to these strong questions.

The weakest of them all are the nonanswers, the silences, and the taken for grantedness of the new common sense about the mission of the university. This is a situation that we should overcome as soon as pos-sible. The danger is to convert really mediocre achievements into brilliant leaps forward, to disguise resignation under the mask of consensus, to orient the university toward a future in which there is no future for the university.

In my mind, we are at a juncture which our complexity scientists would characterize as a situation of bifurcation. Minimal movements in one or other direction may produce major and irreversible changes. Such is the magnitude of our responsibility. We all know that we never act upon the future; we act upon the present in light of our anticipations or visions of how the future will look like. The strong questions indicate that there is no single, consensual anticipation or vision to be taken for granted, and that is why the questions invite deep reflection.

I suggest that we are before two alternative visions and that their co-presence is the source of the tensions running through our university system today. They both invite two opposing imaginary visions of a retrospective evaluation of the reforms under way. That is, they look from the future at our present.

According to one of them, our reform efforts were indeed a true reform, as they succeeded in preparing the university to confront the challenges of the twenty-first century effectively—by diversifying its mission without giving away its authenticity, by strengthening institutional autonomy, academic freedom, and social responsibility under the new and very complex conditions of Europe and of the world at large. Thus, the European university was able to rebuild its humanistic ideal in a new internationalist, solidary, and intercultural way.

According to the other, imaginary, retrospective vision, the Bologna Process was, on the contrary, a counterreformation, as it blocked the reforms that the universities in different European countries were undertaking individually, and each one according to its specific conditions to face the above mentioned challenges; furthermore, the Bologna Process forced a convergence beyond a reasonable level. It did this with the purpose of disabling the university from the mechanisms that would allow it to resist against the business and market imperatives in the same manner as it resisted in the past against the imperatives of religion and later of the state.

In order not to end this essay on a pessimistic note, I will start by briefly detailing the second retrospective vision and then turning to the first one. The second vision, the vision of the counterreformation, displays before us a dystopic scenario with the following features.

As we realize that the financial crisis has unveiled the dangers of creating a single currency without putting together public and fiscal policies and state budgets, it may well happen that, in the long run, the Bologna Process turns out to be the euro of European universities. Here are the foreseeable consequences: the principles of solidary university internationalism and respect for cultural diversity will be discarded in the name of the efficiency of the European university market and competition; the weaker universities (gathered in the weaker countries) will be dumped by the university rating agencies into the ranking garbage bin. Though claiming to be rigorous, university ranking will be, in a great measure, arbitrary and subjective. Most universities will suffer the consequences of fast decrease of public funding; many universities will be forced to close down.

As is happening in other levels of education, the wealthy students and their parents will search throughout many countries for the best quality/price ratio, as they are already doing in the commercial malls which universities are also becoming, while the poor students and their parents will be confined to the poor universities existing in their poor countries or neighborhoods. The internal impact will be overwhelming: the relation between research and teaching, highly advertised by Bologna, will be a very paradise for the universities at the top of the ranking (a scarce minority) and perfect hell for the large majority of the universities and their scholars. The commodification criteria will reduce the value of the different areas of knowledge to their market price. Latin, poetry, or philosophy will be kept only if some informatic McDonald recognizes in them any measure of usefulness. University administrators will be the first ones to internalize the classifying orgy, an orgy of objective maniacs and indicators maniacs; they will excel in creating income by expropriating the students' families or robbing the faculty of their personal lives and leisure. They will exert all their creativity to destroy university creativity and diversity, to standardize all that is standardizeable and to discredit or discard all that is not. The faculty will be proletarianized by the very means of educational production of which they are supposedly owners — that is, teaching, assessment, and research. They will end up being zombies of forms, objectives, evaluations that are impeccable as to formal rigor but necessarily fraudulent in substance, work packages, deliverables, milestones, bargains of mutual citation to improve the indices, evaluations of where-you-publish-what-I-couldn't-care-less, careers conceived of as exhilarating but flattened at the low positions in most situations. For the younger faculty the academic freedom will be a cruel joke. The students will be as masters of their learning as they will be slaves of their indebtedness for the rest of their lives. They will enjoy autonomy and free choice in curricular matters with no idea of the logic and limits of the choices presented to them, and will be guided, in personalized fashion, toward a mass alternative of professional employment or of professional unemployment. Tertiary education will be finally liberalized according to the rules of the World Trade Organization.

According to the other, imaginary, retrospective vision, the Bologna Process was, on the contrary, a counterreformation, as it blocked the reforms that the universities in different European countries were undertaking individually, and each one according to its specific conditions to face the above mentioned challenges; furthermore, the Bologna Process forced a convergence beyond a reasonable level. It did this with the purpose of disabling the university from the mechanisms that would allow it to resist against the business and market imperatives in the same manner as it resisted in the past against the imperatives of religion and later of the state. In order not to end this essay on a pessimistic note, I will start by briefly detailing the second retrospective vision and then turning to the first one. The second vision, the vision of the counterreformation, displays before us a dystopic scenario with the following features.

As I said, none of the above has to happen. There is another retrospective vision, and in our hearts and minds we very much hope that it will prevail. But for it to happen, we should start by recognizing and denouncing that the supposed new normalcy of the state of affairs in the above description is in fact a moral aberration and will entail the end of the university as we know it. Let us consider now the other retrospective vision, the vision which, looking from the future into our present, evaluates the Bologna Process as a true reform that changed the European university deeply and for the better. Such vision will emphasize the following features of our current undertakings.

First, the Bologna Process was able to identify and solve most of the problems that the pre-Bologna university was suffering and unable to confront, such as: established inertias that paralyzed any reformist effort; endogamic preferences that created aversion to innovation and challenge; institutional authoritarianism under the guise of scholarly authority; nepotism under the guise of merit; elitism under the guise of excellence; political control under the guise of democratic participation; neofeudalism under the guise of department or school autonomy; fear of being evaluated under the guise of academic freedom; low scientific production justified as an heroic resistance to stupid terms of reference or comments by referees; and generalized administrative inefficiency under the guise of respect for tradition.

Second, in so doing the Bologna Process, rather than discrediting and throwing overboard the self evaluation and reformist efforts that were being undertaken by the most dedicated and innovative professors and administrators, provided them with a new framework and powerful institutional support, to the extent that the Bologna Process could become an endogenous energy rather than an outside imposition. In order to succeed in this, the Bologna Process managed to combine convergence with diversity and difference, and developed mechanisms of positive discrimination to allow for the different national university systems to cooperate and compete among themselves in fair terms.

Third, the Bologna Process never let itself be taken over by the so-called international tertiary education experts with the capacity of transforming subjective, arbitrary preferences into self-evident truths and inevitable public policies. It kept in sight two powerful intellectual views of the mission of the university produced in the early years of the past century and unequivocally took sides between the two.

One was formulated by Ortega y Gasset and Bertrand Russell, two intellectuals with very different political ideas, but who converged in denouncing the political instrumentalization of the university; the other was formulated by Martin Heidegger in his inaugural lecture as rector of Freiburg University in 1933, in which he invited the university to contribute to the preservation of the German strengths of soil and blood. The Bologna Process unequivocally adopted the first and refused the second.

Fourth, the reformists never confused the market with civil society or the community and urged the universities to keep a broad conception of social responsibility, encouraging action research as well as extension projects aimed at bettering the lives of the more vulnerable social groups trapped in systemic social inequality and discrimination, be they women, the unemployed, young and elderly people, migrant workers, ethnic and religious minorities, and so on.

Fifth, the reform Process made it very clear that universities are centers of production of knowledge in the broadest possible sense. Accordingly, it promoted interculturality, heterodoxy and critical engagement in the best liberal tradition which the pre-Bologna Process university had abandoned in the name of political or economic correctness. In the same vein, it encouraged internal scientific pluralism and, most importantly, granted equal dignity and importance to knowledge with market value and knowledge with no possible market value. Moreover, the reformists understood clearly all along that in the field of research and development, cost/benefit analysis is a very crude instrument and may kill innovation instead of promoting it. In fact, the history of technology amply shows that the innovations with highest instrumental value were made possible with no attention to cost/benefit calculations.

Sixth, the Bologna Process managed to strengthen the relationship between teaching and research, and, while rewarding excellence, it made sure that the community of university teachers would not be divided between two stratified segments: a small group of first-class university citizens with abundant money, light teaching loads, and other good conditions to carry out research, on the one hand, and, on the other, a large group of second-class university citizens enslaved by long hours of teaching and tutoring with little access to research funds only because they were employed by the wrong universities or were interested in supposedly wrong topics. It managed to combine higher selectivity in recruitment and strict accountability in the use of teaching time and research funds with a concern for really equal opportunities. It conceived of the rankings as the salt in food: too little makes it unpalatable; too much kills all the flavors. Moreover, at a given point it decided that what had happened in international rankings elsewhere could be applied to the university system as well. Accordingly, as the GDP index exists today side by side with the index of human development of the UNDP, the Bologna Process managed to insert internal plurality in the ranking systems.

Seventh, the Bologna Process ended up abandoning the once fashionable concept of human capital after concluding that the universities should form full human beings and full citizens and not just human capital subjected to market fluctuations like any other capital. This had a decisive impact on the curricula and on the evaluation of performances. Furthermore, the Bologna Process managed to convince the European Union and the European states that they should be financially more generous with the public universities not because of corporatist pressures but rather because the investment in an excellent public university system is probably the best way of investing in the future of a Europe of ideas, so the only way for Europe to remain truly European.

Finally, the Bologna Process expanded exponentially the internationalization of the European university but took good care to promote other forms of internationalism than commercial internationalism. In this way, the European area of higher education ceased to be a threat to the academic freedom and intellectual autonomy of universities throughout the world to become a loyal and powerful ally in keeping the ideas of academic freedom, institutional autonomy and knowledge diversity well and alive in a world threatened by the *pensée unique* of market imperatives.

I have presented you with two alternative visions of our future. There is no doubt in my mind that all of us here wish that our future be molded by the retrospective vision I just described. It is in our hands to make that happen.

NOTES

1. This piece is originally published in *Human Architecture: Journal of the Sociology of Self-Knowledge,* 10 (2012): 7–16. Reprinted with kind permission of the editor.

2. Please visit the following site for more information: www.ond.vlaanderen.be/hogeronderwijs/bologna/.

3. See Amilar Cabral, "The Role of Culture in the Struggle for Independence," in *The African Liberation Reader* (London: Zed Books, 1982), 197–203.

BIBLIOGRAPHY

Cabral, Amilar. "The Role of Culture in the Struggle for Independence." In Aquino de Bragança and Immanuel Wallerstein (eds.), *The African Liberation Reader*. London: Zed Books, 1982, 197–203.

Heidegger, Martin. "The Self-Assertion of the German University: Delivered on the Solemn Assumption of the Rectorate of 1933/34: Facts and Thoughts." Translated with introduction by Karsten Harries, *Review of Metaphysics* 38(3), (1985): 467–502.

Ortega y Gasset, José. *Mission of the University*. Princeton: Princeton University Press, 1944.

Russell, Betrand. "Freedom or Authority in Education." *The Century Magazine*, (1924): 172–180.

Part II

Decolonizing the Westernized University in Europe, the United States, and Latin America

TWO

About Them, But Without Them

Race and Ethnic Studies Relations in Dutch Universities

Kwame Nimako

Universities are organized to teach, research, and produce knowledge.[1] But knowledge is not produced in isolation, and knowledge about race and ethnic relations is no exception. Historically, social forces and events in Europe have given rise to policies to combat racism and racial discrimination. Among other things, racist events in Britain between 1958 and 1963 gave the United Kingdom the oldest and the most extensive anti-racism and anti-discrimination regulation in Europe.[2] The British Race Relations Act of 1965 was adopted before the United Nations Convention on the Elimination of All Forms of Racial Discrimination on December 21, 1965.[3] Anti-racism and anti-discrimination regulations entered continental Europe via the United Nations in the 1970s. The British Race Relations Act 1965 went almost unnoticed in continental Europe. In the formulation of Stuart Hall, "Western Europe did not have, until recently, any ethnicity at all. Or didn't recognize it had any."[4]

In continental Europe, white middle-class social upsurge in the form of university student revolts in May 1968 in Paris gained significant attention. The Paris student revolts had spinoffs in Amsterdam and elsewhere, which in turn facilitated the democratization of the universities, gender "equality" and democratization of lifestyle. The counterpart of these upsurges in relation to race and ethnic relations in the Netherlands was the uprising of the Moluccans in 1976. Formal and systematic regulation of race and ethnic relations was in response to the Moluccan uprising and took the form of the establishment of the department of minorities

17

affairs within the Dutch Ministry of Home Affairs, which in turn culminated in the publication of the ethnic minorities' policy document or
report (*Minderhedenbeleid*) of 1983; this in turn laid the foundations of
formal ethnic studies within the universities.

In this chapter I examine the nature and articulation of some of these
processes in the Netherlands and document the small but rising body of
institutional and ideological opposition to them. In this way I reveal the
various knowledge-production processes, the limitations of each, and the
ways in which challenges are being mounted. I also reveal the ways in
which international exchange, especially across programs with African
Diasporic studies and other programs of critical analysis contribute to the
developing patterns in Europe in general and the Netherlands in particular.

SHADOWS OF FORTRESS EUROPE

Fortress Europe overshadows ethnic studies in the European Union. The
proliferation of race, ethnic, and immigrant studies and research in the
Netherlands took off after the establishment of the department of minorities' affairs within the Ministry of Home Affairs in the late 1970s. The
active role of the government in institutionalizing research to support the
development of Minorities' Policy is expressed in the notion of Minorities' Research (*Minderhedenonderzoek*). Virtually all research on ethnic minorities is funded directly by government departments or, indirectly, via
(state-funded) university-related institutes and professional NGOs. It is
safe to assume that the majority of Dutch universities with major social
science faculties conduct some studies on immigrants or ethnic minorities
groups. However, the core of Dutch migration and ethnic studies is located in three centers or institutes within three universities, namely, the
Institute for Migration and Ethnic Studies (IMES) at the University of
Amsterdam (UvA), the European Research Centre on Migration and Ethnic Relations (ERCOMER) at Utrecht University, and the Institute for
Sociological and Economic Research (ISEO) at Erasmus University in Rotterdam.

The Institute for Migration and Ethnic Studies (IMES) is the precursor
of the Centre for Race and Ethnic Studies (CRES). Established in 1984 at
the University of Amsterdam by Chris Mullard, a citizen of the United
Kingdom, and then director of the Race Relations Policy and Practice
Research Unit at the University of London, the Institute of Education
(CRES) was the first major center or institute devoted to the study of race
and ethnic relations in the Netherlands. Chris Mullard was not only the
first professor of education and ethnic studies in the Faculty of Education
and Pedagogy and the first director of the Centre for Race and Ethnic
studies (CRES) but also the first professor of ethnic studies in Europe.

The mission of CRES (1984–1991) was to develop race-critical research in relation to other class, gender and other ordering principles. Chaired by a black director, Chris Mullard, staff, faculty, and affiliates consisted of a mix of different racial, ethnic, and majority populations, a degree of gender and race-ethnic integration that, to date, has not found its match in another university institute in the Netherlands. In his earlier publications, prior to his arrival in the Netherlands, Chris Mullard had noted that "race as a sociocultural category has appeared historically to be relatively independent of class."[5] Flowing from this analysis, issues of equal opportunity, anti-racism, anti-discrimination, and social mobility remained at the core of black scholarship. These insights were taken into account at CRES.

As professor of education and ethnic studies, Chris Mullard located CRES in the Faculty of Education and Pedagogy. However after the formal objections of the decision-makers of the Faculty of Education and Pedagogy to its location in the Faculty, CRES was closed down by a university board decision in 1991. A year later it was reopened and renamed IMES, with more financial resources, under a new director, Rinus Penninx. A former civil servant at the Ministry of Social Affairs and professor of research methodology at the Free University of Amsterdam, Penninx was appointed professor of migration and ethnic studies at the University of Amsterdam. He also chaired the production of the first report of the WRR (Scientific Council to the Government) on minorities in 1979. On its current official website, however, the Institute for Migration and Ethnic Studies is referred to as an interdisciplinary research institute of the University of Amsterdam which has existed since 1994.

CRES was not only the first race and ethnic studies center in the Netherlands but it was also the first institute to include both people and issues in race and ethnic studies. The closure of CRES and the emergence of IMES was not just a matter of the changing of the guard. It led to a shift of focus away from race and ethnic studies to immigration studies. This in turn followed a state policy shift from ethnic minorities' policy to "aliens' policy." Aliens' policy came into effect in 1989 and classifies "ethnic" groups on the basis of two categories, namely, "natives" and "nonnatives." Since the concept of "race" is rejected in official and academic usage, "natives" came to mean "whites."

According to the IMES website, the research program promotes the polder model of encounter and — where possible — integration of different perspectives, and therefore cooperates with a range of other University of Amsterdam departments: Anthropology, Sociology, Communication Science, Political Science, Social Geography, Economic Geography, Econometrics, Administrative Law, and Social and Economic History. The research program consists of the following themes: international migration; multiculturalism and integration in modern Western societies, including citizenship in multicultural democracies; history of immigration and immigrants in the Netherlands in Western European perspective; immigrants and the urban economy; structural and sociocultural integration of immigrants in welfare states.

Other important institutes in the Netherlands include the European Research Centre on Migration and Ethnic Relations (ERCOMER) of Utrecht University and the Institute for Sociological and Economic Research (ISEO), Erasmus University in Rotterdam. Among other things ERCOMER focuses on comparative international migration and ethnic relations within a European context, whereas ISEO monitors social inequality in education and the labor market in relation to ethnic minorities for the state. What stands out in this mode of research is the use of the insider outsider paradigm—"us versus them"—as the starting point. The "us" represents "white" Europeans; the "them" represents the "Other." In other words the researchers consider themselves as insiders and their object of research, namely, the migrants and ethnic minorities, as outsiders. The implication of this mode of operation is that the "us" has become the consumers of their own knowledge production. The objects (i.e., "them") of research are hardly interested in the knowledge production of the subjects (i.e., "us").

PARALLEL KNOWLEDGE PRODUCTIONS

The closure of CRES prevented the institutionalization of anti-racism education and research within universities, but it does not mean that those interested in race and ethnic relations research have not moved on outside the universities. It is worth noting that Chris Mullard coined the term "Black Britain" in his book of the same title in 1973. Contrary to the debate on immigration in Britain then prevalent in the 1960s, "Black Britain" reminded us that a new generation of Black Europeans had come of age; namely, those who were born in Britain, and for that matter in Europe, who knew no other country than the countries in which they were born.[6] In turn, Stuart Hall drew our attention to a new culture that was unfolding as a consequence of these developments.[7] This constituted parallel knowledge productions. As we shall note below, it took about three decades before the notion of Black Europe appeared on the public agenda.

In the Dutch context, official minorities' policy (1983–1989) was accompanied by budgetary support for ethnic specific welfare organizations. Some of these welfare organizations became the main source of employment for some blacks. The change from minorities' policy (*minderhedenbeleid*, 1983) to aliens' policy (*allochtonenbelied* 1989) went hand in hand with the withdrawal of state funding for welfare organizations and the breakdown of those organizations. Parallel to these developments were the rise of claims by predominantly Dutch people of Surinamese and Antillean origin for attention to slavery and historic injustice, and the absence of this part of Dutch history in Dutch schoolbooks. These claims gave rise to social movements that culminated in the emergence of the National Institute for the study of Dutch slavery and its Legacy (NiNsee), which was founded in 2003 and began operations in 2004.

The emergence of NiNsee may be seen as a progressive step forward, but it actually paralleled developments in the frame of education that are relevant to this discussion. The establishment of an institute that would serve to document and discuss the legacy of slavery and commemorate the victims of the transatlantic slave trade and slavery would arise only at the insistence and thanks to the petitioning of the Afro-Surinamese community in the Netherlands. To understand why this is the case, one must first understand the national self-consciousness of the Dutch with regard to their involvement in slavery and the slave trade. For a long time in the Netherlands, it was taken for granted that the Atlantic "slave" trade and slavery took place long ago in some distant countries—Africa, the Caribbean, and the Americas. The Dutch did not see the numerous ways in which Dutch society at home—in economics, politics, cultural, museums, ideologies—was implicated in slavery and shaped by it. With the mass migration from the former plantation colony of Surinam that took place when that country gained independence in 1975, the legacy of slavery was literally delivered to the Netherlands' front door. The migrant population included thousands of descendants of enslaved people. This Afro-Dutch community was the seedbed for the development of organizations in the major cities of Amsterdam, Rotterdam, and The Hague that organized events on the first of July with the primary objective of commemorating the legacy of slavery and celebrate its abolition.

In 1998, the Afro-European Women's organization Sophiedela created plans for a national monument. Sophiedela presented a petition to the Lower House. The petition, entitled *Sporen van slavernij* (Traces of Slavery), requested the building of a national monument to commemorate the Dutch slavery legacy. This petition was discussed in the House in February 1999. Since that time, first of July committees have been established in other major cities, such as Rotterdam. The annual *Bigi Spikri* ("big mirror") parade, where the descendants of enslaved people parade past shop windows (mirrors) in traditional costumes in order to display their beauty, always attracts thousands of visitors. On the first of July 1999, the Rotterdam committee presented a petition to the municipal council requesting that it use its influence in the Cabinet to declare July 1 a national holiday.

The many initiatives at the grassroots level went into high gear when the Cabinet granted the request in the Sophiedela petition and the new Minister for Integration, Roger van Boxtel, adopted the idea of a national slavery monument and made it a spearhead of his policy geared to the promotion of the social integration of ethnic minorities. The various Afro-

Surinamese, Antillean, Aruban, and African organizations and organizations of maroons and indigenous peoples joined forces at the insistence of the Ministry of the Interior. This umbrella organisation—the *Landelijk Platform Slavernijverleden* (LPS, National Platform on the Legacy of Slavery)—then consulted with the government during the process.

The developments in the Netherlands relating to the slavery legacy ran parallel with international initiatives to combat repression and exclusion, including the World Anti-Racism Conference held in Durban, South Africa, in 2001. At that conference, the then Minister for Integration Van Boxtel spoke on behalf of the Dutch Cabinet on the approach to the struggle against racism and racial discrimination.

It was only due to the efforts of the Black community in the Netherlands that the Dutch slave legacy was placed on the political agenda. This brought the discourse on the legacy of slavery into the public domain and simultaneously gave it an emotional charge. Once in the public domain, this movement culminated in the unveiling of the *National Monument Slavernijverleden* (National Monument to the Legacy of Slavery) on July 1, 2002, in the Oosterpark in Amsterdam. This static monument was unveiled in the presence of Queen Beatrix.

Let us continue this narrative with two observations. First, the minister made this statement without support from major mainstream Dutch public intellectuals—there was by no means a general political or academic shift in the views on slavery and racism. At that time, dominant public intellectuals were preoccupied with issues of multiculturalism and Islam. Meanwhile, black academics and intellectuals started going outside the university system to design their own programs, conferences, and networks.

With financial support from Volkswagen, Peggy Piesche and her friends and colleagues took the initiative to develop a Black European Studies (BEST) Network, at the Johannes Gutenberg Universitat in Mainz, Germany. This led to a series of international conferences in Germany between 2003 and 2006. Some of the top scholars of race and ethnic relations, including scholars that focused directly on gender, from across Europe, were involved in these conferences. There were also very significant contributions from scholars of race and ethnic relations based in the United States. The BEST initiatives, financed by Volkswagen, were not institutionalized after funds dried up. However, many of the scholars, on both sides of the Atlantic, continue to carry out research and publish on these topics.[8]

Running parallel to the initiative of BEST were the "Racial Configuration in post-9/11 era" workshops organized by Ramón Grosfoguel and his colleagues at the Maison des Sciences de l'Homme in Paris in June 2004 and June 2005. In April 2006 Darlene Clark Hine and Trica Danielle Keaton organized a conference on Black Europe and the African Diaspora held at Northwestern University (United States). What these conferences, workshops, and summer school have in common is the production of knowledge that is uncommon in mainstream European universities, namely, knowledge production that challenges the parameters, epistemologies, and methodologies of research being carried out within the university frameworks, and that challenges the limitations prescribed for research that is funded by the state. It also involved significant commitments to anti-racist education. These developments culminated in the organization of the first international Black Europe Summer School in Amsterdam in June 2008, initiated and founded by Kwame Nimako and Amy Abdou.

The organizers of this program had originally approached the University of Amsterdam, home of the IMES, for support for the program and an academic anchor. This was in concert with other summer programs that were developed through the International School for Humanities and Social Sciences, a division of the University of Amsterdam. The program was rejected for its emphasis on race, as opposed to immigration, and for its critical nature. At one juncture, the then dean of the International School suggested that it would be more feasible to establish a program that examined the role of Islam in the current debate over immigration. Such a suggestion should not be understood in isolation. It forms part of what I call frontier social science, which refers to a particular research tradition that follows official policy of progressive control, of which more below. The Summer School on Black Europe is an intensive summer program that takes place in the Netherlands each year and seeks to address the dimensions of race and ethnic relations that are unique to Europe. The program examines the ways in which conceptions of the other are institutionalized and reproduced; the rise of xenophobia in various EU countries; the legal definitions and discourse surrounding the conceptualized other; and the ways in which each country has dealt with issues of race and national identity. The program engages in international comparison and provides an historical overview of the developments within a variety of European countries via case studies and an analysis of antidiscrimination laws. In this sense, the Netherlands provides an interesting setting for a discussion of the disparity between antidiscrimination law and the philosophy behind critical race studies.

As we noted above, the formal and systematic regulation of race and ethnic relations was adopted in response to the Moluccan uprising; not only did this culminate in official ethnic minorities policy but it also laid the foundations of formal ethnic studies within the universities. The point of departure of formal ethnic studies is the identification of the object of study as "problem." In response to these so-called "problem groups," social science researchers assigned to study the groups shift their focus to new frontiers. Thus, the Moluccan "problem" was superseded by the "Surinamese problem," followed by the "Antillean problem" and the "Moroccan problem," as determined by major state agencies. After September 11, 2001, Islam became the new frontier on research on immigration and ethnicity. It was against this backdrop that it was suggested to us to "follow the research money," because policy priority and the allocation of resources favored the study of Islamic groups. This also constitutes Progressive Control, a dynamic process which, observed in and endorsed by policies, practices, official statements, and the like, is oriented and continuously moves toward newer forms of control which, in turn, are called for as a result of changes in the material and structural conditions, consciousnesses, and resistances that distinguish the character of a Europeanized society at any given time.[9]

While it refused to affiliate itself with the program officially, the University of Amsterdam took the position that if the organizers were capable of funding the program externally and locating an academic anchor outside the university, they would be willing to rent classroom space and student housing to the organizers. Thus the program was established in 2008 through the financial and institutional support of NiNsee.

After the first year, the program was then taken over by the National Institute for the study of Dutch slavery and its legacy (NiNsee). The Vrije Universiteit (VU) became the academic anchor, although the VU does not contribute to the financing of the program. The Black Europe Summer School received its third group of students and scholars in June 2010. This program was enhanced by the development of the Black European Research Network, a collective of researchers, professionals, and practitioners in the field of Black European Studies that was developed in conjunction with the yearly meetings in Amsterdam.

In addition, NiNsee has since established an annual symposium on Trajectories of Emancipation and it collaborates with the Center for Global Studies and Humanities (CGSH, Duke University) and the Institute for Postcolonial and Transcultural Studies (INPUTS, University of Bremen) in organizing an annual series of symposia. A series of these meetings has already taken place, both in the Netherlands and in the United States.

Finally it should be mentioned that parallel knowledge production has a long tradition and is tied to knowledge production itself. In recent years intellectuals and academics who found no place within the mainstream universities have gone their way to form alternative institutes such as the Transnational Institute (TNI) based in Amsterdam; they have also developed forms of knowledge production and set up alternative publishing outlets such as the *Monthly Review Press, Pluto Press, New Left Review, Race and Class,* and *Review.*

CONCLUSION:
FROM RACE RELATIONS TO BLACK EUROPEAN STUDIES?

The politics of research on race and ethnic relations in the Netherlands have been more or less similar to developments in other (Western) countries: competition between oppositional and mainstream paradigms, between *critical race research* (which in this context focus on de- and neo-colonization, race, racism, intertwined systems of domination, transnationalism, diversity) and what has come to be called in the Netherlands *minority research*). The two directions are not completely mutually exclusive; there is some overlap where oppositional paradigms meet the critical end of mainstream research, notably in the advocacy of transnationalism and (cultural) diversity.[10]

Traditionally, however, race relations research in Europe has been about white Europeans studying and representing Black Europeans. This is no exception in Dutch universities. This is problematic for both political and intellectual reasons. On the one hand, politically this mode of knowledge production is also power projection. On the other hand, academically it is a (mis)representation of the "other." Both tend to be rejected or invalidated by Blacks. The emphasis on immigration studies, the exclusion of Black Europeans from academia amid a significant Black presence, has given rise to the emergence of Black European studies outside the universities. In the United States, Black studies take place in universities; in Europe, Black studies operate the shadows of Fortress Europe.

NOTES

1. This piece is originally published in *Human Architecture: Journal of the Sociology of Self-Knowledge,* 10 (2012): 45–52. Reprinted with kind permission of the editor.

2. See Robert Miles and Annie Phizacklea, *WhiteMan's Country: Racism in British Politic*(London: Pluto Press, 1984). Also see Stephen Small and John Solomos, "Race, Immigration and Politics in Britain. Changing Policy Agendas and Conceptual Paradigms, 1940s–2000s," *International Journal of Comparative Sociology* 47 no. 3–4 (2006): 236–257.

3. See www.ohchr.org/EN/ProfessionalInterest/Pages/CERD.aspx.

4. See Stuart Hall, "What Is This 'Black' in Black Popular Culture?" in *The Black Studies Reader* (New York: Routledge, 2004), 255–263.

5. See Chris Mullard, "Racism, Ethnicism and Etharchy or Not? The Principles of Progressive Control and Transformative Change" in *Minority Education: From Shame to Struggle* (Clevedon: Multilingual Matters Ltd., 1988), 7.

6. See details in Stephen Small, *Police and People in London II: A Group of Young Black People* (London: Policy Studies Institute, 1983).

7. See Stuart Hall, "What Is This 'Black' in Black Popular Culture?" in *The Black Studies Reader* (New York: Routledge, 2004), 255–263.

8. See Darlene Clark Hine, Trica Danielle Keaton, and Stephen Small (eds.) *Black Europe and the African Diaspora* (Urbana Champaign: University of Illinois Press, 2009).

9. See Chris Mullard, Kwame Nimako, and Glenn Willemsen, *De Plurale Kubus: Een Vertoog Over Emancipatiemodellen en Minderhedenbeleid* (The Plural Cube: Discourse on Emancipation Models and Minorities Policy),('s-Gravenhag: Warray, 1990).

10. See Philomena Essed and Kwame Nimako. "Designs and (Co)-incidents: Cultures of Scholarship and Public Policy on Immigrants/Minorities in the Netherlands." *International Journal of Comparative Sociology,* 47 (2006): 281–312.

BIBLIOGRAPHY

Essed, Philomena, and Kwame Nimako. "Designs and (Co)-incidents: Cultures of Scholarship and Public Policy on Immigrants/Minorities in the Netherlands." *International Journal of Comparative Sociology,* 47 (2006): 281–312.

Hall, Stuart. "What Is This 'Black' in Black Popular Culture?" In: Jacqueline Bobo, Cynthis Hudley and Claudine Michel (eds.), *The Black Studies Reader.* New York: Routledge, 2004.

Hine, Darlene Clark, Trica Danielle Keaton, and Stephen Small. (eds.) *Black Europe and the African Diaspora.* Urbana Champaign: University of Illinois Press, 2009.

Miles, Robert, and Phizacklea, Annie. *WhiteMan's Country: Racism in British Politic.* London: Pluto Press, 1984.

Mullard, Chris. *Black Britain.* London: Allen & Unwin, 1973.

———. "Racism, Ethnicism and Etharchy or Not? The Principles of Progressive Control and Transformative Change." In: T. Skutnabb-Kangas and J. Cummins (eds.) *Minority Education: From Shame to Struggle.* Clevedon: Multilingual Matters Ltd., 1988.

Mullard, Chris, Kwame Nimako, and Glenn Willemsen. *De Plurale Kubus: Een Vertoog Over Emancipatiemodellen en Minderhedenbeleid* (The Plural Cube: Discourse on Emancipation Models and Minorities Policy),'s-Gravenhag: Warray, 1990.

Muller, Jerry. "Us and Them: The Enduring Power of Ethnic Nationalism." *Foreign Affairs,* March–April 2008.

Murray, Nelson, Chris Mullard, and Kwame Nimako. "Demographic and Legal Status of ACP Migrants in Europe: ACP General Guide Book," Volume 1, Focus Consultancy: Wiltshire, UK, 1997.

Nimako, Kwame, and Stephen Small. "Theorizing Black Europe and the African Diaspora: Implications for Citizenship, Nativism and Xenophobia." In: Hine, Darlene Clark, Danielle Keaton, Trica, and Small Stephen (eds.), *Black Europe and the African Diaspora.* Urbana Champaign: University of Illinois Press, 2009.

Small, Stephen (ed.). *Black Europe and the African Diaspora.* Urbana Champaign: University of Illinois Press, 2009, 212–237.

———. *Police and People in London II: A Group of Young Black People.* London: Policy Studies Institute, 1983.

Small, Stephen, and John Solomos. "Race, Immigration and Politics in Britain. Changing Policy Agendas and Conceptual Paradigms, 1940s–2000s." *International Journal of Comparative Sociology,* 47 (2006): 3–4, 236–257.

THREE

The Dilemmas of Ethnic Studies in the United States

Between Liberal Multiculturalism,
Identity Politics, Disciplinary Colonization,
and Decolonial Epistemologies

Ramón Grosfoguel

Ethnic studies in the United States represents a contradictory space within which two hegemonic discourses (identitarian multiculturalism and disciplinary colonization) and a counter hegemonic one (decolonial epistemologies) condense and enter into debate and struggle.[1] In contrast to other parts of the world, ethnic studies in the United States emerged as a part of the civil rights movement for racialized minorities. In the late 1960s and early 1970s, a number of student strikes and university occupations were organized by these minorities, leading to the creation of African-American, Puerto Rican, Chicano, Asian, and indigenous studies programs in many universities all over the United States. This epistemic insurgency was key to the opening of spaces in universities for professors from ethnic/racial groups suffering discrimination and/or with non-Western epistemologies in areas which were up to that point monopolized by white professors and students and Eurocentric epistemologies privileging the Cartesian "ego-politics of knowledge."[2]

In contrast to the Eurocentric epistemology in Westernized universities which is characterized by the privileging of a Western male canon of thought and the study of the "other" as an object rather than as a knowledge-producing subject—concealing at the same time the geo-politics and the body-politics of knowledge through which white academics and intellectuals think—the entry of professors of "color" through affirmative action programs and the creation of ethnic studies programs aimed at studying the problems confronting oppressed minorities constituted an important change in the production of academic knowledges. At that time (late 1960s and early 1970s), many of those minority professors were activist intellectuals who privileged the "geo-politics of knowledge" and the "body-politics of knowledge" over the "ego-politics of knowledge" in the production of knowledges. This represented a break, for the first time in Westernized universities, with the subject-object dichotomy of Cartesian epistemology. Instead of a white male subject studying non-white subjects as "objects of knowledge," assuming a neutral, privileged viewpoint not situated in any space or body—that is, the "ego-politics of knowledge," which allows the subject to claim a false objectivity and epistemic neutrality—we have a new situation in Westernized universities in the United States in which subjects from racialized minorities study themselves as subjects who think and produce knowledges from bodies and spaces (the "geo-politics" and "body-politics" of knowledge), approaches which have been routinely subalternized and inferiorized by Westernized racist/sexist epistemology and power. Moreover, it can also be said that their work questioned the hegemonic white understanding of racialized minorities which sought to make the latter responsible for the marginalization and poverty they experience in the United States (for example, the paradigms of "the culture of poverty" and "modernization theory"), thereby concealing the rampant racism of that society. Not only did this challenge the epistemic racisms/sexisms that recognize only the production of theory by white/male Western subjects while non-whites are assumed to produce only folklore, mythology, or culture but never knowledge equal to that of the West, it also opened up the potential for the decolonization of knowledge, by also challenging the Cartesian "ego-politics of knowledge" of Western social sciences/humanities and counterposing to this the "geo-politics" and "body-politics of knowledge" of subaltern subjects. I say "potential," because this decolonial process is not complete and faces several obstacles. This article seeks to identify these obstacles which ethnic studies still confront. However, it is necessary first to clarify some concepts that are indispensable for our discussion.

EPISTEMIC RACISM/SEXISM AND THE WESTERNIZED UNIVERSITIES IN THE WORLD-SYSTEM

The "Modern/Colonial Capitalist/Patriarchal Westerncentric/Christian-centric World-System" is composed of a heterarchy or intersectionality of multiple global power structures beyond the sole economic and political structures frequently identified in world system analysis and neo-Marxist political-economy perspectives more generally.[3] In my work on decolonizing paradigms in political economy, I identify about fifteen global power structures of the world system. In this section I would like to discuss one of these structures: the global epistemic hierarchy in the world system. This hierarchy produces and reproduces the same structure of the global racial/ethnic hierarchy and the global Judeo-Christian gender/sexual hierarchy of the world system—that is, it privileges as superior Western male knowledges and treats as inferior knowledges that are women-centered and non-Western. This racist/sexist hierarchy of knowledge operates on a world scale with variations and particularities in different regions of the world according to the diverse colonial and local histories. As will be discussed below, this global epistemic hierarchy is not merely a "superstructure" but is constitutive of capitalist accumulation at a world scale. Without it, there would be no historical capitalism as we know it today.

This epistemic hierarchy has its own discourses, ideology, and institutional framework. Eurocentrism is the global discourse/ideology of the epistemic hierarchy. Eurocentrism as an epistemic perspective privileges the knowledges, memories, and histories of the Westernized male colonizers throughout the world. This epistemology is institutionally globalized around the world through the Westernized university. The Westernized university is organized around a canon of thought that is both Western and masculine. Nearly all disciplines in the social sciences and the humanities, with very few exceptions, privilege in their canon of thought Western male thinkers. Not even Western women are included within the canon, while non-Western males and women are excluded from it. This is not a question of representation or recognition, but rather one of how Western universities are provincial in their scope while claiming to be valid for all humanity beyond time and space—that is, while pretending to be universal.

The main problem is that the Westernized university model, with its provincial sexist/racist structure of thought and its nineteenth-century liberal disciplinary divisions of knowledge, is institutionally globalized around the world. The provincialism of Westernized universities, with their Eurocentric sexist/racist foundation of knowledge, is taken as the normality everywhere it goes. Non-Western social scientists, historians, philosophers, and critical thinkers, thinking from different geo-politics and body-politics of knowledge and/or from different cosmologies/epistemologies, are considered inferior to Western male epistemologies and, thus, excluded as valid knowledge from the Westernized university. Thus, the Westernized university is a machine of global mass production of *Eurocentric fundamentalism*. Any critical thinking or social scientific development produced by and from a non-Westernized perspective/epistemic location is inferiorized, received with suspicion and considered as not serious or not worthy of being read in the Westernized university.

We find the same structure of knowledge in Westernized universities everywhere in the world, no matter where they are located. Be they in Dakar, Buenos Aires, New Delhi, Manila, New York, Paris, or Cairo, they have fundamentally the same disciplinary divisions and the same racist/sexist canon of thought. Thus, in terms of global capitalism, the Westernized university produces the Westernized political and economic elites all over the world, without which the world system would be unmanageable. Through this mechanism, the core powers of the world system are able to form the Westernized Eurocentric fundamentalist elites that will suppress any alternative way of thinking beyond the system and will carry to every corner of the world its epistemic racist/sexist knowledge structures and policies. This monocultural, monoepistemic, and mono-cosmological Eurocentric fundamentalist framework is what defines who is a valid social agent, who is a terrorist, who is a plausible candidate to win an election, and who is a valid interlocutor in the globe today. Moreover, the Westernized university is a machine of "epistemicide." It inferiorizes and destroys the epistemic potential of non-Western epistemologies.[4]

The absurdity of this epistemic structure has been demonstrated very well in the work of Portuguese social scientist, Boaventura de Sousa Santos.[5] He has pointed out many times that if we examine what is called social theory in the social sciences of Westernized universities today, it comes fundamentally from Western male thinkers of only five countries: Italy, France, Germany, England, and the United States. The claim is that the social theory created to account for the social experience and history of these five countries, which comprise only 12 percent of the world's population, should be taken as valid and universal for the rest of the countries of the world, which account for 88 percent of humanity. This structure throws away the social experience of most of humanity.

Epistemic racism/sexism is one of the most hidden forms of racism in the "modern/colonial capitalist/patriarchal Westerncentric/Christiancentric world system" we inhabit.[6] To move beyond this structure would require not a university (where one epistemology defines for the rest the questions and the answers to produce a colonial, universal social science and humanities) but a pluriversity (where epistemic diversity is institutionally incorporated into necessary inter-epistemic dialogues in order to produce decolonial, pluriversal social sciences and humanities). This is why Boaventura de Sousa Santos calls for an "ecology of knowledges" as a point of departure to decolonize knowledge and the Westernized university.[7] According to Sousa Santos, the "ecology of knowledges" is an opening to a new decolonial space of epistemic diversity where Western social sciences are not the only source of valid knowledge but one among others.

ETHNIC STUDIES FACE WESTERNIZED UNIVERSITIES: IDENTITIES IN POLITICS AND TRANSMODERNITY

For the first time in 500 years of globalization of the Westernized universities (first Christian-centric, then secular Eurocentric, and, more recently, the corporate university), the eruption of the US civil rights struggles for the decolonization of the US empire penetrated the Westernized university at the center of empire, challenging its knowledge production in a radical way. Ethnic studies, women studies, queer studies, and so on, were founded within the United States' Westernized universities, in response to the demands of people of color, women, and gay/lesbian movements. The goal of these programs is not to produce a particular knowledge that will be "added on" in order to supplement the social sciences and humanities today, but *to produce a pluriversal decolonial social science and humanities*. Pluriversal decolonial social sciences would have epistemic diversity guiding their processes of knowledge production. The kinds of knowledges ethnic studies, women studies, and queer studies have produced challenge the racist/sexist capitalist/patriarchal Western canon of thought and epistemology. In opposition to white male hegemonic identity politics, which are hidden as the norm within the process of knowledge production, these subalternized subjects developed via a struggle against identity politics. However, this does not mean that there are small groups inside these new fields of knowledge that reproduce a subaltern kind of identity politics.

Identity politics sets out from an identitarian and culturalist reductionism that ends up essentializing and naturalizing cultural identities. In these identitarian projects there is a powerful suspicion toward groups whose ethnic/racial origin differs from their own. This epistemic closure of walled identities is what characterizes the *Eurocentric fundamentalism* of the hegemonic identity politics of Western male epistemology, which produces phobia and rejection of non-Western epistemologies and knowledges.

Identity politics usually maintain closed identitarian frontiers even among oppressed groups themselves that practice a subaltern form of identity politics, making dialogue and political alliances among them impossible. In some cases they end up inverting hegemonic racism and reproducing an inverted racism by making the subaltern ethnic/racial group into one which is culturally and/or biologically superior to whites.

In sharp contrast to such identity politics, there are what Angela Davis called "identities on politics."[8] The latter are based on ethico-political-epistemic projects which are open to all regardless of ethno/racial origin. For example, the Zapatistas in the southwest of Mexico are an insurgent indigenous movement that thinks epistemically from an Amerindian epistemological/cosmological points of view. These are open to all people and groups who support and sympathize with their political proposals as

well as those who criticize them in constructive ways. Within the Zapatista movement there are whites and mestizos. The movement led by Evo
Morales in Bolivia is an indigenous movement that thinks from the perspective of the Ayllú cosmology of the Aymara communities. This movement counts, among its leaders and in its ranks, both white and mestizo
activists who have assumed the Aymara ethico-political-epistemic political project as well as those who provide constructive critiques to the
movement.

Another example would be African spiritual practices in the Americas
that, while setting out from cosmologies/epistemologies of African origin,
are nevertheless open to the participation of all. That is to say, there is no
correspondence between the ethico-epistemic identity of the project (in
this case its indigenous or African origin) and the ethnic/racial identity of
the individuals who participate in the movements. As a result, these
movements are quite distinct from "identity politics," since they exclude
no one who supports their project for reasons of ethnic/racial origin.

If Eurocentrism seeks to disqualify these alternative epistemologies in
order to inferiorize, subalternize, and discredit them—thereby constructing a world of "unitary thought" that does not allow us to think of "other" possible worlds beyond "white, masculine, neo-liberal capitalist globalization"—the project proposed here would be one that transcends the
Eurocentric epistemic monopoly of the "modern/colonial capitalist/patri-
archal Western-Centric/Christian-centric world-system." To recognize
that there exists an epistemic diversity in the world poses a challenge to
the existing modern/colonial world. It is no longer possible to construct a
global design through a single epistemology as a "single solution" to the
problems of the world, be it from the left (socialism, communism, etc.) or
from the right (developmentalism, neo-liberalism, liberal democracy,
etc.). On the basis of this epistemic diversity there are various anti-capitalist, anti-patriarchal, anti-colonial, and anti-imperialist proposals that
offer different ways of confronting and resolving the problems produced
by the sexual, racial, spiritual, linguistic, gender, and class power relations within the current "modern/colonial capitalist/patriarchal world-
system."[9] This diversity of proposals rooted in "other" epistemologies
that have been subalternized and silenced by Eurocentric epistemology
would provide ways of transcending Eurocentered modernity that go
beyond those proposals involving the culmination of that modernity or
the development of postmodernity. The latter represent Eurocentric critiques of Eurocentrism.[10]

What we are speaking of, then, is developing what the philosopher of
liberation Enrique Dussel calls "transmodernity"—the utopian project for
the fulfillment, not of modernity or postmodernity, but rather of the incomplete and unfinished project of decolonization.[11] "Trans" is used here
in the sense of "beyond." In a utopian transmodern world there exist as
many proposals for the "liberation of women" and "democracy" as there

are epistemologies in the world. Parisian "feminists of difference" cannot impose their solutions or their forms of struggle against patriarchy on Islamic feminists in Iran, indigenous Zapatista feminists in Mexico, or black feminists in the United States, just as the Western world cannot impose its liberal concept of democracy on indigenous, Islamic, or African forms of democracy. Zapatismo sets out from Tojolabal cosmology to redefine democracy as "command [while] obeying," and its institutional practice constitutes the community spaces known as "caracoles" ("shells"). Such concepts are very different from Western democracy in which "those who command do not obey and those who obey do not command," and in which the practical institutional forms are parliaments or national assemblies.

Transmodernity is not an "everything goes" relativism, since we are speaking of a critical anti-capitalist, anti-patriarchal, anti-Eurocentric (never anti-European), anti-colonial, and anti-imperialist perspective that is born from the epistemic diversity of the world. For decolonial thought there is no single epistemology that can claim a monopoly over critical thinking on the planet as imperialism has sought to do for Western thought in the last 500 years of the world system. My proposal here is to redefine ethnic studies departments/programs as "transmodern decolonial studies."

ETHNIC STUDIES IN THE UNITED STATES

Ethnic studies in the United States is at present torn between two problems of the coloniality of global power: (1) the "identity politics" of liberal multiculturalism in the United States and (2) the disciplinary colonization of the Western colonial human sciences (social sciences and the humanities) over these spaces.

Furthermore, those forms of "identity politics" that absolutize and privilege the "identities" and "projects" of their own ethnic/racial group at the expense of other racialized/inferiorized subjects lead them to view other ethnic/racial groups with suspicion and as competitors, including those who share a similar situation of ethnic/racial discrimination. The scholars who promote the worst forms of "identity politics" in ethnic studies programs end up: (1) celebrating their own identity while leaving ethnic/racial hierarchies as such intact; or 2) emphasizing their own ethnic/racial group, gazing at their own navel and, as a result, considering themselves to be in constant competition with other groups that are equally discriminated against, thereby contributing to the reproduction of a system of "divide and conquer" which also maintains intact the status quo of ethnic/racial hierarchies. Thus, both "identity politics" positions—that of "liberal multicultural identitarians" as well as that of "militant identitarians"—end up in complicity with the ethnic/racial hierarchies of white supremacy by leaving the status quo intact. Beginning with the first point: the organization of ethnic studies departments and programs takes place on the basis of ethno/racial identities (African-American, Asian-American, Latino, indigenous, etc.) in the United States. A minority of scholars in the field of ethnic studies uses this structure to reproduce the worst kind of "identity politics." Rather than decolonial studies, "identity politics" tend to reproduce colonial relations that manifest two main tendencies: one based in Anglo-American "light" liberal multiculturalism and the other based on the chauvinist and nationalist absolutization of one's own ethnic/racial identity to the detriment of dialogue and alliance with other racially oppressed groups. Hegemonic liberal multiculturalism allows each racialized group to have its space and celebrate its identity/culture, as long as they do not question the ethnic/racial hierarchies of white supremacist power and as long as they leave the status quo intact. This privileges certain elites within the racialized/inferiorized groups, granting them a space and resources as "tokens," "model minority," or "symbolic showcases," thereby giving a cosmetic multicultural tinge to white power, while the majority of these populations victimized by this rampant racism experience the coloniality of power on a daily basis. Condoleezza Rice is one of the most extreme examples of this policy. This African-American woman has been one of the architects of the racist foreign policy of the Euro-American empire (white capitalist elites) in the Middle East and Iraq, thereby giving an anti-racist and multicultural face to what otherwise are racist imperial policies.[12]

The other tendency of the coloniality of knowledge is the academic disciplinary colonization of ethnic studies.[13] Disciplinary colonization occurs when the fields of knowledge within ethnic studies are divided on the basis of the disciplinary specializations of the human sciences (social sciences and the humanities) and ethnic studies are carried as thinking "on" or "about" rather than thinking "from," "with," and "alongside" the ethnic/racial groups in question. Instead of producing knowledge from the *critical* thought created by racialized/inferiorized subjects, these disciplines impose the Western canon of thought and the Western Cartesian "point zero" epistemology—the point of view that does not assume itself as a point of view, that is, the "God's-eye view" that has characterized modern Western philosophy from Descartes to the present in the Western human sciences.[14] This has affected the production of knowledges in ethnic studies departments/programs because instead of producing knowledges "from" and "with" these ethnic/racial groups and aimed at their liberation, such a perspective privileges the production of knowledges "about" the "others" according to the colonial epistemological tradition, from sixteenth-century Christian missionaries to present-day Cartesian social scientists. This tradition makes of the racialized/inferiorized subject an "object of study" to control and exploit. This raises the following questions: Knowledge for what and for whom? Is it possible to produce neutral knowledges in a society that is divided in racial, sexual, spiritual, and class terms? If epistemology has not only color but also sexuality, gender, cosmology, spirituality, class, and so on, it is not possible to assume the myth or false premise of neutrality and epistemological objectivity (the "point zero" of the "ego-politics of knowledge") as the Western sciences claim to do.

Furthermore, that current which hopes to make ethnic studies into "interdisciplinary studies" reproduces the same problems mentioned above. Interdisciplinarity maintains disciplinary identities intact (with their canon and Eurocentric epistemology) and only opens up an interdisciplinary dialogue within Western epistemology, closing itself off to a trans-modern dialogue between various epistemologies. If we think not from academic disciplines but instead from the notion of "transdisciplinarity" in the sense of going beyond disciplinary knowledges, then the ethnic studies project would be opened up to epistemological diversity instead of the current monotopism and monologue of the dominant Western Eurocentric fundamentalist epistemology that refuses to acknowledge any other epistemology as a space for the production of critical or scientific thought. The disciplinary colonization of ethnic studies constitutes an epistemic colonization since these academic disciplines privilege a Eurocentric epistemic canon.

CONCLUSION

My point is not to dismiss the important and useful critical work produced from within the disciplinary fields of Western academia. I am simply questioning the colonial Eurocentric nature of mainstream disciplines and, thus, the appropriateness of creating ethnic studies departments/programs, if these are reduced merely to studying the sociology of race, the anthropology of ethno/racial identities, the history "of" (not "from" or "with") blacks, the economics of the insertion of indigenous labor, and so on. To colonize ethnic studies through the Western disciplines does not constitute an innovation in the field of knowledge production. It was already possible to do so through the respective academic disciplines of the human sciences, and it requires neither ethnic studies departments nor programs.

It would be a different story if ethnic studies departments or programs proposed to open themselves up to transmodernity, that is, to the epistemic diversity of the world, and redefine themselves as "transmodern decolonial studies," offering to think "from" and "with" those "others" subalternized and inferiorized by Eurocentered modernity, offering to define their questions, their problems, and their intellectual dilemmas "from" and "with" those same racialized groups. This would give rise to a decolonial methodology very different from the colonial methodology of the social sciences and the humanities.[15] It would also imply a transmodern dialogue between diverse ethico-epistemic political projects and a thematic internal organization within ethnic studies departments/programs, one based on problems (racism, sexism, xenophobia, Christian-centrism, "other" epistemologies, Eurocentrism, etc.) rather than either ethnic/racial identities (Blacks, indigenous, Asians, etc.) or Western colonial disciplines (sociology, anthropology, history, political science, philosophy, arts, economics, etc.).[16]

Ethnic studies, once redefined as "transmodern decolonial studies," would make an extremely important contribution not only to the decolonialization of the production of academic knowledge toward a decolonial transmodern social sciences and humanities, but also to liberation as the political project toward the (epistemic, social, political, economic, and spiritual) decolonization of those groups oppressed and exploited by the "Western-centric/Christian-centric capitalist/patriarchal modern/colonial world-system."[17]

NOTES

1. This piece is originally published in *Human Architecture: Journal of the Sociology of Self-Knowledge,* 10(1), (2012):81–90. Reprinted with the kind permission of the editor.

2. See Ramon Grosfoguel, "Para descolonizar os estudos de economia política e os estudos pós-coloniais: Transmodernidade, pensamento de fronteira e colonialidade global," *Revista Crítica de Ciências Sociais,* numero 80(março), (2008): 115–147.

3. For a justification of this characterization of the contemporary world-system and the cartography of power implied in this large phrase, see the online English version of this article originally published in Portuguese in: "Decolonizing Political Economy and Postcolonial Studies: Transmodernity, Border Thinking and Global Coloniality." See www.eurozine.com/pdf/2008-07-04-grosfoguel-en.pdf.

4. See Boaventura de Sousa Santos, *Epistemologías del Sur* (Mexico: Siglo XXI Editores, 2010).

5. See Boaventura de Sousa Santos, *Epistemologías del Sur* (Mexico: Siglo XXI Editores, 2010).

6. See Ramón Grosfoguel, ""Para descolonizar os estudos de economia política e os estudos pós-coloniais: Transmodernidade, pensamento de fronteira e colonialidade global," *Revista Crítica de Ciências Sociais,* numero 80(março), (2008): 115–147.

7. See Boaventura de Sousa Santos, *Epistemologías del Sur* (Mexico: Siglo XXI Editores, 2010).

8. See Angela Davis, "Interview" in *The Politics of Culture in the Shadows of Capital* (Durham: Duke University Press, 1997).

9. See Ramón Grosfoguel, "Para descolonizar os estudos de economia política e os estudos pós-coloniais: Transmodernidade, pensamento de fronteira e colonialidade global," *Revista Crítica de Ciências Sociais,* numero 80(março), (2008): 115–147.

10. See Walter Mignolo, *Local Histories: Global Designs: Coloniality, Border Thinking and Subaltern Knowledges* (New Jersey: Princeton University Press, 2000).

11. See Enrique Dussel, *1492: El encubrimiento del otro. Hacia el origen del mito de la modernidad* (La Paz: Plural Editores, 1994).

12. The same could be said of the Obama administration. Although Obama came to power as part of a mass movement discontent with eight years of the Bush administra-

tion that led to domestic and international chaos and a new Great Depression, his commitments with Wall Street, Transnational Corporations and the Pentagon make the present US imperial state (with a Black President in charge) "a white power imperial structure with a black face." This is part of what I have described elsewhere as the twenty-first century, post-civil rights new apartheid (neo-apartheid) imperial structure in place in the United States.

13. See Edgardo Lander, *La colonialidad del saber* (Buenos Aires: CLACSO, 2000).

14. See Santiago Castro-Gomez, *La Hybris del Punto Cero: ciencia, raza e ilustración en la Nueva Granada (1750–1816)* (Bogotá: Editorial Pontífica Universidad Javeriana, 2006).

15. See Smith, Linda Tuhiwia, *Decolonizing Methodologies: Research and Indigenous Peoples* (London: Routledge, 1999).

16. Here I am not implying that Latino studies, African-American studies, Asian American studies, or Native American studies should not exist as such. To maintain these programs is important in order to focus on the particular contributions the experience of each of these groups brings toward the decolonization of the world. What I am saying here is that inside each of these programs, the focus of research should be primarily based on problems rather than on affirming "identity politics."

17. For a perspective very close to that which I am proposing here, see Maldonado-Torres (2006).

BIBLIOGRAPHY

Castro-Gomez, Santiago. *La Hybris del Punto Cero: ciencia, raza e ilustración en la Nueva Granada (1750–1816)*. Bogotá: Editorial Pontífica Universidad Javeriana, 2006.

Davis, Angela. "Interview." In *The Politics of Culture in the Shadows of Capital*; edited by Lisa Lowe and David Lloyd. Durham: Duke University Press, 1997.

de Sousa Santos, Boaventura. *Epistemologías del Sur*. Mexico: Siglo XXI Editores, 2010.

Dussel, Enrique. *1492: El encubrimiento del otro. Hacia el origen del mito de la modernidad*. La Paz: Plural Editores, 1994.

Eze, Emmanuel. "The Color of Reason: The Idea of 'Race' in Kant's Anthropology," *Postcolonial African Philosophy: A Critical Reader*, editado por E. C. Eze. Cambridge: Blackwell, 1997.

Grosfoguel, Ramón. *Colonial Subjects*. Berkeley: University of California Press, 2003.

———. "Para descolonizar os estudos de economia política e os estudos pós-coloniais: Transmodernidade, pensamento de fronteira e colonialidade global," *Revista Crítica de Ciências Sociais*, numero 80(março), 2008a: 115–147.

———. "Latinos and the Decolonization of the US Empire in the 21st Century." *Social Science Information* 47 (2008b): 605–622.

Habermas, Jürgen. "La modernidad, un Proyecto incomplete." Edited by Hal Foster. *La Posmodernidad*. Barcelona: Editorial Kairos, 1985.

Lander, Edgardo. *La colonialidad del saber*. Buenos Aires: CLACSO, 2000.

Maldonado-Torres, Nelson. "The Topology of Being and the Geopolitics of Knowledge: Modernity, Empire and Coloniality." *City* 8 (2004): 29–56.

———. "Pensamento crítico desde a subalteridade: os Estudos Étnicos como ciências descoloniais ou para a transformação das humanidades e das ciências sociais no século XXI." *Revista Afro-Asia* 34 (2006): 105–130.

Mignolo, Walter. *Local Histories: Global Designs: Coloniality, Border Thinking and Subaltern Knowledges*. New Jersey: Princeton University Press, 2000.

Smith, Linda Tuhiwai. *Decolonizing Methodologies: Research and Indigenous Peoples*. London: Routledge, 1999.

FOUR

The Crisis of the University in the Context of Neoapartheid

Nelson Maldonado-Torres

An often-neglected consideration in reflections about the crisis of the university and the humanities today is that some of the most intractable challenges and perverse consequences that the university and the humanities face are not only due to the influence of global capitalism or neoliberalism simpliciter, but more specifically to racial neoliberalism, global coloniality, and neoapartheid.[1] Spelling out the current crisis of public education and the challenge that the humanities face today in terms of neoliberalism alone is a repetition of the same mistake that others have committed when they have aimed to articulate every problem as simply an emanation of capitalism, without seeing how capitalist exploitation is inextricably connected with multiple forms of dehumanization, many of them based on the colonial enterprises of European civilization (slavery, the modern gender system, racism, and Orientalism, among others).

This reductive understanding of the current crisis is partly rooted in theoretical perspectives that consider racialization and coloniality secondary to the power of commodification and to the expansion of the market logic and value system, and partly due to the definition of the humanities as the heart and soul of liberal university education and to their perception as useless when observed through the lenses of neoliberalism. When one departs from those premises, the disinvestment on the humanities and their consideration as useless, cosmetic, or merely optional appears as the most devastating dimension of the current crisis at the university. Lost from view is that, while the humanities and the interpretive social sciences are often devalued as fields that do not produce profit, areas such as ethnic studies are straightforwardly rendered illegal and perceived as dangerous.[2] Likewise, the critiques of the modern Western university and its liberal form of education that have emanated from fields such as ethnic studies are also ignored or left aside as unimportant or as too temporary to have any substantial value. And so, the great crisis of the age at the level of the university is presented in terms of an encounter between the liberal humanities and neoliberalism, a duality that preserves the presuppositions that keep interdisciplinary and emancipatory fields like ethnic studies as a temporary complement of the humanities, or as a threat. This is without a doubt one of the most disconcerting and unfortunate aspects of analyses of the crisis of the university today, and one that must be corrected not only for the sake of social and cognitive justice, but also for the preservation of what is best in the humanities and other areas in the university.[3]

Based on the previous considerations, I submit that in order to respond to the current crisis the humanities have to insist not only on how important they are for a robust democracy and for the formation of an educated citizenry, but also to:

a. take stock of how they have been complicit with neoliberalism (in terms of over-professionalization, etc.) as well as with different forms of dehumanization, segregation, and apartheid;

b. enter in a closer relationship with interdisciplinary formations that focus on the critical examination of race, gender, and other markers of dehumanization and consider the possibility that a formation like "ethnic studies" could actually become a matrix for the transformation of the humanities through engagement with questions and issues that have typically remained excluded from it, as Johnella Butler (2001) aptly describes.[4] I conceive of "ethnic studies" as a name for a particular expression of a project that precedes the formation of "ethnic studies" in the academy and that has gone with different names in different places and spaces. These different projects can be seen as part of an unfinished project of decolonization after the end of formal desegregation in the academy. What we find today, though, are multiple attempts to intensify the colonization of knowledge and the segregation of peoples in society. One only has to compare census projections on the one hand, which anticipate that people of color, and possibly Latina/os alone, will become majority in the country sometime in the twenty-first century, and the dismal reports of, for instance, Latina/os having "the lowest rate of high school completion and the lowest level of educational attainment of any minority group" or Black students having "the lowest college persistence rate of any racial group."[5] In face of this, one could argue that neither the humanities nor the social sciences should aim to remain "neutral." But this only means that they have to take sides with the emancipatory and decolonial forms of knowledge production today, and being willing to change in the process;

c. Consider entering into a different relation with social movements, and develop methods that simultaneously legitimize those movements and provide new lenses for work in the humanities, the social sciences, and the university at large (e.g., Boaventura de Sousa Santos' theorization of the World Social Forum and his proposal for changes in existing research universities and the creation of a Popular University for Social Movements.[6];

d. Seek to empower the population that is expected to become the majority in the United States by engaging the problems that they face and that are common to other long-standing populations in the country who have always been considered to be outside the norm.

The humanities have more chance of saving what is most important about them by showing their relevance in critical analysis and by pursuing the most constructive lines of inquiry that I have indicated above, than by rehearsing the typical arguments about its constructive role in educating the citizen subject, and so forth—lines of argument that do not take sufficiently into consideration the extent to which the problem that we face is neoapartheid, and not just economic neoliberalism.

"HUMANITIES METHODS IN ETHNIC STUDIES": A VIEW FROM UC BERKELEY

Now I would like to give a more concrete account of some of the main points that I have made. I will primarily take a local perspective and focus on the present, without ignoring history or global dynamics. I will highlight the value of the humanities, but do so via a circuitous route that does not necessarily end in the humanities as we have known them. As to a focus on the present and the local context, I will begin with a reflection on a course that I taught for seven years at UC Berkeley, where I first offered these reflections.

The course in question was entitled "Humanities Methods in Ethnic Studies." The approach that the course presupposes poses the humanities as the source of tools for the study of "ethnic" populations, which in the field of ethnic studies does not mean people who have an ethnicity in general, but those who by virtue of their language, culture, or place of origin are not conceived as part of the norm and are rather perceived as dispensable populations. As worthy as this kind of study is, my approach was different. What I decided to do with the course was to focus on the questions and methods explored by a number of intellectuals, the majority of whom are of color, and who are attentive to multiple forms of dehumanization, oppression, and exploitation. It was this work, for the most part inter- and trans-disciplinary, that served as a foundation to raise the question of method and simultaneously think about the meaning and significance of the humanities. That is, the course focused not so much on already existing humanities tools or methods, but on how ethnic studies both demands and provides tools for a renewed and reconceptualized form of humanities.

I taught this course several times at UC Berkeley, and it became perhaps the most successful course that I taught there, as measured by the number of study groups that were formed and by student organizing (organizing film series, doing free tutorials for other students, etc.) that continued well after the course had finished. The course begins with a discussion of Cathy Davidson and David Theo Goldberg's "A Manifesto for the Humanities in a Technological Age," which appeared in the *Chronicle of Higher Education* in 2004.[7] In that essay, Davidson and Goldberg identify certain elements in the crisis of the humanities and argue for a renewed conception of humanities work that more fully embraces the challenges brought up by digital technologies, interdisciplinarity, and questions about value, meaning, and significance in the design and implementation of research in all areas and policy issues.

Davidson is John Hope Franklin Institute Professor of Interdisciplinary Studies and the first vice provost for Interdisciplinary Studies in the nation, if not ever. John Hope Franklin was an eminent African American historian with a long record of research in African American and US American history, as well as a leader in the struggle for civil rights and social justice in the United States. So, Davidson and, as I will show, Goldberg as well are not only humanities scholars, but also intellectuals whose vision is shaped by foundational literature and figures in ethnic studies. I dedicated the first week of the course to discussing Davidson's and Goldberg's "Manifesto," reading it with the lenses of the traditional humanities and assessing it from the angle of ethnic studies scholarship. I'll try to give you a taste of this now, but be mindful that it takes several hundred pages and long hours of lecturing to take students to a level in which they are able to understand the different layers of the arguments just quickly outlined here.

It is quite significant that Duke, a southern university, decided to link its agenda for interdisciplinary studies in the academy with the work of an African American scholar. This agenda became solidified with the creation of the John Hope Franklin Center for Interdisciplinary Studies and the John Hope Franklin Humanities Institute at Duke, both of which were cofounded by Cathy Davidson and African Americanist Karla Holloway. In my view, the John Hope Franklin Center for Interdisciplinary and International Studies and the Humanities Institute are places originally conceived to do interdisciplinary, international, and humanities work "in color," by which I mean, not just for African Americans and people of color, but oriented by imperatives of social justice, fully aware of the significance of dehumanization and race for the very constitution of modern society and scholarship, and inspired by horizons of possibility that envision the emergence of a decolonized humanity. Isn't something like this what also inspires the Kantian-Humboldtian liberal arts and the sciences that are at the core of the modern Western university? Well, not exactly. The John Hope Franklin Humanities Institute takes its point of departure from elsewhere (the US south and the underside of modernity rather than just the European Enlightenment and its characteristics ideas of nature, society, and reason), even as it is also inscribed in the modern Western research university. But let me turn now to the co-author of the "Manifesto," David Theo Goldberg.

David Theo Goldberg is director of the Systemwide University of California Humanities Research Institute at UC Irvine. Davidson and Goldberg are, indeed, conscious of the relevance of their positions as directors of humanities institutes, and they wrote their "Manifesto," "as scholars with experience as directors of two interdisciplinary humanities institutes—one on the West Coast and one on the East Coast, one at a public university system and one at a private university."[8] But they share more than they willingly admit in the essay, as Goldberg, just like Davidson, has a record of commitment with a scholarly vision grounded on attending to social justice issues and anti-racist work. To be sure, we all know that Goldberg is one of the foremost theoreticians of race and racism, and one strongly committed to an anti-racist vision, to showing the conceptual viability of the concept of race, and to the rejection of color-blind racism, which is the dominant form of racism today. Less known is that before being the director of the UC Humanities Research Institute, he directed the School for Social Justice, known today as the School for Social Transformation at Arizona State University. I am going to take a moment to at least mention some features of that School because, just like Duke University's John Hope Franklin Institute, it represents a place where the humanities and the social sciences are being reconfigured, rather than simply revalued, in a direction that can ultimately make what we call "the humanities" more productive and relevant.

The School for Social Transformation is driven by the tasks of revealing "intersecting forms of injustice based on race, gender, class, sexual orientation and legal status, among other factors," engaging "multiple visions of justice," and transformation, by which they mean using "multidisciplinary social inquiry" to allow scholars and community leaders to translate lessons learned during one historical moment or location to solutions appropriate for emerging social justice concerns."[9] The goals and principles of the School for Social Transformation seem to be in line with other contemporary efforts such as Boaventura de Sousa Santos' proposal for a Popular University of Social Movements.[10] Santos is arguably the foremost theoretician of the World Social Forum, and a strongly respected intellectual and scholar-activist in parts of Africa, Asia, and Latin America. He has written amply about the crisis of the university since at least the 1990s, if not before. And in addition to developing a proposal for a Popular University of Social Movements, he argues that research universities can become sources of "counter-hegemonic global-ization-as-public-good," but this entails for him a radical transformation from fixation on northern epistemologies to openness to southern episte-mologies, from university to pluriversity knowledge, and, from speaking about the liberal arts and their value to focusing one's reflection on global social and cognitive justice.[11]

At stake in Santos' reflections is a critical intervention in the conceptu-alization of the university, and a shift away from the monopoly that the liberal arts have had at the time of articulating the relevance and princi-ples of education, even as they are being challenged by corporate criteria. The shift in question complicates debates on the dominant principles and oppositions between fact and meaning, prediction and interpretation, and explanation and understanding. Here we see, rather, an emphasis on emancipation and social transformation that invites us to formally intro-duce concepts such as emancipation and decolonization in our discussion about education, well beyond the limits imposed by the traditional sci-ences and the humanities with their typical insistence on explanation and understanding. This is part of what I want to put on the table for discus-sion here, and part also of the fundamental claims of the "Decolonizing the University" conference, which took place in the spring of 2010 at UC Berkeley and celebrated the forty years of ethnic studies on that cam-pus.[12]

CONSERVATIVE AND LIBERAL RESPONSES

It is not difficult to imagine how conservative and liberal quarters react when faced with these possibilities, concepts, and frameworks. From the conservative side, in 2006 David Horowitz wrote a series on "Indoctrina-tion," the third installation of which targeted the School of Justice and Social Inquiry at Arizona State University. He wrote that the school "is not a department whose course of study is devoted to legal concepts of justice or discussions of the same. Quite the contrary. The department's self-description makes it clear that the agenda is specifically designed to introduce students to the concepts of 'economic justice' and 'social jus-tice,' which are ideological terms associated with the political left. The department's self-description specifically (and deceptively) claims that its approach is empirical and objective."[13]

It is instructive that the first piece in Horowitz's "Indoctrination" se-ries is dedicated to the University of Colorado at Boulder and that it begins by making reference to its Ethnic Studies Department's former chairperson Ward Churchill.[14] Ethnic studies, to be sure, is typically first in line when it comes to conservative attacks, even as it has sometimes been forced to survive only in the form of primarily social scientific studies about race and ethnicity, or as a companion to area studies, which are arguably reductionist conceptions of the field. I would argue, instead, that what we have come to call ethnic studies is one of the most important interventions in academic settings and that it challenges the division of knowledge based on the primacy of explanation and understanding and the European and US American-oriented humanities and sciences. That is, ethnic studies is yet another example of an intellectual and scholarly space that challenges the humanities and aims to make humanities' work simultaneously more rigorous and relevant. To be sure, those committed with the liberal arts curriculum and division of knowledge tend to see ethnic studies as an undesirable field whose relation to social movements make it suspect; as an unsophisticated scholarly space that is haunted and fundamentally limited by feelings of nostalgia, cultural nationalism, or ethnic essentialism; or, at best, as a temporary space to be either maintained at a minimum, phased out, or folded into discipline-based departments and the standard divisions between the humanities, the social sciences, and other areas.

The difference between the two realities is to some extent captured in a piece by Stanley Fish entitled "The Crisis of the Humanities Officially Arrives" when compared with Roberto Rodríguez's column "Arizona: This Is What Apartheid Looks Like."[15] The first article addresses the proposed elimination of French, Italian, Classics, Russian, and theatre programs from the State University of New York at Albany and calls for political action in defense of the liberal arts. The second focuses on laws SB 1070 and HB 2281, and calls attention to a social reality of apartheid that affects bodies as well as knowledges and cultures. The issues are quite different: the crisis of the liberal arts vis-à-vis the near-criminalization of certain forms of knowledge with HB 2281. And, yet, one must reflect on how these two realities relate to each other. While ethnic studies disturb and challenge the existing division of knowledge and conceptions of the humanities in the university, they appear even more as a threat to other forms of hegemony out of the university. There is no better evidence of this today than the passing of state law HB 2281 in Arizona, which bans Raza studies from Arizona's public schools classrooms. This law is a companion to another piece of legislation, SB 1070, which allows police to interrogate suspects about their citizen status on the basis of "reasonable suspicion." While humanists complain about the lack of recognition of the value of their fields, and their evaluation according to metrics that belong to the corporate sector and that seek efficiency rather than understanding, Raza and ethnic studies scholars face not only the menace of neoliberalism, but also persecution and illegality. That is, while the humanities are facing the pressure of neoliberalism, ethnic studies is facing the pressure of both neoliberalism and neoapartheid in context where the people and their memories, knowledges, questions, and perspectives are rendered illegal.

From the perspective of a number of humanists, the relation is clear and prioritizes the crisis of the humanities even as it shows concerns for apartheid: one must demonstrate how the humanities are important for the education of ethno-racialized populations, particularly those that are growing demographically. The argument claims that these populations deserve the humanities, and that the humanities deserve support from the state in compensation for their function of enlightening the population. The implicit view here is that it is better for the state and for ethno-racialized populations to value and support the humanities, since they can pay a role in better prepare people for life in the nation and, doing this, they help reduce the apparent need for apartheid. This argument, though, is not much different from liberal views that propose unidirectional assimilation in response to the more conservative ones that tend to justify apartheid. But unidirectional assimilation and its demoralizing and marginalizing effects are precisely what Raza studies classes in Arizona high schools are combating.

If youth of color and other sectors who have been crucial to the creation of ethnic studies and related units in the university thought that investment in the humanities was what would have best responded to their needs, they would have sought direct support for them. Rather, they found a situation where "Arts and Sciences" have been understood for the most part as "White Arts and Sciences," and where the divisions of knowledge within the university, and between knowledge and praxis, are not up to the task of responding to their questions and their concerns. Prioritizing the defense of the humanities in a context of rising apartheid and the near criminalization of academic spaces focused on reflecting on people of color's ideas, questions, and concerns is another form of erasure and subalternization. A better response to the challenges of the time would be for the humanities to take more seriously the questions and critical insights from decolonial and emancipatory epistemological formations, such as ethnic studies, Raza studies, and other projects, and thereby seek to respond to the questions of value and relevance that they face today, even if this means fundamental changes in the humanities themselves. But crises often strengthen the urge for self-preservation, which can lead to ignoring other realities even if those realities are far more dangerous. If responding to the challenge posed by neoliberalism is difficult, it is even more difficult for the humanities to increase their scope and challenge that very limited understanding of the crisis that we face, while seeking to strengthen their ties with the multi- and transdisciplinary epistemological projects that are most closely related to those who are the objects of neoapartheid.

Now, there are other ways to understand the relation between the crisis of the humanities and the emergence of neoapartheid. One interesting consideration that ties these two realities together is that the humanities are facing in the current context the kind of questioning that communities of color have usually faced: they do not produce value and must constantly attempt to prove their right to exist and receive support from the state, and they are ultimately dispensable. Neoliberalism thus seems to be informed by the logic of racism. And as the humanities suffer the brunt of racial logic, people of color and the forms of knowledge most relevant to them become not merely unproductive, but outright dangerous. Through this process the university becomes more and more "white," that is, it keeps certain bodies and knowledges away, or in minimum form, while hastening the incorporation of corporate values and racial logic into the very perception and evaluation of the remaining fields.

The temptation for the humanities would be to show that they are the depositories of a better form of whiteness (without ever calling it that, or recognizing it as such) than the one that is now putting the humanities at the level of "unproductive" people of color. The international financial crisis represents, among other things, a crisis of Western hegemony and a limit to the expectations of certain groups of people precisely at moments of increased migratory flows from the South to the North and significant demographic changes in countries such as the United States. It would be a fundamental mistake to critically evaluate the attack on the university today, and the position that the humanities face, only in relation to economics or neoliberalism. Race, racism, and neoapartheid are equally important considerations, as well as the legacies of colonialism, slavery, and hetero-patriarchy, and all these must be looked at in interconnected ways. Doing so is part of the very analytic framework that ethnic studies and related fields often follow. As a result, and contrary to the desire of self-preservation, it seems to me that what the humanities can better do is to expand their analytic vision well beyond the opposition between liberal education as public good and neoliberalism, recognize the racial logic operating in the context of increasing apartheid, and take emancipatory and decolonial epistemological projects more seriously, even to the point of considering a transition from the emphasis on liberal arts training to the cultivation of emancipatory and decolonial acting and thinking.

As I noted previously, it is not only conservatism and neoliberalism that seek to undermine ethnic studies and projects such as the School of Social Transformation at Arizona State. It is also liberalism. Liberals typically defend the humanities and, of course, the liberal arts in face of neoliberalism and conservatism, while at best tolerate areas like ethnic studies and seek to keep them at their very minimal level of expression. I'll give a few succinct examples, drawn in part from the UC Berkeley campus, with which I am most familiar:

- The path from the third world strike and the demand of a third world college to the creation of an ethnic studies department with "ethnic" programs under the division of the social sciences.
- The path from the demand of an ethnic studies requirement on campus to the establishment of an American cultures requirement. Note the path here in designations, which go from "third world" to "ethnic" to "American"; and the transition from a demand for a College with departments to the reality of a department with various "ethnic" programs within the School of Social Sciences. A contestatory nomenclature is converted into an ethno-national project within the established division of knowledge in the university.
- The path from projects for empowerment by faculty and students in ethnic studies programs, on the one hand, and universities' interest in "civic engagement" and "university community partnerships," on the other, after massive disinvestment from the former and with the expectation that the former would fold into the latter.
- The path is from desegregation and decolonization of society and knowledge, to initiatives for equity and diversity, as in the Berkeley Diversity Research Initiative, and other such initiatives in the country. Diversity is a concept that can have some usefulness in post-affirmative action California, but it must be properly situated alongside other less ambiguous concepts and within an emancipatory and decolonial rather than a liberal framework. Consider that David Horowitz's campaign prides itself for trying to bring diversity to university campuses. To be sure, the diversity that concerns him is the presence of conservatives and conservative ideas in the liberal arts. It is also instructive that the academic standards that Horowitz explicitly adopts "to measure what is an appropriate curriculum is provided in a classic statement by the longtime president of the University of California, Berkeley, Robert Gordon Sproul, who defends the freedom of the university and the "right to prevent exploitation of its prestige by unqualified persons or by those who would use it as a platform for propaganda." [16] This is, I submit, the way in which ethnic studies is usually considered in the academy: at most, they are good for diversity (understood in a liberal form) and good enough for them to be able to exist within the humanities or the social sciences, but not good enough to lead agendas for wider transformation.

Coming back to Davidson and Goldberg, I submit that their eloquent defense of the humanities as well as their commitments and work are testimony to the power of ethnic studies and related fields. Their "Manifesto" can be seen in part as a Trojan horse of sorts, which consists of reconceptualizing the humanities and putting them more in line with areas such as ethnic studies while defending them. The defense is clearly necessary, particularly as their main target is humanities scholars and, particularly, administrators who make decisions about funding and support for the humanities. I often wonder, though, how they would have written their "Manifesto" with another audience in mind. What if they wrote it directly to those who inspired their work—for example, John Hope Franklin and other, numerous anti-racist authors? I wonder whether they would have gone beyond a defense of the humanities and a description of ethnic studies as a field within them, and whether they would have sided with Johnella Butler, who proposes that we see ethnic studies along with gender and women's studies and other emancipatory fields as matrixes for changing the humanities and the social sciences.[17]

I myself take Butler's path, and join Boaventura de Sousa Santos, who distills important epistemological and socially transformative principles from the World Social Forum and similar projects. But joining these efforts would have sent the message that administrators, and directors of humanities institutes should not just be looking at each other and to how the humanities work in the Ivy League or prestigious research universities. They would have sent the message that sometimes the best keys for transformation come from what has been systematically excluded, and from spaces that remain in the margins or altogether outside the university. Ironically perhaps, if humanities scholar leaders took this turn they might increase their chances of getting more support by socially conscious foundations, as well as by the growing number of legislators of color in different states.

I would like to conclude by stating that rethinking the university through the careful consideration of neoapartheid and "racial neoliberalism" instead of solely in reference to neoliberalism *simpliciter*, conservatism, or capitalism—along with serious consideration of the epistemological principles in ethnic studies and related projects, has the potential of both addressing the most fundamental problems of the age and gaining the hearts and minds of the neocolonized and segregated populations who make up the majority of people in the world and are expected to become the majority in California (between 2030 and 2040) and in the United States (in the second half of this century).[18] And if the public university in California and the United States makes itself relevant to those who become the majorities in the state and the nation, maybe that very public will support it.

I believe that at least some public universities are becoming aware of this, but they are responding to the challenges through the same liberal logic that they have always tended to use, being unable to challenge the roots of the problems that we observe. Perhaps it is time to seriously engage other approaches, particularly those that the segregated populations themselves have often produced and strongly supported, even if that means that we have to dramatically change the university and reconceptualize the organization of the humanities, the social sciences, and the university as a whole. The humanities are welcome to join and support this so far primarily "southern" conversation (counting ethnic studies as a southern epistemological space within a northern setting), and maybe, in that way, maintain, and even radicalize, what is best about them in opposition to neoapartheid and in favor of a more fully decolonized world.

NOTES

1. This piece is originally published in *Human Architecture: Journal of the Sociology of Self- Knowledge,* 10(1), (2012): 91–100. Reprinted with kind permission of the editor. Also for explorations of racial neoliberalism and global coloniality see Goldberg (2008) and Grosfoguel (2002), respectively.

2. See Roberto Cintli Rodríguez, "Arizona: This is What Apartheid Looks Like," *Truthout*, April 28, 2010. Accessed: October 19, 2010. www.truth-out.org/roberto-cintli-rodriguez-arizona-this-is-what-apartheid-looks-like58955.

3. See Boaventura de Sousa Santos, "The University in the Twenty First Century: Towards a Democratic and Emancipatory University Reform," *Eurozine* July 1, 2010. Accessed January 22, 2010. www.eurozine.com/articles/2010-07-01-santos-en.html.

4. See Johnnella Butler, "Ethnic Studies as a Matrix for the Humanities, the Social Sciences, and the Common Good," in *Color-Line to Borderlands: The Matrix of American Ethnic Studies,* (Seattle: University of Washington Press, 2001), 18–41.

5. See Peter Schmidt, "Educational Difficulties of Men and Immigrants Hinder Efforts to Improve College Attainment," in *Chronicle of Higher Education*, October 20, 2010. Accessed January 22, 2010. chronicle.com/article/Educational-Difficulties-of/125015.

6. See Boaventura de Sousa Santos, "The Popular University of Social Movements: To Educate Activists and Leaders of Social Movements, as Well as Social Scientists, Scholars and Artists Concerned with Progressive Social Transformation," Accessed on January 22, 2010. www.ces.uc.pt/universidadepopular/Popular%20University%20 of%20the%20Social%20Movements.pdf Also see Boaventura de Sousa Santos, "The University in the Twenty First Century: Towards a Democratic and Emancipatory University Reform," *Eurozine* July 1, 2010. Accessed January 22, 2010. /www.eurozine. com/articles/2010-07-01-santos-en.html.

7. See Cathy Davidson and David Theo Goldberg, "A Manifesto for the Humanities in a Technological Age," in *The Chronicle of Higher Education*, 50 no. 23 (2004): B7.

8. See Cathy Davidson and David Theo Goldberg, "A Manifesto for the Humanities in a Technological Age," in *The Chronicle of Higher Education*, 50 no. 23 (2004): B7.

9. See justice.clas.asu.edu/about accessed January 22, 2011.

10. See Boaventura de Sousa Santos, "The Popular University of Social Movements: To Educate Activists and Leaders of Social Movements, as Well as Social Scientists, Scholars and Artists Concerned with Progressive Social Transformation," (2003) Accessed on January 22, 2010. www.ces.uc.pt/universidadepopular/Popular%20 University%20of%20the%20Social%20Movements.pdf.

11. See Boaventura de Sousa Santos, "The University in the Twenty First Century: Towards a Democratic and Emancipatory University Reform," *Eurozine* July 1, 2010. Accessed January 22, 2010. www.eurozine.com/articles/2010-07-01-santos-en.html.

12. See vimeo.com/15729523.

13. See David Horowitz, "Indoctrination in One Department at Arizona State—Third in a Series," (2006a) Accessed January 22, 2010. www.discoverthenetworks.org/Articles/indoctatarizonastatedhorowitz.html.

14. See David Horowitz, "Indoctrination U: Colorado," (2006b) Accessed January 22, 2010. www.discoverthenetworks.org/Articles/indoctudh.html.

15. See Stanley Fish, "The Crisis of the Humanities Officially Arrives," *The New York Times*, October 11, 2010. Accessed October 19, 2010. opinionator.blogs.nytimes.com/2010/10/11/the-crisis-of-the-humanities-officially-arrives/?pagemode=print. Also see Rodríguez, Roberto Cintli. 2010. "Arizona: This is What Apartheid Looks Like" *Truthout*, April 28. Accessed: October 19, 2010. www.truth-out.org/roberto-cintli-rodriguez-arizona-this-is-what-apartheid-looks-like58955.

16. See David Horowitz, "Indoctrination U: Colorado," (2006b) Accessed January 22, 2010. www.discoverthenetworks.org/Articles/indoctudh.html.

17. See Johnnella Butler, "Ethnic Studies as a Matrix for the Humanities, the Social Sciences, and the Common Good," in *Color-Line to Borderlands: The Matrix of American Ethnic Studies* (Seattle: University of Washington Press, 2001), 18–41.

18. See David Theo Goldberg, *The Threat of Race: Reflections on Racial Neoliberalism* (Malden: Wiley-Blackwell, 2008).

BIBLIOGRAPHY

Butler, Johnnella. "Ethnic Studies as a Matrix for the Humanities, the Social Sciences, and the Common Good." In *Color-Line to Borderlands: The Matrix of American Ethnic Studies*, edited by Johnnella Butler, 18–41. Seattle: University of Washington Press, 2001.

Davidson, Cathy and David Theo Goldberg. "A Manifesto for the Humanities in a Technological Age." In *The Chronicle of Higher Education*, 50 no. 23(2004): B7.

Fish, Stanley. "The Crisis of the Humanities Officially Arrives" *The New York Times*, October 11, 2010. Accessed October 19, 2010. opinionator.blogs.nytimes.com/2010/10/11/the-crisis-of-the-humanities-officially-arrives/?pagemode=print.

Goldberg, David Theo. *The Threat of Race: Reflections on Racial Neoliberalism*. Malden: Wiley-Blackwell, 2008.

Grosfoguel, Ramón. "Colonial Difference, Geopolitics of Knowledge, and Global Coloniality in the Modern/Colonial World-System." *Review* 25 no. 3(2002): 203–24.

Horowitz, David. "Indoctrination in One Department at Arizona State--Third in a Series." (2006) Accessed January 22, 2010. www.discoverthenetworks.org/Articles/indoctatarizonastatedhorowitz.html.

———. "Indoctrination U: Colorado."(2006) Accessed January 22, 2010. www.discoverthenetworks.org/Articles/indoctudh.html.

Rodríguez, Roberto Cintli. "Arizona: This Is What Apartheid Looks Like." *Truthout*, April 28. 2010. Accessed: October 19, 2010. www.truth-out.org/roberto-cintli-rodriguez-arizona this-is-what-apartheid-looks-like58955.

de Sousa Santos, Boaventura. "The Popular University of Social Movements: To Educate Activists and Leaders of Social Movements, as Well as Social Scientists, Scholars and Artists Concerned with Progressive Social Transformation." (2003) Accessed on January 22, 2010. www.ces.uc.pt/universidadepopular/Popular%20University%20of%20the%20Social%20Movements.pdf.

———. "The University in the Twenty First Century: Towards a Democratic and Emancipatory University Reform." *Eurozine* July 1, 2010. Accessed January 22, 2010. www.eurozine.com/articles/2010-07-01-santos-en.html.

Schmidt, Peter. "Educational Difficulties of Men and Immigrants Hinder Efforts to Improve College Attainment." In *Chronicle of Higher Education*, October 2010. Accessed January 22, 2010. chronicle.com/article/Educational-Difficulties-of/125015/.

FIVE

Dropouts as Delinkers from the Modern/Colonial World System

Ernesto Rosen Velásquez

When thinking about education statistics, not so much in terms of their use as evidence to support a general claim about a group of people but in terms of the interpretation, a complication emerges. Sometimes evaluative interpretations of a statistic can be mystifying when it is common parlance to cast a problem based on statistical evidence. Our understanding of statistical trends can lead to misrepresentations of the education crisis, when from one perspective, some data is seen as a sign of vitality, while from another standpoint the same data is often quickly perceived as an indicator of decadence. Consider the following statistics on Latina/o enrollment rates from the Pew Research Center:

> A record seven-in-ten (69%) Hispanic high school graduates in the class of 2012 enrolled in college that fall, two percentage points higher than the rate (67%) among their white counterparts, according to a Pew Research Center analysis of new data from the US Census Bureau. This milestone is the result of a long-term increase in Hispanic college-going that accelerated with the onset of the recession in 2008.[1] The rate among white high school graduates, by contrast, has declined slightly since 2008. The *positive* trends in Hispanic educational indicators also extend to high school. The most recent available data show that in 2011 only 14% of Hispanic 16- to 24-year-olds were high school dropouts, half the level in 2000 (28%). Starting from a much lower base, the high school dropout rate among whites also declined during that period (from 7% in 2000 to 5% in 2011), but did not fall by as much [italics mine].[2]

Let's put aside theories that attempt to partially explain these numbers. Let's not be concerned with sample size, the identities of those referred to by the data, or whether the best label is "Latina/o or Hispanics." Instead, let's consider the evaluative status of the trends that high school dropout rates among Hispanics are declining while they increasingly are enrolling in college at higher rates than their white counterparts. These facts are identified as positive trends. Even though the research data does not say why these trends are identified as such—it is taken for granted—the question emerges: why are these trends interpreted in this way? There are many reasons. The ones mentioned are not intended to be exhaustive but to be explicitly put on the table. Each of these reasons has complications. I do not intend to argue against these grounds for interpreting the trend as positive; however, I wish to show some of the conceptual constellations informing why the trends may be interpreted as positive. I raise ambiguities that begin to open up a conceptual space for another way of interpreting certain statistics that are raised in education discourses about minorities and also reframes the way the stay-in-school/dropout binary gets taken up in the US context. Let's focus solely on increased enrollment in college.

First, we seem to think Latina/o students should complete high school and enroll in college because there is evidence that students believe it is important. In a 2009 Pew Research Center survey, 88 percent of Latinos of ages sixteen and up agreed that a college degree is necessary to get ahead in gaining economic benefits—attaining salaried positions with health care benefits and greater independence in the better-rewarded sectors of the organized US economy. Upward economic mobility also can entail accruing social benefits—prestige, epistemic credibility, efficient access to goods, services, housing, and spaces of leisure. Latinas/os who educate themselves by enrolling in college and lift themselves out of poverty can function as role models for other minorities, showing they also can make it if they work hard. At a social symbolic level, this supports the idea that the basic structure of society is just, and if others drop out or don't make it, then it is their fault. But just because going to a university is construed as a means of upward socioeconomic mobility, it does not necessarily imply the students want to go to school, the basic structure of society is fair or that higher enrollments in universities indicate a positive trend independent of preparing to attain higher paying positions in the labor market. Students want to get ahead, and it seems attending a university and obtaining a degree is a primary means to accomplish this goal. The idea of getting ahead is fueled by views of staying behind; students do not want to face situations where the only viable occupations are in the black market or underground economies. Whether or not universities generally achieve the goal of preparing students to acquire the knowledge and skills they need to attain better-rewarded positions within a sector of the organized economy is not my concern. Interestingly, student expressions of interest are made without exploring or critically question-ing what it might mean to get ahead. If getting ahead is about securing a salaried position with health care benefits, is this a worthwhile pursuit? Should higher education try to prepare students to enter higher-wage sectors of the labor market so they can be integrated into the organized sectors of the global economy in ways that enable them to not only live within the modern/colonial world system but also to sustain it? We should not assume this should be the aim of higher education. Instead we should critically evaluate it and uncover the reasons behind it.

Second, the US federal government echoes the Latina/o students proc-lamation when it announced its desire to compete in the world market in science, technology, engineering, and math (STEM). One strategy to achieve this nation building goal is increased minority interest and en-rollment in STEM programs. By being competitive in the world market, US minorities can help secure the economic well-being of the nation's future. The worry here is the uncritical acceptance that the primary goal of education should be to secure the economic well-being of the nation's future. The state and the Latina/o students provide a link between knowl-edge, power, and capital. Furthermore, Western European epistemology is the main vehicle toward reaching this financial goal: other epistemolo-gies, if extracted from other locations and integrated into the corporate westernized university, will be used in the service of that fundamental economic objective. Therefore, the ambition to strive for the commodifi-cation of all knowledge production is present. The students want to learn mainly because it is a means to acquire a salaried position and univer-sities have experts that disseminate knowledge to meet these students' demands. There is no immediate problem with students getting jobs, especially for those who are raised in a condition of scarcity while the dominant society is overly materialist and judges one's self-worth finan-cially or in terms of the number of possessions. The challenge is the uncritical acceptance of the link between knowledge, power, and capital. How can knowledge be disentangled from power and capital?

Third, lower dropout rates can indicate less dependency on social welfare and prison programs due to teen pregnancies, juvenile delin-quency, and incarceration rates from zero-tolerance policies. The dog-whistle politics that frets over higher dropout rates uses non-racial lan-guage at a surface level to appear beyond race, yet invokes all sorts of racial associations, ranging from the black welfare queen and the black urban ghetto criminal thug to the brown, undocumented, illegal immi-grant.[3] Therefore, the concept of the dropout is one, highly charged, neg-ative concept within a constellation of other stigmas tethered to racialized minority identities. When coupled with the federal government's pro-nouncements, two minority identity formation processes can be iden-tified: criminalization/welfare dependency and assimilation. With forced, unidirectional, upward assimilation identity change for minorities can occur in such a way that various dimensions of one's social identity—race, ethnicity, sex, gender, class—are either diminished so they become indistinguishable from their white, heterosexual, middle-class American counterparts that function as mediators between the West and the rest or they enter the labor market as ethnoracial ornaments in situations where there is a tendency toward inoculation of difference whereby individuals protect themselves from spaces of alterity and are able to consume small doses of difference; to enjoy and tolerate but only to a level that does not puncture the inoculated one's sense of self.

Fourth, low dropout rates can suggest schools perhaps are doing something right; they are actually meeting the primary aims of education expressed by students and the federal government. Additionally, they are getting ahead economically, as the nation takes steps toward greater wealth. Maybe student's education needs in STEM are being met. Maybe STEM programs provide students the proper attention and respect they deserve. Maybe there are lesser amounts of overcrowded classrooms with non-effective teachers, less trauma, and less chance of falling behind in their work. The statistics may indicate Latina/o families are stable since they support the value of higher education and make them fit as a new model minority like some white ethnic groups. The concern is the uncritical acceptance of what it means for schools to be doing something right. Let me offer some reflections that complicate matters by considering some indigenous universities in Latin America.[4]

NONAUTONOMOUS INDIGENOUS UNIVERSITIES

Anders Burman makes a distinction between two kinds of indigenous universities: non-autonomous and autonomous.[5] He focuses on the heterogeneity of the former by thinking through the following question: what constitutes the indigeneity of an indigenous university? He addresses this by reflecting on the state controlled universities in Bolivia, such as la Universidad Indígena Boliviana Aymara "Tupak Katari" (UNIBOL "TK") and la Universidad Indígena Tawantinsuyu (UTA). While these universities may have some combination of either indigenous faculty, students, or knowledge production and practices based on other epistemic and ontological premises, the indigeneity of these universities is not reduced to any one of these features. Institutional self-identification, that challenges dominant academia and creates universities for another society is fundamental for Burman. This two-pronged institutional self-identification paradigm finds expression in its answer to the perennial question posed in Western European philosophy of education: what should be the goals of education?

The Bolivian Ministry of Education answer: to be decolonizing. To have the language of decolonization at the state level, in the constitution and in other government documents is no small feat. There is a long, complex, bloody history of struggle leading up to the rise of indigenous movements stepping onto the world stage after the collapse of the Soviet Union which I do not go into because of this paper's focus. Instead, while recognizing the significance of the discourse of decolonization in Bolivian jurisprudence, it bears noting that, according to Burman, there are two broad senses of decolonization set up in this context: one externally to an international audience and one internally in Bolivian state politics and government discourse. The former understands decolonization involves a challenge to Eurocentric paradigms of development and knowledge production, as well as a serious turn toward indigenous knowledge, social, and economic practices. The latter is decolonization as national sovereignty based on infrastructural modernization, technological progress, and natural resource extraction. These two senses of decolonization frame the debates in Bolivian higher education in such a way that pose at least six challenges to the various kinds of indigenous universities in Bolivia; this begins with the less indigenous universities and then proceeds along a continuum to the predominately more indigenous ones.

First, some universities take decolonizing education goals to mean giving all people equal access to a high-quality university education without discrimination. These indigenous, nonautonomous universities are indigenous related to just student composition. They provide vocational-tech offerings to Indians that reinforce racist stereotypes of them as naturally fit for manual labor and not thought, theory, or philosophy. This also reproduces the epistemological structure of the westernized university and is more cosmetic—a kind of Benetton model of diversity where faces are different but the thought and knowledge production is the same. This is hardly a decolonizing education goal in the sense that takes seriously the value of substantial epistemic diversity.

Second, with the less and predominately more indigenous universities, there is state involvement in micromanaging the labor force. When serious attempts are made to challenge the Eurocentric paradigm, the state ends up colonizing the objectives of some thick indigenous universities by its insisting to have them produce engineers, nuclear physicists, oil prospectors, and other experts resulting from STEM fields. This keeps the epistemic hierarchy intact by making indigenous knowledge a diversity add-on that one could learn on the side while mastering the real knowledge emerging from the Western European sciences. It also reproduces an expert certificate system of professionals that tracks graduates to meet the needs of the labor market and does so in a way that reproduces discrimination in the job market: the knowledgeable experts with degree and the less-knowledgeable nonexperts without degrees. Are degrees necessary?

Third, some of the thicker indigenous universities are caught in a performative contradiction. On the one hand, these centers of learning are working to challenge and transform extractivist economies that not only perform a kind of epistemic violence on indigenous cosmovisions but produce rural poverty and the physical destruction of everything that has life. On the other hand, these universities depend on the state for revenues resulting from these extractivist policies, a kind of extractivism as a means for social transformation. The special tax on natural gas collected in Bolivia is what funds UNIBOL and other universities. Could there be other nonextractivist ways of decolonizing education and the state? Why turn to the state when it is linked to extractivist policies and practices?

Fourth, some nonautonomous indigenous universities such as the Indigenous Intercultural Univeristy Amwatay (UIAW) of Ecuador had their accreditation withdrawn by the state when they were reviewed in 2009.[6] This is because while these universities are thickly indigenous, the accreditation criteria are still colonial. Therefore, these institutions are delegitimized in society in a way that implements an epistemic disauthorization of their institutional self-identification as universities. This can produce a disjuncture between these indigenous universities' self-understandings and the way they are perceived in the wider society. The lack of institutional backing in the wider society in the face of their self-identification as indigenous universities produces activity without agency.[7] This challenge has been defused somewhat because, in 2012, the Higher Education Council of Ecuador announced that the re-accreditation of UIAW would incorporate intercultural criteria and considerations. However, it is not clear what these criteria are and how satisfying the accreditation will be determined. And even if these questions are answered sufficiently, the question remains, why seek validation from the state? If it is partly to lend legitimacy to the degrees granted by those universities, the problem of the certificate system still remains. Furthermore, does agency require institutional backing of the state? Could there be other forms of agency, that is, institutional backing beyond the state?

Fifth, with thicker indigenous universities, there is the concern over the way indigenous knowledge is used. It is not only the state that thwarts certain decolonizing objectives but corporate indigenous universities themselves run the risk of using indigenous knowledge production in an extractivist way. When indigenous lifeworlds and pedagogical practices are institutionalized they run the risk of being use by pharmaceutical companies, and health and food industries in ways that take a cosmovision—with its intermeshed ethical-spiritual-epistemological, political, ontological dimensions—and compartmentalize this knowledge into information packages separate from their ethical-spiritual orientations, epistemological methods and geo-historical context. This situation results in no substantive procedural change in education. This is a limitation of indigenous, nonautonomous universities that take decolonizing education objectives to incorporate indigenous knowledge and faculty, resulting in the transformation of syllabi.

Sixth, some of the thicker indigenous universities are librocentric. The concern here is when critical epistemologies are taught, the nonindigenous faculty who teach them tend to assume citational practices which prioritize knowledge learned from books over knowledge gained from relational experiences with other human beings or other non-human knowledge-producing subjects. Birds, mountains, rivers, landscapes, and all other forms of life are not taken as knowledge bearers. For instance, Burman notes how the Aymara students in University of La Paz have trouble understanding why a professor who speaks Spanish and not Aymara will lecture about someone like Karl Marx, who died several hundred years ago, and talk about him as if he knew him.[8] Without knowing Aymara data source tracking, the students perceive the teacher with suspicion and confusion because in Aymara epistemology, personal, experiential knowledge is given priority, vis-à-vis, knowledge acquired through books and knowledge acquired from nonpersonal sources. The faculty pedagogy ends up recycling the same colonial epistemological asymmetries of knowledge transmission and consumption procedures as found in the westernized university.

These are six related limits involving racism, micromanagement, performative contradiction, accreditation, extractivism, and librocentrism. Is there a way indigenous universities can avoid these limits? To explain other ways of navigating these challenges, I want to build on Burman's distinction between indigenous nonautonomous universities and indigenous autonomous universities by investigating the conceptual contours of the latter in light of la Universidad de la Tierra also known as Centro Indígena de Capacitación Integral (CIDECI) in San Cristobal de Las Casas, Chiapas, Mexico. Through this investigation, we can get a sense of what decolonizing education goals mean in another locale and identify some of the distinct challenges this type of indigenous university might face. What is autonomous about this type of indigenous university?

UNIVERSIDAD DE LA TIERRA:
AN AUTONOMOUS INDIGENOUS UNIVERSITY

As I opened the large metal door to the Universidad de la Tierra entrance, I heard my feet crunch the soil as I took my first step on the other side. Some things you experience in this space: sheep grazing in the grass, classrooms, the smell of sweet rolls, rabbits, hand-carved seminar tables and chairs with an indigenous flair, vegetable and spice gardens, libraries, clay ovens, Mayan students playing basketball in the warm sun, the dean with a tank top and hedge clippers trimming the plants that are growing in various directions, a collage of Malcom X, Vandana Shiva,

Ghandi, Steve Biko, Subcommandante Marcos, Martin Luther King, Romero, Frantz Fanon, and other intellectual activists from all over the world.

Being immersed in this environment affects you. The semiotics of the space disrupt the barrage of images groups of upper-middle-class white American parents and their children might experience on their typical campus tour: expensive recreational facilities, parking lots, libraries, labs, dining options, bas reliefs of Plato, Aristotle, and St. Thomas Aquinas interspersed with a token woman or black thinker. When you walk into CIDECI, you are stepping into another world. This is a university without deans, professors, tenure-track processes, undergraduate or graduate programs, dining halls, classrooms, or electricity. There is a sense we lack the sufficient vocabulary to describe accurately and best capture the processes unfolding in this learning space. It is not accredited by the state or any of its apparatuses, nor is anything a commodity in this space. Its philosophy of education is fueled, in part, by a backward gaze to understand when this historic, modern/colonial world system was established. It is firmly planted in Mesoamerican histories, Spanish and Mayan languages — Tzotzil, Tzeltal, Chol, and Tojolabal — and the colonial histories of oppression and resistance. Its gaze also turns to the present and future enlightened by an ethical horizon, which includes a negative ethics that is anti-capitalist, anti-Eurocentric, anti-imperialist, anti-racist, anti-sexist, as well as a positive ethics that involves notions of *pachamama* (Mother Earth) and *buen vivir* (living well). Mother Earth and living well differ respectively from the Western European notions of nature as being out there distinct from man and the notion of *vivir mejor* (live better). The latter notions are constitutive of the goals of the corporate westernized university.

Universidad de la Tierra has no dean as is typical in westernized universities. I use the term "dean" and other normalized vocabulary in higher education discourses to suggest various transgressions of identities, praxis and processes which are not merely inversions of western binaries but moves beyond them. For example, the person with the hedge clippers is not the gardening staff but the dean. In westernized universities we are not in the habit of perceiving the dean in this way. Your preconceptions of what a professor, student, and all of the other identities and objects populating a westernized university space are disrupted if not shattered. A professor or student on a westernized university campus might walk past gardening staff fifty times a semester on their way to class and not even notice the gardener; they are seen as a background figure. The coordinator of the university is not wearing a suit and tie but a tank top. He is not in a salaried position. There is no job posting. The coordinator does not revise curriculum, or generate new graduate programs (there are no degrees granted as we typically understand them). The coordinator of Indigena De Capacitación Integral (CIDECI) does not give talks that take stock of a university's accomplishments, challenges, and charts of a future trajectory and other duties that come with being a dean. The man with the hedge clippers coordinates all parts of the university system.

This education site is not in a mimetic relation with colonial European universities such as the University of Bologna (1088), the University of Oxford (1096), and the University of Salamanca (1134); nor is it their colonial surrogates in the Caribbean, Latin America, and the United States such as the University of Santo Domingo (1538), the University of San Marcos (1551), the Royal and Pontifical University of Mexico (1551), and Harvard University (1636). Indigenous universities mark a spatial-temporal epistemic fracture within the linear developmental track of the history of the Western European scholastic medieval and Kantian Humboldtian modern universities.[9]

There are no professors who are hired by the university through the typical application, search, interview, selection, and recommendation processes. By contrast, people who teach in indigenous universities are there voluntarily and are not paid biweekly. There is no tenure clock or the expectation to publish a certain number of articles within a certain time, nor is there preparation of a tenure binder. This site does not have a graduation ceremony that grants bachelor's or master's degrees to a mass of students who have all reached the end of a process after completing the required courses and electives, receive their degree(s), leave after their graduation ceremony, and hopefully enter the labor market. This university does not try to disseminate knowledge so students can gain a salaried position with health care benefits and incrementally move up the socioeconomic ladder. CIDECI does not prepare you for this scenario. It does not prepare you to become a businessman, a senator, or the president of the United States. In this university knowledge is shared so people can return to their communities and organizations to address specific issues. After the student's peers think they are competent enough in a specific trade, they will make them a homemade diploma that symbolizes their commitment to their community instead of their right to demand high salaries or fringe benefits. It is not used to try and impress a person you find attractive or to condescendingly degrade others who do not have a diploma. It is not used to ask for a job or any privilege or to make you feel more secure as you enter a competitive labor market with other graduates. It is an expression of their autonomy and social recognition not offered by the westernized university. As Gustavo Esteva, one of the founders of Universidad de la Tierra says, "Many of our students are surprising us, however, by not asking for any diploma. They do not feel the need for it."[10] In this sense CIDECI and the various indigenous students enrolled there are aware that objectives of the university are consistent with a long, slow process of delinking from the modern/colonial world system.

Universidad de la Tierra does not have a dining hall where students, faculty, and staff select from a variety of ethnic foods and then pay the cashier for the weight of the food on their trays. CIDECI's food-production is not linked to large grocery stores or usual food-production processes. This university does not have a conventional dining hall. The food and coffee at the Universidad de la Tierra are free. The university organically and locally grows their own food—to a certain degree, they are not dependent on energy companies for electricity and heat. The university does not pay electricity and heating bills because electricity and heat are not viewed as commodities. They have a generator to light the rooms and fire-operated clay ovens. This university is generally energy sufficient. Each building brick was laid not by government contracts but by the people's hands; the land, buildings, every hand-carved chair and table, communally built clay oven, basically, everything that goes into making this space was completed in a slow, continual process, that is not so dependent on the complex modern/colonial world system.

Universidad de la Tierra is not accredited by the state or some other agency. In an act of self-determination, the university did not seek state validation. This breaks away from the westernized university certificate system—a global structure of power that manages the modern/colonial world system through the production of westernized elites. These experts are placed in the organized economy to manage and replicate the system. Since knowledge is produced and shared in CIDECI they are a university, as well. The knowledge shared in that space also has value, even if experts who monopolize the authority of knowledge and expression may disagree. CIDECI is an education site that strives to keep people close to the earth, in the service of others, and share knowledge which will allow them to strengthen their habitat in order to survive, to resist.[11] All of these material ways of delinking from the modern/colonial world system can be seen as multiple, intertwined attempts to engage in what Burman aptly identified in his contribution to this collection as ontological disobedience.[12] This is distinct from, though not necessarily opposed to, the related concept Mignolo identified as epistemic disobedience.[13] Because Universidad de la Tierra is delinking from the modern/colonial world system in these various respects, I identify this as an indigenous, autonomous university as opposed to an indigenous, nonautonomous university tied to the state and the modern/colonial world system. But what is autonomous about this indigenous university?

First, CIDECI is not state-controlled. It turns away from the state. It does not run the risk, identified by Burman, of being subject to state aspirations to regulate what kind of experts should be produced in this learning site. It moves toward undoing the performative contradiction by not depending on state funding from extractivist policies. It bypasses accreditation concerns that either take for granted colonial criteria or reify intercultural criteria in a bureaucratic way that assumes a quantification model of value. Instead of this politics of recognition CIDECI has taken a step in self-determination by acknowledging that it disseminates knowledge so it is justified in self-identifying itself as a university. Why does CIDECI need state recognition to determine whether or not it is really a university? Since CIDECI is not focused on granting degrees it does not fall into the trap of reproducing the certificate system of discrimination based on the experts/nonknowers binary of epistemic disauthorization linked to the reproduction of the racial/sexual political economy. Since one of the goals of education at CIDECI is to learn so the knowledge acquired can be used in local communities, it reduces the risk of instrumentalizing knowledge in a way that is linked to pharmaceutical companies, health care, and other industries that may use indigenous knowledge production in an extractivist sense. Because knowledge is not a commodity at CIDECI, it marks a fundamental break with the corporate, westernized university. As the coordinator of CIDECI, Raymundo Sanchez Barraza remarked, "we say everything of ours here is free."[14] This does not imply the people in CIDECI do not ask for reciprocity. Students sweep floors, farm, clean rooms, cook, and work on projects to keep the place functioning.

From a Western European philosophy of education standpoint, CIDECI marks a break from the Platonic idea that the state should have the authority to determine education matters because the philosopher king knows the good. Since the Mexican state has ignored and marginalized Indians for over four hundred years, why should they believe that the state in its allegedly greater wisdom is necessary to establish harmony between individual virtue and the social good? In light of colonial considerations the Platonic reason for grounding educational authority in the state is idealized. The alleged philosopher king has actually historically been a violent racist/sexist Eurocentric colonial tyrant.

Furthermore, an appeal to a nonplatonic grounding that bases the state's educational authority on its status as a political parent of all its citizens is also not convincing. Historically, the state has demonstrated to the Indians it is not a fit political parent but an abusive one. Why should indigenous people habitually treated as subhuman noncitizens think of the state as an artificial parent that has sustained the conditions for raising and educating them, binds them to an implicit social contract? Although in the *Crito*, Socrates disagreed with the courts death sentence to drink hemlock for allegedly corrupting the youth and in the face of his friends help for him to escape with impunity, he made this paternalist early social contract appeal in his defense to stay in prison. Indians who were never asked nor agreed to the reality of the racial/sexual contract do not have the privilege of making the argument Socrates offers their own.[15] It flies in the face of their lived experience. This runs directly counter to one of Amy Gutman's reasons for grounding partial educational authority in the state when she says "because children are members of both families and states, the educational authority of parents and of polities has to be partial to be justified."[16] A parent is not reduced to a biological relation but is a moral one which involves at the very least protecting the child from harm, and providing nourishment and care. In this sense just as it would not make sense to say a biological parent who abuses, beats, and nearly starves their child is not justified in claiming parental status in any meaningful sense, similarly the Mexican state should not be naturalized in a way that assumes it is a political parent of all its citizens. The state doesn't recognize her majesty's other children: Indians are not children of the state.

Plus, CIDECI's political philosophy that is not dependent on the state is not in sync with an interventionist ground for the state's authority in education matters. Even if the state has historically intervened to protect children's autonomy from their parents in cases where families are inclined to pass on their opinions to their children, teaching them to be disrespectful or intolerant of other views, this does not imply that, "History suggests that without state provision or regulation of education, children will be taught neither mutual respect among persons or rational deliberation among ways of life."[17] The people in CIDECI treat each other with mutual respect and they rationally consider ways of life; yet they have turned away from the state. It is too extreme to claim that mutual respect and moral deliberation are dependent on the state. For Gutman to claim, "many parents would teach racism, for example, in the absence of political pressure to do otherwise" overinflates the power of the state in human relations.[18]

Is it true that without the state more parents would teach their kids racism? It does not seem so. Right now, if you go anywhere around the world—Mexico City, Lima, Buenos Aires, Chicago, London, or Barcelona—and open the doors of a university in any of these locations, when you enter, as a general rule, you will find, a canon of thought that consists primarily of white, heterosexual, upper-middle class males from five countries: England, France, Italy, Germany, and the United States.[19] When you combine these five countries, their populations make up roughly 12 percent of the world's population. Consequently, the social historical experience from which theories emerge represents 6 percent of the world's population, excluding Western European women. The standards of canonicity emerged from this small percentage of the population and is now universal across the globe. The other 94 percent of humanity is perceived to have no theory. They are perceived as either having nothing to contribute in terms of articulating standards of excellence or in addressing the world's most pressing crises and offering solutions. This is a high level of parochialism—people all over the world are supposed to learn and master this canon and apply it globally in a top-down fashion, regardless that those other regions have different histories, peoples, languages, philosophies, cultures, and life experiences. This epistemic racism/sexism at the foundation of the westernized university has been the norm for about 450 years, not long after Columbus sailed in 1492. States have not exerted pressure to resist Western European colonial expansion; therefore, it seems inaccurate to think the state exerts pressure on people in such a way that makes families less racist. On the contrary, the state has played and continues to play a part in the production and reproduction of racism.

It's a hard sell for people considered nonbeings—people who experience systematic racism, genocide, epistemicide, enslavement, criminalization, and colonization of language, history, and memory—to believe à la Gutman that the state should have partial authority in education matters because it makes freedom of "choice possible by teaching its future citizens respect for opposing points of view and ways of life."[20] Given the 400-year-plus life span of the modern/colonial world system which relegates Indians to the periphery why believe à la Gutman that the state "makes freedom of choice meaningful by equipping children with the intellectual skills necessary to evaluate ways of life different from that of their parents"?[21] Historically, the state has functioned to not only block the possibility for Indians to emerge and be free, it has either diminished choice or defined the parameters of choice in a violent way, such as in the *reconocimiento* when the Spanish colonizers declared to the Indians that they have the choice of either converting to Christianity or becoming enslaved.[22] How is this way of using choice that diminishes their dignity an indication that intellectual skills are being implemented to evaluate different ways of life? To claim the state equips students with the tools needed to evaluate different views takes for granted there is a diversity of views; in fact, as mentioned earlier, there is conceptual parochialism in the westernized university. If there is diversity, it is in a peculiar sense that is internal to the Western European intellectual tradition. A kind of "I do diversity because I teach Descartes, Hume, and Kant, different views" model of diversity. CIDECI is not simply a counterexample to Gutman's claims, but represents a process that moves toward liberation and a meaningful life in a way that need not depend on the state.

Another reason why CIDECI is not state controlled is because it is not interested in transforming the world by working to change the historic modern/colonial world system itself, from the inside. To do this is a difficult, if not a practically impossible task in light of its roughly 450-year life. Instead, it tries to transform the world by creating another world. This runs counter to Gutman's democratic theory of education which claims, "conscious social reproduction is the primary ideal of democratic education."[23] The limitation of Gutman's view is it is not clear how it involves substantive, procedural changes and it takes for granted a notion of representative democracy as the model for understanding governance. CIDECI complicates discussions that too quickly connect education to political philosophy with its privileging of the state. Therefore, it challenges discussions that assume the legitimacy of the state and questions the role the government should play in education matters.

There is no requirement to have a high school diploma, GED, or other certificate; dropouts are welcome in CIDECI. However, some students don't return to their communities. They enter the labor market after continual pressure from family and the wider dominant society to integrate themselves into the economy—what do you have to show for what you are doing; how much is in your bank account; do you have a professional career, job security, health care benefits; do you own a home, a new car? This is a struggle facing this type of autonomous indigenous university. How can other centers of meaning be built from below in such a way that the charms offered in the modern/colonial world system are decentered? How can conditions be created where the student can offer meaningful reasons to value CIDECI when pressured? How can a situation be created where the student's reasons carry weight because the dominant standards of valuation have been decentered? How can an atmosphere be generated by which the parents and other friends exerting pressure to leave CIDECI instead become excited about learning in, with, from and alongside the people at CIDECI? These are some of the challenges facing an autonomous indigenous university such as CIDECI. Nevertheless, how does the discussion of an autonomous indigenous university and its challenges connect to the stigmatized concept of dropouts in the United States introduced at the outset?

CONCLUSION

There is a tendency to interpret statistical facts about black and Latina/o high dropout rates as part of the education problem in the United States. The causes point to either the youth or the education system or some combination of them. Instead, when we turn to the autonomous indigenous university south of the US border—Universidad de la Tierra—it is a learning space that offers living proof for rethinking the stigmatized notion of dropouts perpetuated in US national and academic discourses. This other concept of dropouts opens up the possibility to begin viewing these populations labeled as problem people differently—not so much as lazy, ignorant, criminal, sexually irresponsible, immature youth but as courageous, politically conscious delinkers. Viewed in this way, dropouts could regain their dignity in a modern/colonial world system whose westernized university structure fundamentally organizes and perpetuates continuing this historic world system by creating westernized elites who view those outside of the mainstream in the underdeveloped past as needing to catch up with the first-world modern nations. The westernized university houses a culturally irrelevant curriculum with amnesiac methodologies; it creates greater poverty and allows a few token minorities to move up to become upper-middle class consumers. Based on the discussion that builds on the distinction between nonautonomous indigenous universities and autonomous indigenous universities, I wish to create a conceptual space for another view of dropouts as delinkers from the modern/colonial world system. This is my modest conceptual prescription: we should not think of dropouts simply in negative terms. Even though the dropouts in indigenous universities face their unique challenges, there is a positive yet nonromanticized notion of dropouts that can reframe future education issues. I do not want to imply an ethical prescription: that students currently enrolled in US universities should individually or dropout en masse because it is not clear that, at this writing, there are others forms of sociality established for many people to take part in the United States. Nor do my critical remarks about the westernized university imply that it cannot play a role the process of decolonization. We need to meet people where they are at—as they are positioned within westernized universities or outside them or in both spaces. To deny that the westernized university cannot play any role will not just be a performative contradiction on my part given my imbrication within it but may also reinscribe the same westernized logic of extermination that tries to destroy the other—which in this case would be the westernized university. My hope is my conceptual offering invites us to consider not so much alternative schools but alternatives to school. [24] This paper builds on the work of people who already have struggled to bring other modes of organization into existence. I also find the following claim problematic: Universidad de la Tierra is so particularly tied to its locale— its geography, histories, languages, heterogeneous populations, and other features of its unique circumstance—that it is troublesome to try to universalize anything from it into a different context such as the United States. The problem with this claim is it seems to imply that say people in the United States cannot learn anything from something happening south of the border or elsewhere. We can learn something from Universidad de la Tierra; aspects of its philosophy of education can be relevant in the United States, not as a franchise—that is my worry—but as an opportunity to create the conditions for the possibility of another education option created from the ground up and focused on distinct histories, heterogeneous peoples, languages, cultural forms, and geography. Autonomous indigenous universities in the United States may seem difficult to bring to fruition in the modern/colonial world system, given our preoccupation with money, pleasures, comforts, and excesses. Yet, it seems the reasons we offer or tell ourselves to justify our inaction or indifference are privileged problems. How is it that the richest economy on the planet—currently estimated at 17 trillion dollars—has difficulty allowing autonomous indigenous universities to flourish in the United States yet Mexico, our southern neighbor perceived as a poor, third world country has struggled and emerged an alternative to education? It is hard to believe we can land on the moon but we can't create an autonomous indigenous university in the United States. These questions, as painful and embarrassing as they are for me to ask, must be faced.

NOTES

1. See Richard Frye and Mark Hugo Lopez, "Hispanic Student Enrollments Reach New Highs in 2011: Now Largest Minority Group on Four-Year College Campuses," *Pew Research Center Hispanic Trends*, August 20, 2012: www.pewhispanic.org/2012/08/20/hispanic-student-enrollments-reach-new-highs-in-2011/.

2. See Richard Frye and Paul Taylor, "Hispanic High School Graduates Pass Whites in Rates of College Enrollment," *Pew Research Center Hispanic Trends*, May 9, 2013: www.pewhispanic.org/2013/05/09/hispanic-high-school-graduates-pass-whites-in-rate-of-college-enrollment/.

3. See Ian Haney López, *Dog Whistle Politics: How Racial Codes Have Reinvented Racism and Wrecked the Middle Class* (Oxford University Press, 2015).

4. While the name and idea of Latin American has been identified as an eighteenth-century French invention to identify romance language affinity and to contrast it with Anglo America I use it for purposes of communication. The name *Abya Yala* is used to refer to the continent of the Americas prior to the arrival of Columbus. Walter Mignolo, *The Idea of Latin America* (Blackwell Publishing, 2005).

5. See Anders Burman, "Damnes Realities and Ontological Disobedience: Notes on the Coloniality of Reality in Higher Education in the Bolivian Andes and Beyond," eds. Ramón Grosfoguel, Roberto D. Hernández, and Ernesto Rosen Velásquez, *Decolonizing the Westernized University: Interventions in Philosophy of Education from Within and Without* (New York: Lexington Press, 2016).

6. See Skye Stevenson, "Green Light for Indigenous Intercultural University Amawtay Wasi of Ecuador," August 7, 2012: cpnn-world.org/cgi-bin/read/articlepage.cgi?ViewArticle=891.

7. See Maria Lugones, *Pilgramajes and Peregrinajes: Theorizing Coalitions Among Multiple Oppressions* (Rowman Littlefield, 2003).

8. See Anders Burman, "Places to Think With, Books to Think About: Words, Experience and the Decolonization of Knowledge in the Bolivian Andes," *Human Architecture: Journal of the Sociology of Self-Knowledge* 10 (2012): 103.

9. See Walter Mignolo, "Globalization and the Geopolitics of Knowledge: The Role of the Humanities in the Corporate University," *Nepantla* 4 (2003): 97–119.

10. See Gustavo Esteva, "Reclaiming out Freedom to Learn," *Yes! Magazine* August 7, 2007: www.yesmagazine.org/issues/liberate-your-space/reclaiming-our-freedom-to-learn.

11. See Nic Paget-Clarke Interview with Raymundo Sanchez Barraza by *In Motion Magazine* on September 30, 2005, in San Cristobal de Las Casas, Chiapas.

12. See Anders Burman, "Damnes Realities and Ontological Disobedience: Notes on the Coloniality of Reality in Higher Education in the Bolivian Andes and Beyond," eds. Ramón Grosfoguel, Roberto D. Hernández, and Ernesto Rosen Velásquez, *Decolonizing the Westernized University: Interventions in Philosophy of Education from Within and Without* (New York: Lexington Press, 2016).

13. See Walter Mignolo, "Epistemic Disobedience, Independent Thought and Decolonial Freedom," *Theory, Culture and Socety*, 26 (2009): 1–23.

14. See Nic Paget-Clarke Interview with Raymundo Sanchez Barraza by *In Motion Magazine* in San Cristobal de Las Casas, Chiapas on September 30, 2005.

15. See Carol Pateman and Charles Mills, *The Domination Contract* (Polity Press, 2007).

16. See Amy Gutman, "Democratic Education" in Steven M. Cahn (ed.) *Classic and Contemporary Readings in the Philosophy of Education.* (Oxford University Press, 2012), 333.

17. See Amy Gutman, "Democratic Education" in Steven M. Cahn (ed.) *Classic and Contemporary Readings in the Philosophy of Education.* (Oxford University Press, 2012), 333.

18. See Amy Gutman, "Democratic Education" in Steven M. Cahn (ed.) *Classic and Contemporary Readings in the Philosophy of Education.* (Oxford University Press, 2012), 334.

19. See Ramon Grosfoguel, "Decolonizing the University" 2nd Decolonial Days Berlin 2011: youtu.be/LKgL92yqygk.

20. See Amy Gutman, "Democratic Education" in Steven M. Cahn (ed.) *Classic and Contemporary Readings in the Philosophy of Education.* (Oxford University Press, 2012), 333.

21. See Amy Gutman, "Democratic Education" in Steven M. Cahn (ed.) *Classic and Contemporary Readings in the Philosophy of Education.* (Oxford University Press, 2012), 333.

22. See Linda Alcoff, *Visible Identities: Race, Gender and the Self* (Oxford University Press, 2005), 98.

23. See Amy Gutman, "Democratic Education" in Steven M. Cahn (ed.) *Classic and Contemporary Readings in the Philosophy of Education* (Oxford University Press, 2012), 341.

24. The distinction between alternative schools as opposed to alternatives to school is an extension of the more general distinction between alternative modernities and alternatives to modernity introduced by Arturo Escobar. See Escobar, *Encountering Development: The Making and Remaking of the Third World* (Princeton University Press, 2005).

BIBLIOGRAPHY

Alcoff, Linda. *Visible Identities: Race, Gender and the Self.* New York: Oxford University Press, 2005.

Burman, Anders. "Damnes Realities and Ontological Disobedience: Notes on the Coloniality of Reality in Higher Education in the Bolivian Andes and Beyond." In Ramón Grosfoguel, Roberto D. Hernández, and Ernesto Rosen Velásquez (eds.) *Decolonizing the Westernized University: Interventions in Philosophy of Education from Within and Without.* New York: Lexington Press, 2016.

———. "Places to Think With, Books to Think About: Words, Experience and the Decolonization of Knowledge in the Bolivian Andes." *Human Architecture: Journal of the Sociology of Self-Knowledge*, 10 (2012): 103.

Escobar, Arturo. *Encountering Development: The Making and Remaking of the Third World.* Princeton: Princeton University Press, 2005.

Esteva, Gustavo. "Reclaiming out Freedom to Learn." *Yes! Magazine*, August 7, 2007: www.yesmagazine.org/issues/liberate-your-space/reclaiming-our-freedom-to-learn.

Frye, Richard, and Lopez Hugo, Mark. "Hispanic Student Enrollments Reach New Highs in 2011: Now Largest Minority Group on Four-Year College Campuses." *Pew Research Center Hispanic Trends*, August 20, 2012: www.pewhispanic.org/2012/08/20/hispanic-student-enrollments-reach-new-highs-in-2011/.

Frye, Richard, and Taylor, Paul. "Hispanic High School Graduates Pass Whites in Rates of College Enrollment." *Pew Research Center Hispanic Trends*, May 9, 2013: www.pewhispanic.org/2013/05/09/hispanic-high-school-graduates-pass-whites-in-rate-of-college-enrollment/.

Grosfoguel, Ramon. "Decolonizing the University." 2nd Decolonial Days Berlin 2011: youtu.be/LKgL92yqygk.

Gutman, Amy. "Democratic Education." In Steven M. Cahn (ed.) *Classic and Contemporary Readings in the Philosophy of Education*. New York: Oxford University Press, 2012.

Lopéz, Haney Ian. *Dog Whistle Politics: How Racial Codes Have Reinvented Racism and Wrecked the Middle Class*. New York: Oxford University Press, 2015.

Lugones, Maria. *Pilgramajes and Peregrinajes: Theorizing Coalitions Among Multiple Oppressions*. Landham: Rowman Littlefield, 2003.

Mignolo, Walter. "Epistemic Disobedience, Independent Thought and De-colonial Freedom." *Theory, Culture and Society*, 26 (2009): 1–23.

———. *The Idea of Latin America*. Malden: Blackwell Publishing, 2005.

———. "Globalization and the Geopolitics of Knowledge: The Role of the Humanities in the Corporate University." *Nepantla*, 4 (2003): 97–119.

Paget-Clarke, Nic. Interview with Raymundo Sanchez Barraza by *In Motion Magazine* in San Cristobal de Las Casas, Chiapas on September 30, 2005.

Pateman, Carol and Mills, Charles. *The Domination Contract*. Malden: Polity Press, 2007.

Stevenson, Skye. "Green Light for Indigenous Intercultural University Amawtay Wasi of Ecuador." August 7, 2012: cpnn-world.org/cgi-bin/read/articlepage.cgi?ViewArticle=891.

SIX

Damnés Realities and Ontological Disobedience

Notes on the Coloniality of Reality in Higher Education in the Bolivian Andes and Beyond

Anders Burman

DECOLONIZATION UP FOR NEGOTIATION

Lifting one's eyes from the noisy and crowded street-life in the commercial center of the "rebel city" of El Alto, one can see a homemade black-and-red placard in one of the windows on the fourth floor of a smutty building. It says "Escuela de Pensamiento Pacha." On Saturday afternoons a small group of indigenous Aymara university students and intellectuals gather there in a small, chilly room to discuss philosophical queries and concepts and to produce knowledge for a radical "indianization" of society and being. This is a space, I argue in this text, not only for *epistemic* disobedience but also for *ontological* disobedience in which historically subalternized beings and ontologically informed lifeworlds—"*damnés* realities"—are being unfolded and making themselves present through concrete and situated practices and conversations, by no means in isolation from a dominant world, but in spite of it, in defiance of it, in the face of it. For more than a decade now, I have participated in these activities and maintained a continuous and deeply engaging and critical conversation with the two brothers who constitute the core of the group, the charismatic Aymara activists and intellectuals René Acarapi and Freddy "Pachakuti" Acarapi.[1]

In June 2015 I was invited to give a talk at the annual conference organized since 2010 by the Escuela de Pensamiento Pacha and the Acarapi brothers in their rural hometown of Tiwanaku under the motto "Reconstituting the State of Tawantinsuyu." The conference has grown with each year and the last few years it has attracted indigenous Aymara, Quechua, and Mapuche intellectuals and activists from Bolivia, Peru, Chile, and Argentina as speakers and a nearly thousand-headed audience. Central themes of the conference are "indigenous knowledge" and "decolonization," be that of political power, history, or higher education. At the inauguration Pachakuti spoke: "This is a special day . . . to strengthen the thinking, the knowledge . . . of the Indian nations of this continent."

Though among the most radically critical, the Acarapi brothers are far from alone in discussing the decolonization of higher education in relation to indigenous knowledges. Rather, there is a diverse set of actors who play a role here, such as the Bolivian state and the Ministry of Education, indigenous organizations, activists, intellectuals, and university lecturers, but also ritual specialists and other knowledgeable indigenous men and women. Thus, this text deals with notions, practices, and, ultimately, realities that collide, coexist, and coalesce in the colonial and decolonial dynamics surrounding higher education in contemporary Bolivian society. Since 2006 and the coming to power of Evo Morales and the Movimiento al Socialismo (MAS), "decolonization" has been avowed as the ideological lodestar of governmental politics and "indigeneity" has been used as a rhetorical device and a legitimizing symbolic capital in governmental discourse and state ceremony. From day one, education was identified as a key area for the implementation of decolonizing politics. In the new Education Law, passed in 2010, Bolivian education—from kindergarten to postgraduate studies—was envisioned to be "decolonizing, liberating, revolutionary, anti-imperialist, depatriarchalizing." In the same law, state-controlled indigenous universities were given the task of: "Developing processes of recovery, strengthening, creation and recreation of the knowledges . . . and languages of the indigenous, originary [*"originario"*] and peasant nations and peoples" (my italics and translation).

Apart from such legislative measures and the rhetoric recognition of indigenous peoples and their knowledges, Evo's coming to power also implied an "ontological opening" in national political practices and debate; "earth beings" that had been suppressed and subjected to colonial extirpation efforts since the Spanish invasion but had lingered on in stigmatized "Indian" rituals and agricultural practices and as suggestive political symbols of ancestral power evoked by the Andean indigenous *indianista-katarista* movement were all of a sudden integral parts of governmental discourse and state ceremony. Lifeworlds and beings that supposedly had been, as it were, buried under centuries of colonial, Eurocentric, and racist dust, reemerged, were remodeled and gained formal political relevance. Concepts developed by critical indigenous intellectuals, such as *suma qamaña*, and concepts of cosmopolitical significance, such as *pachakuti*, were acknowledged in state discourse and incorporated into formal counter-narratives against Eurocentric, reductionist notions of development, economic growth, and reform.

Likewise, higher education experienced an opening of the ontological and epistemological conditions for producing legitimate knowledge. Aymara *yatiris* and *amawt'as* ("shamans"/"wise ones") were not only positioned as key actors in the ceremonial protocol of the new Bolivian state, but were also invited as lecturers to the indigenous Aymara university, Universidad Indígena Boliviana Aymara "Tupak Katari" (UNIBOL "TK") founded in 2008, and were, even in the eyes of many nonindigenous urban people, to a certain extent relieved of their historically ascribed depreciatory identity as superstitious witchdoctors and were rather regarded as knowledgeable men and women or, in more romanticizing and exotifying terms, as "guardians of tradition" or even "guardians of Mother Earth." Conventional academic disciplines and scientific practices were contrasted with, and in certain contexts and to a certain extent even challenged by, other ways of producing knowledge. Over centuries of colonial oppression, such "knowledges otherwise" or "Othered ways of knowing" have persistently been generated from within concrete and situated practices, struggles, and experiences, but never before had they been embraced by state authorities and incorporated into formal higher education. In the eyes of many indigenous intellectuals and activists, state policies that aimed at the decolonization of knowledge production and the establishment of indigenous universities were indeed encouraging initiatives. Even radical *indianista* critics like the Acarapi brothers were moderately enthusiastic.

However, hardly had any serious state-endorsed decolonizing attempt at engaging other ontologies and epistemologies in higher education begun before a tidal wave of critical voices flooded the public debate, starting in 2010. Any attempts at seriously articulating a political or cultural critique in languages other than Spanish, using concepts other than those intelligible to non-indigenous intellectuals, or based on ontological or epistemological premises or pedagogical practices other than those sanctioned by modernity, were brushed aside as exercises in romanticizing exoticism without any "revolutionary potential" (according to the left) or as an expression of dangerous, dissident and irreverent indigenist tendencies (according to the right); it was characterized as a quasi-esoteric form of Andean essentialist culturalism and was soon pejoratively labeled "*pachamamismo*," in reference to the Andean deity Pachamama. To be sure, similar, but quite marginal, voices had made themselves heard ever since the coming to power of Evo and the government's first efforts of incorporating indigenous ritual practices and concepts into governmental discourse and state ceremony. However, this time the critique had serious repercussions, because this time it was articulated by actors who were identified as critical, leftist thinkers who were perceived to be seriously worried about the path taken by the MAS government, and who moreover managed to tap hegemonic social theory of its deconstructivist, postmodernist, and anti-essentialist potential in a critique of any political project claiming "ancestral knowledge" or "indigeneity." The starting point for this critical tide wave was Pablo Stefanoni's short 2010 polemic piece "¿Adonde nos lleva el pachamamismo?"[2] ("Where is *pachamamismo* taking us?") in which it is argued that

> the process of change is all too important to be left in the hands of *los pachamámicos*. The pose of ancestral authenticity . . . does not seem capable of contributing anything significant in terms of constructing a new state, of establishing a new model of development, of discussing a viable model of production or of new forms of democracy and mass [*"popular"*] participation. Rather, in a philosophy that would supposedly be an alternative to the Western one, *el pachamamismo* . . . dissolves the profound concerns for change which Bolivians nurture. [my translation]

Accidentally or not, more or less at the same time as Stefanoni scorned anyone who articulated political visions or made epistemological claims from other ontological premises than the ones embraced by himself and his likes, the semantics and semiotics of "decolonization" in state politics and governmental discourse started to change. As I have argued elsewhere, "decolonization" is indeed a multivocal concept—something of a floating signifier in Bolivian political debate—which is filled with different meanings by different actors in different political and social contexts. A few years after Evo's coming to power, the conceptualization of decolonization as a challenge to Eurocentric paradigms of development and forms of knowledge production and as a serious turn toward "indigenous knowledges" and subalternized social and economic practices in search for alternative societal paradigms was increasingly challenged by the conceptualization of decolonization as a project aimed at national sovereignty based on industrialization, infrastructural modernization, technological progress, and natural resource extraction. These two differing conceptualizations managed to coexist in state politics and governmental discourse for quite a few years. With time, however, the contradictions became overwhelming, and the latter conceptualization became dominant in state politics and governmental discourse directed at the national public, while the former lingered on in governmental discourse directed at the international community and in some spectacular events organized by, for instance, the Vice Ministry of Decolonization. This "turn" in state politics and governmental discourse—which Rivera in the subtitle of a recent book calls "the colonial turn of the MAS government"—became blatantly manifest in the conflict between indigenous and environmentalist movements and the Bolivian state over a projected highway in the Bolivian Amazon, that is, the so-called TIPNIS conflict which materialized in 2011 and still agitates Bolivian politics. Moreover, this turn also had serious repercussions for higher education: Universities—be they indigenous, public, or private—were increasingly urged by state authorities to produce engineers with technological skills; an emphasis on the production of nuclear physicists and oil prospectors replaced earlier rhetorical appraisal of "ancestral knowledge" and "indigenous wisdom."

The "ontological opening" transformed, I would argue, into an ontological *ch'akhi*, an ontological hangover, a backlash, a recoil. In order to understand how and why this happened, in this text I draw attention to how the MAS government have used certain representations of indigeneity to justify its hold of power and to legitimize its supposed identity as an "indigenous government." Moreover, and especially so in relation to higher education, I situate this "turn" in the context of what I call "the coloniality of reality" and I discuss it in terms of an "ontological conflict" as rewardingly theorized by Blaser. Last but not least, in a context in which the implications and the very nature of "decolonization" are up for negotiation, the decolonization of knowledge and the production of decolonial knowledges from ontological premises other than the ones sanctioned by a hegemonically modern university and a colonial, capitalist world-system, are discussed in terms of "ontological disobedience."

POLITICAL ONTOLOGY AND THE COLONIALITY OF REALITY

To assess the so-called "ontological turn" in social theory is far beyond the scope of this text. However, I use the concept "ontology" quite profusely throughout these pages and a few words on the rationale for this would not be amiss. "Ontology" as an analytical category is used in different ways by different authors. On the one hand, drawing on Heidegger and others, "ontology" is used to discuss existential and phenomenological dimensions of being (or even "Being") and to draw our attention to the nature of being in the sense of "being *qua* being" or in the sense of "the self" (or even "the Self"). On the other hand, it is used to discuss the nature(s) of reality in the sense of the world(s) in which the self exists and unfolds. While finding much of interest and inspiration in the former usage of the concept, my usage of the concept in this text is more directly related to the latter. However, in order not to forego the importance of lived experience, situated practice and the relational nature of existence and in order not to reify the existence of multiple realities as discrete world-objects, I employ the somewhat phenomenologically oriented concept "ontologically informed lifeworlds."

Critics of the ontological turn have convincingly pointed out the meager prospects for theorizing power and articulating a radical critique of the capitalist world-system from within a seemingly relativist turn toward a notion of the multiplicity of realities and a "complete dissolution of the notion of an objective, universal nature." Indeed, how do we articulate a critique of fossil-fueled capitalism if the causal chains behind climate change as identified by science are no more objectively and universally real than, say, the autonomous agency of ancestral spirits in Andean mountains? Blaser addresses such problems by framing the debate as one of "*political* ontology" and by attending to ontological differences without losing sight of sociopolitical struggles and global asymmetric relations of political and economic power. While depending on one's analytical objectives there might be, or not, a point in maintaining an *analytical* distinction between "nature" and "society" and thereby maintaining "an objective, universal nature," current *political* dynamics in Bolivia and elsewhere reveal that any clear-cut distinction between material/political and cognitive/ontological conflicts is based on a moot dichotomy. Ontological and epistemological dimensions of human existence are at the center of struggles over resources and power and struggles against racism, sexism, ecocide, and exploitation, since these are simultaneously struggles over being, struggles over knowledge, struggles over reality, over "what there is."

One could certainly make a critical argument about coloniality, that is, that which Mignolo once called "the less visible side of modernity," or "the hidden face of modernity . . . and the condition of its possibility" as de Oliveira Andreotti et al., drawing on Mignolo, succinctly put it and the asymmetries of power involved in higher education without referring to "ontology." However, I believe some fundamental aspects of the dynamics at work here are rewardingly discussed in terms of "political ontology." Ontology is, after all, not "just another word for culture" nor is the so-called ontological turn merely a sophisticated technique to get away with essentialist claims or homogenizing ethnographic narratives. A turn toward ontology does not by implication constitute the ideal paradigm for neoliberal social science, nor does it by definition imply a turn away from political economy—and even less so away from political ecology—a dogmatic assertion of the multiplicity of reified realities, or a retreat into a Heideggerian version of "fundamental ontology." I rather think of it as an intellectual project of serious engagement with "radical difference" and the situated practices that generate different ontologically informed lifeworlds—"ways of worlding" in Blaser's words—and of taking seriously that which is serious to the people with and among whom we work. This implies acknowledging the real realities of our partially connected lifeworlds and existences. Hence, I would argue, it is a project—not the only one, not the ultimate one, but still—that, if combined with a serious attention to the power asymmetries instituted and reproduced by a colonial, capitalist world-system, may reveal dynamics of colonial domination that go deep into the very nature(s) of reality and being(s).

Elsewhere, drawing on Mignolo and others, I have referred to the "coloniality of knowledge" in order to discuss the epistemic dimension of colonial domination and to draw attention to epistemic violence as an integral part of the colonial relations of power that characterize the world since 1492. Nevertheless, I believe there is an essential dimension that is missing in many contributions (including my own) to the prolific debate on the coloniality of knowledge. What is missing is the fundamental discussion about "what there is" and the mechanisms by which a dominant reality imposes itself on other realities in an ontocidal process of colonial ontological warfare, "not a war of words . . . but an ongoing war of worlds." Or as Maldonado-Torres argues: "Colonization and racialization are not only political and social events or structures. They also have metaphysical and ontological significance." In other words, while "a review of what should be known, for what purpose, how to know it, and what should be the criteria to legitimize knowledge" is an indispensable component of any project aimed at contributing to the decolonization of knowledge and decolonial knowledge production, it is not enough. I would add a number of other questions: What is there to know? What realities are unfolded/enacted/catalyzed into being by different knowledge generating practices and learning processes? Within which ontologically informed lifeworlds and in which relational fields are knowledges produced and by whom? How and by which mechanisms are the partial connections between different ways of producing knowledge and of generating and experiencing realities transformed into spaces of conflict, domination and resistance? These are questions of an ontological nature; questions dealing with "what there is," with what kind of actors there are and what kind of beings compose the relational fields—the communities of being—within which knowledge production, learning, and political struggle take place.

Ontological conflicts could either be conceptualized as conflicts over what there is, that is, conflicts over the nature of reality, or as conflicts between different realities. These are two quite different things. While the former would imply a multiplicity of perspectives on one single reality, the latter would imply a multiplicity of realities, the existence of different worlds, in Strathern's words a "pluriverse," or in Viveiros de Castro's words "multinaturalism." The concept of "realities" in the plural could easily lead one to think in terms of reified, discrete, and mutually excluding worlds supposedly tied to likewise reified, discrete, and mutually excluding ethnic groups or "cultures." However, if we think of ontology not as the hermetically sealed property of a neatly defined group, but as a formation of premises concerning the nature(s) of being or the nature(s) of reality and if we think of "being" and "reality" as transforming and transformative processes—biophysical and sociopolitical, sociophysical and biopolitical—generated by concrete and situated practices and in concrete relational fields, then there is nothing necessarily essentialist, static or reductionist in discussing intersecting, partially connected and partially overlapping different realities. Knowledge production and learning processes are, just like political activism or ritual practice, ways of coming into being in a world—and being brought into being *by* a world—that is concomitantly being brought into being by one's practices, and, of course, those of others (and this is important, since otherwise "worlding" would be a solipsistic activity without any relation to the activities of powerful actors—be they transnational corporations, states, universities, or ancestral beings—in the sociophysical formation of our realities). In other words, if knowledge production and learning are ways of enacting and unfolding realities, they necessarily take place within and in relation to already enacted and unfolded realities. Knowledge production and learning are not only ontologically generative processes, that is, processes in which the loose ends of practices, materialities, and knowledges are twined together to form realities; they take place in already ontologically informed lifeworlds and are therefore also ontologically cognizant. While it is true, as Restrepo argues, that "different knowledges create diverse worlds, because they result in actions that shape the way in which cultures manage their materiality, time and space," it would be deceptive to portray the relation between "knowledges" and "realities" as a one-way process of causality. Realities are generated in concrete and situated practices, and knowledge production and learning are indeed practices. However, as such they are embedded in concrete lifeworlds and are therefore ontologically informed, and materially conditioned, practices. Hence, knowledges and realities are mutually formative, playing major roles in constituting each other. These are the power-infused dialectics of reality and knowledge/reality generation. Or, in the words of de Sousa Santos, Arriscado Nunes, and Meneses: "The very action of knowing . . . is an intervention in the world, which places us within it as active contributors to its making."

In relation to this understanding of "realities," and if we understand ontological conflicts as conflicts between different ontologically informed lifeworlds over anything from "what there is," the proper ways of engaging with the world(s) and the morally correct ways of acting in society and in relation to "the environment" (or, in terms of an other ontology: "Pachamama") to the meanings and implications of social and environmental justice, exploitation and decolonization, it is evident that ontological conflicts involve severe asymmetries of power and that they cannot be understood in isolation from the power asymmetries that characterize the current colonial, capitalist world-system, or in Grosfoguel's words, the "Capitalist/Patriarchal Western-centric/Christian-centric Modern/Colonial World-System."

In Bolivia, the decolonization of higher education was supposed to establish a shared middle-ground of knowledge production and learning at the university; different knowledges ("indigenous"/"ancestral" and "universal" as they tend to be labeled in policy documents) were supposed to meet and "complement" each other. However, the university is a logocentric, librocentric four-wall institutionalized setting which in this context therefore constitutes a *colonial* middle-ground where not only one specific form of knowledge production is given preference, but also one specific reality—with its grotesque asymmetries of power; "a world with masters and slaves" with "cannibal economies, consuming the lives of some for the luxury of others"—is naturalized and legitimized, generated, and reproduced. Hegemonic academic processes of learning and knowledge production are not practices that simply describe a pre-existing reality; they rather contribute to the *generation* of a specific reality. Academic institutions are thereby quite resilient to change, since they not only define reality, but are accomplices in generating it. This was made manifest in the seventeenth century when "New Science" created a new reality; God's creation was transformed into brute biophysical matter and, with time, "nature" turned into "natural resources" and "ecosystem services." The "realities" I refer to in this text, then, are not reified world-objects but rather realities-in-the-becoming that can be transformed, enacted and unfolded in relation to and by human knowledge producing practices.

It has been convincingly argued that universities reproduce and reinforce the "colonial difference" in an epistemological sense, and de Sousa Santos and Grosfoguel discuss this in terms of "epistemicide." Relating this debate to Blaser's project of "political ontology," however, it could be likewise argued that the "colonial difference" is reinforced by the hegemonic university also in an ontological sense. Hence, the attention to the "coloniality of knowledge" would need to be accompanied by a critical attention to the "coloniality of reality."

THE COLONIALITY OF HIGHER EDUCATION AND ATTEMPTS AT DECOLONIZATION

All Latin American universities, public and private, are predominantly white, segregated, and racist institutions that reproduce exclusively the Eurocentric model of knowledge developed in the West in the modern period.[3]

This claim should be critically assessed, not in order to be dismissed, but rather to be nuanced, and to explore the prospects for a university otherwise and the assessment of factual concrete attempts of doing things otherwise in higher education. De Carvalho and Flórez-Flórez have probably never visited the Universidad Indígena Tawantinsuyu (UTA), founded in the late 1990s by a group of radical Aymara intellectuals and activists in the small rural town of Laja but operating in the city of El Alto since more than a decade. But if they would have, they would have encountered a small and alternative institution that is quite far from the "predominantly white, segregated, and racist" university (be that the Humboldtian university or the neoliberal corporate university) that reproduces "exclusively the Eurocentric model of knowledge." They would have found an institution that offers academic programs such as "Andean Theology and Philosophy," "Indigenous Rights," and "Aymara Linguistics and History"; among its lecturers they would have found Aymara intellectuals, *indianista* activists and *yatiris* and *amawt'as* and among the students they would have found anything from young urban *indianista* activists and second-generation rural-urban Aymara migrants, to *yatiri* apprentices and public school teachers; actually, they would have found many of the members of the Escuela de Pensamiento Pacha referred to above. Although a university, rather than a racist institution UTA is a reaction to colonial academia, a decolonial attempt in a racist world, an attempt at carving out another epistemological and ontological space in the very coloniality of reality of higher education. Or in the words of a former UTA student in her late twenties, who also studied at the school of education ("La Normal"):

> There is a huge difference between UTA and La Normal. UTA was like our own home . . . ; we treated ourselves . . . like in family, like we do in the community, but in La Normal the treatment was very different . . . , it was like in the city: no respect. Because they always think that anything coming from the West or from the *gringos*, from "the intelligent ones" as they tend to think, that they are superior to us.

As such, UTA is not the first, nor the most recent, critical attempt at establishing an institution of education otherwise in Bolivia, in which indigenous and other subalternized knowledges and practices are placed at the very foundation of the learning process. In 1931, the legendary "Escuela Ayllu de Warisata" was established in the heart of rural Aymara society. The communities provided land, building materials, and labor, while the state provided teachers and economic funding to a school project that would flourish and spread throughout the country, and that would become a quasi-mythical educational model that was not only *directed* at indigenous people (in itself a quite radical project at the time) but that also had as its pedagogical point of departure the harsh reality of rural Aymara people (i.e., racism, discrimination, poverty, serfdom) and their knowledges and practices. La Escuela Ayllu thrived less than a decade before it was closed down by the political regime; students and teachers were pursued and education was not to return to rural communities until the mid-1950s, but then not as an emancipatory initiative but rather as an assimilationist project of the new *patria mestiza*.

During the era of neoliberal multiculturalism of the 1990s and early 2000s, a quite defanged educational reform was implemented and policy documents were sprayed with buzzwords such as *"interculturalidad"* and *"educación bilingüe"*; nevertheless, "decolonization" was not on the agenda. Moreover, the reform targeted basic education and nothing or very little spilled over into higher education. It was not until the new educational law (*Ley de Educación "Avelino Siñani-Elisardo Pérez"* named after the founding fathers of La Escuela Ayllu) was passed in 2010 that "decolonization" and "education" were formally combined in legislative measures and governmental discourse. However, many authorities of private and public universities alike saw with mistrust upon their new role as promoters of a higher education that would be

> decolonizing, liberating, revolutionary, anti-imperialist, depatriarchal-izing, and transformative of the economic and social structures; orient-ed towards the cultural reaffirmation of the indigenous, originary [*"originario"*] and peasant nations and peoples. [my translation]

Most university boards paid lip service to interculturality, decolonization, and so on, and then continued business as usual, referring to their legally recognized university autonomy. By this time, though, in order to secure a space for decolonized and decolonizing higher education, the Bolivian state had already founded three indigenous non-autonomous universities, one of them (Universidad Indígena Boliviana Aymara "Tupak Katari" or UNIBOL "TK") in the village of Warisata, in the very premises of La Escuela Ayllu. One of the intellectual authors of the indigenous Aymara university, Carlos Callisaya, explained its aims to me: "To us, the indigenous university . . . is the vanguard to transform higher education, and to turn education into the engine of productive development."

UNIBOL "TK," currently with its main campus in the village of Cuyahuani, offers four academic programs: Agronomy, Veterinary and Zoology, Food engineering, and Textile engineering. These are all oriented toward quite practical and technical professions. There is no sociology program, no philosophy program. And many critical voices have been raised against what is argued to be a reflection of racist, colonial stereotypes of *"indios"* as being "naturally fitted" for practical offices and manual labor, and less so for intellectual and theoretically abstract tasks. However, in the words of an *indianista-katarista* intellectual and former lecturer at UNIBOL "TK" in his early forties:

> In the Andes you can't separate practical manual work and technical knowledge from political issues. What we tried to do at the indigenous university was to relate the technical education to political, ideological, religious issues.

At UTA, the curriculum is rather different. There is more direct emphasis on critical theoretical knowledge and more explicit room for issues such as "Andean philosophy" and "Aymara history" as part of a radical ideological debate that permeates the learning process. However, both UTA and UNIBOL "TK" claim to be indigenous universities. This leads us to the question of what it means to be an "indigenous university." In other words, in what does the "indigeneity" of these institutions consist? In a country characterized by a very large indigenous population,[4] the physical presence of indigenous students and lecturers is a quite poor parameter for defining an indigenous university, and if we add to that the changing semantics and semiotics of "indigeneity" over time in Bolivian society, then "indigenous presence" is also an analytically problematic parameter. Moreover, one could arguably claim that even at more conventional public universities such as UMSA in La Paz and, even more so, UPEA in El Alto there is a very strong "indigenous presence." The indigeneity of indigenous universities must, in other words, be sought elsewhere; one option would be to search for it in the institutionally expressed concern for "indigenous knowledges." However, that would only postpone any definite understanding of the indigeneity of indigenous universities since the nature of the indigeneity of indigenous knowledges is far from obvious. Indigenous knowledge can hardly be defined in an essentialist sense as knowledge passed down from one generation to another in an unbroken chain that goes back to precolonial times. However, to define it as any knowledge held by an indigenous person would in this specific case take us back to where we started, that is, defining indigenous universities by pointing to the presence of indigenous individuals. Rather than pinning down a clear-cut definition of "indigenous universities," I would characterize them in a more open way, on the one hand, by pointing to a parameter as basic as the institutional self-identification. This would allow for an understanding of the indigeneity of indigenous universities as diverse and dynamic as that of the indigeneity of "indigenous peoples" in Bolivian society in general. Simultaneously, it would acknowledge "indigeneity" as a space for negotiation and struggle and, in certain contexts, as a politically legitimizing device. On the other hand, I would draw attention to the way these institutions, to varying degrees and in various ways, deal with a certain kind of knowledges (not necessarily "*indigenous* knowledge" in the essentialist sense) and knowledge producing practices that are based on epistemological and ontological premises other than the ones embraced by more conventional universities; these are knowledges and practices that have been subalternized, disregarded and Othered by dominant institutions in Bolivia and by a hegemonic Eurocentric academia on a global level. Thus, "in the current era, an indigenous university must be a challenge to dominant academia and create alternatives for another society" as a former lecturer at the UNIBOL "TK" formulated it.

Moreover, both UNIBOL "TK" and UTA claim to deal with the decolonization of knowledge, and according to the new constitution all Bolivian universities should be dedicated to a general process of decolonization. This leads us to another essential question: What does "decolonization" mean in the context of higher education? In the Bolivian debate, there are two principal standpoints, articulated here in the quotes of two social science students at UMSA: (1) "To decolonize higher education would be to give everyone access to a high-quality university education, without any form of discrimination." (2) "It would mean incorporating indigenous knowledges and knowledgeable indigenous men and women as lecturers and to transform the syllabi completely."

While seemingly ingenuous, the former standpoint, that is, that the "universal" access to higher education would imply its decolonization, could on the one hand partially be corroborated by pointing to the effects within the university system of including formerly excluded sectors, in this case indigenous people. The *indianista-katarista* student movement of the 1970s and 1980s is an example of this. The national revolution of 1952 made it possible for Aymara and Quechua men and women to enter the university and to organize in students' organizations, some of which became radicalized *indianista-katarista* groups in which historical figures such as Bartolina Sisa and Tupaj Katari were recovered from the selective amnesia of dominant nationalist history writing and turned into potent symbols of indigenous liberation. However, the revolution did not eradicate the colonial structures of exclusion and the mechanisms by which the elites secured their privileged positions in Bolivian society and within academia. With time, however, some of these radical indigenous students turned into radical indigenous scholars (for instance Roberto Choque, Simón Yampara, and Esteban Ticona), who insisted on questioning some of the fundaments of colonial academia and, as far as the system permitted, introduced new items in the colonial syllabi. Indeed, this had an effect. On the other hand, however, persistently colonial syllabi and the institutional structures of academia are predisposed to transform the subjectivities of those who access its environments and its knowledges; the Bolivian assimilationist post-revolutionary educational system is an example of this. Dominant Bolivian academia, while to some extent transformed by previously excluded actors, is still a profoundly colonial and marginalizing institution. Consequently, "access" can hardly be synonymous with "decolonization."

The latter standpoint, that is, that decolonization of higher education would imply the incorporation of indigenous knowledges and indigenous knowledgeable men and women as lecturers, is likewise far from indisputable. However, in order to make an informed assessment of this understanding of the decolonization of higher education, the ontological and epistemological foundations of the realities in which such knowledges are produced would need to be assessed in relation to higher education and the coloniality of reality inherent therein.

DAMNÉS REALITIES AND
THE ONTOLOGICAL LOCI OF ENUNCIATION

As I have argued elsewhere, Andean epistemologies—in all their heterogeneity and historicity—are fundamentally experiential, relational, and "of engagement" (Ingold 2000, 216), and have an ontological point of departure in the existence of other-than-human subjectivities and actors, be they *achachila* (male ancestor, embodied in the landscape), *awicha* (female ancestor, embodied in the landscape), *wak'a* ("sacred" place), *uywiri* (local protector/breeder spirit embodied in hills and mountains), or risen to fame through environmentalist discourses tapping Andean worlds of "authenticity" and "exoticism," Pachamama. Knowledge is not produced inside the mind of an autonomous human knower who is detached from the known, but by a knower who is intimately involved in relational fields constituted by human and other-than-human beings—both categories of beings composed by knowledgeable social subjects and intentional actors with agentive efficacy—and within which knowledge is produced, generated or "grown" in situated practices and lived experience. Or as the *amawt'a* and writer Carlos Yujra responded to my question about what will happen to all his knowledge the day he dies and whether he was worried about not having a "disciple" to whom he could pass on his knowledge:

> You still don't get it, do you? I can't pass anything on to anyone. They have to sense it for themselves. I can only point to the places they should go . . . then they will go there and feel and think. If it's a good place, they will think good thoughts.

Aymara epistemologies are relational because they are enmeshed in a relational world; they stem from a relational ontology where "being" is not primarily determined and conditioned by essence but by relation, relation to other human beings and to other-than-human-beings, and fundamentally to "place."[5] However, relational ontologies and epistemologies of engagement are not rewarded within academia. While Aymara epistemologies are based on an ontological premise of oneness, the epistemology that has imposed itself as the hegemonic theory of knowledge stems largely from Cartesian metaphysics and its ontological dualism of two separate worlds: the intentional world of human subjects (the knower) and the world of material things (the known). This epistemology asserts detachment of the known from the knower and the process of knowing. Ingold argues that this is an epistemology that "introjects a division between mind and world, or between reason and nature, as an ontological a priori." Thus, the knower is supposedly able to know the world without being part of the world and to produce knowledge that is universal and independent of context. This hegemonic notion of knowledge engenders discursive scientific practices of knowledge production which generate a dominant reality which, in turn, makes it difficult to think of and from within other realities. There is no room in this hegemonic notion of knowledge for knowledgeable and intentional other-than-human subjects; concurrently, it suppresses anything that actually is produced from other ontologically informed lifeworlds. These suppressed lifeworlds are the *damnés* realities of the subalternized and racialized Other. Fanon coined "*les damnés de la terre*," or "the wretched of the earth," to describe the existential conditions of those who are situated on the darker side of what Mignolo calls "the colonial difference," that is, those who by way of colonial oppression and racist exploitation are positioned in the zone of non-being, "the being who is not there." *Damnés* realities, then, are the realities that are not allowed to be, the ontologically informed lifeworlds that are denied and suppressed in the coloniality of reality that characterizes the current world-system and saturates higher education, in Bolivia and elsewhere. Or in the words of an *indianista-katarista* intellectual and former lecturer at UNIBOL "TK":

> The university is exactly this: *university*, it's "university" in the sense that it reproduces universal schemes, and what the university should be reproducing are not universal schemes, because according to dominant criteria what's "universal" here is Eurocentric. . . . European rationality is denominated as "universal" here. . . . The Bolivian university is in this sense profoundly colonial.

Aymara ontologically informed lifeworlds have for centuries coexisted, and sometimes coalesced in creative constellations, with hegemonic ontological impositions. However, it has been a colonial coexistence in the sense that Aymara ontology has been recognized, not as knowledge of reality in its own right, but as one element in the Cartesian dualism, that is, as the cultural component that projects cultural meaning onto the one and only real reality of brute matter "out there." This way, "Aymara culture" can be reduced to folklore and cultural (mis)representations of reality, and universities can pay lip service to interculturality and multiculturalism without having their epistemological and ontological foundations shaken by "worlds and knowledges otherwise." In a serious process of decolonization, however, these *damnés* realities intend to carve out a space for themselves also in higher education—not as cultural projections but as ontologies—and the lecture room becomes a space of ontological conflicts, a space in which a politics of ontological location is enacted by actors who occupy not only different "epistemic loci of enunciation" but also different ontological loci of enunciation. These actors are students and lecturers engaged in pedagogical interaction, but among them are also authors of textbooks and syllabi who are not there in person. Some of them speak from *damnés* realities, while others speak from a dominant ontology that is enacted and reproduced by academia as a conceptual-ontological straightjacket. A fundamental part of the ontological disobedience referred to at the beginning of this text is to use any ontological opening, any cracks and fissures in dominant reality, to carve out an ontological locus of enunciation different from the one embraced within the coloniality of reality, and to do so from within institutions of higher education. One way to do so would be to claim a space for subalternized and Othered knowledges and subalternized and Othered knowledge producers, such as for instance *yatiris* and *amawt'as*, within academia. However, this is not unproblematic. While it is indeed paradoxical and simultaneously symptomatic that mainly "Western-based masters who embody the decolonial idea are so far present in academia as the authorities in critical thought against neo-colonialism," the incorporation of indigenous knowledges, pedagogical practices, and lifeworlds into colonial academia entails a risk. Instead of decolonizing higher education, there is a risk that indigenous knowledges, pedagogical practices, and lifeworlds are institutionalized, instrumentalized, and thereby colonized and defanged by colonial academia. Hence, incorporating indigenous knowledge and knowledgeable indigenous men and women into a colonial institution of higher education is not by implication a decolonizing act; there is also an urgent need for thoroughgoing structural and institutional transformations. Or in the words of Freddy "Pachakuti" Acarapi: "The university is colonization, whether it's labeled 'indigenous university' or not."

Likewise, though not intending to, separate "indigenous universities" may also play a role in conserving the colonial status quo at conventional institutions of higher education. Public universities may pay lip service to their state-imposed "decolonizing" mission, but since there are state-managed indigenous universities for those who want to "recover indigenous knowledge" and get a technical and practically oriented profession and there is UTA for those who seek radical *indianista* ideological orientation and "ancestral knowledge," conventional public universities seem to be free to continue being "segregated and racist institutions that reproduce exclusively the Eurocentric model of knowledge." Thus, indigenous universities are used to justify and legitimize the status quo at conventional public universities. Moreover, public universities can always refer to their university autonomy, which leaves even the Ministry of Education quite toothless. Serious decolonizing initiatives in the lecture room are therefore not an institutional undertaking at public universities; it is rather up to individual lecturers to implement decolonizing initiatives, but in a conservative institutional setting such initiatives are seldom rewarded.

There is, indeed, much more room for decolonizing pedagogical practices and epistemological and ontological disobedience at UTA. It is a space, like Escuela de Pensamiento Pacha, for the production of knowledge from within a *damné* reality with another ontological locus of enunciation. However, in present-day Bolivian society, any serious engagement with knowledges and realities other than the ones embraced and reproduced by dominant modern academia runs the risk of being ridiculed and delegitimized by powerful actors using the epithet *"pachamamismo."*

PACHAMAMISMO AND THE COLONIAL TURN

As mentioned above, *"pachamamismo"* is used in a general manner since 2010 to criticize what is held to be a quasi-esoteric form of Andean essentialist culturalism, a smokescreen of multiculturalist ritual practices and ceremonial paraphernalia and an indigenist discourse peppered with supposedly enigmatic Aymara concepts. Initially, the criticism was primarily directed at the contradictions between governmental discourse and state ceremony and governmental policies and realpolitik, such as using Pachamama as an environmentalist rhetorical device in governmental discourse while implementing extractivist politics, or speaking of *"Vivir Bien"* as an *"*alternative civilizatory paradigm*"* while executing standard developmentalist projects. According to Rivera, the government has even made a "colonial turn," and the contradictions and inconsistencies have augmented: "the rights of Mother Earth" have been legally recognized and the state agency called the Plurinational Authority of Mother Earth ("Autoridad Plurinacional de la Madre Tierra") has been established to ensure that her rights are respected while the agricultural frontier is simultaneously pushed further and further into the Amazon by state incentives, and deforestation rates and CO_2 emissions have reached unprecedented levels; "ancestral knowledge" is praised by quite peripheral actors within the Bolivian state apparatus while nuclear physics and petroleum engineering are tightly tied to national development and sovereignty in the discourse of governmental representatives in the heart of power; Evo is in state discourse said to represent "the indigenous horizon (which is the negation of modernity)" [my translation] while nuclear plants, highways, industrialization, and natural resource extraction in nature reserves are on the governmental agenda; Aymara ritual specialists give "indigenous legitimacy" to the government in official ceremony while the president questions indigenous peoples' right to prior consultation in any extractivist or infrastructure project that affect them and their territories, by claiming that such consultations are "delaying our development."

Arguably, to veil these contradictions in an essentialist staging of indigeneity and in rhetorical and instrumentalist references to Pachamama is to invite criticism. However, accusations of *pachamamismo* are directed not only at the government, but at nearly anyone who refers to *damnés* realities, beings, and knowledges, not least at actors who try to carve out a space for knowledge production and learning founded on other epistemological and ontological premises within higher education. De Carvalho and Flórez-Flórez argue that "for every area of Indigenous . . . knowledge, Western knowledge has developed a specific mode for dismissing its intrinsic value." Accusations of *pachamamismo* are, I would argue, one such mode of dismissal in which certain knowledges, realities and producers of knowledge are delegitimized while other knowledges and producers of knowledge are legitimized and a certain reality is naturalized and reproduced.

Interestingly, accusations of *pachamamismo* are articulated from radically different political positions: right-wing conservatives, middle-class liberals, Marxists of all kinds, and even certain actors within the *indianista* movement who see no use whatsoever for references to Pachamama and "ancestral knowledge" in their activism directed at the seizure of political power. Their ontological loci of enunciation, however, are quite vicinal. They are, in one way or another, modern. And "modernity itself has conditioned the responses available to its own violence by naturalizing a grammar (i.e., interlinked ontology, epistemology and metaphysics) that captures and reinscribes our attempts to interrupt and resist it."

When Slavoj Žižek visited Bolivia in 2011, invited by Vice President Álvaro García, he articulated a critique of what he saw as New Age elements in Evo's discourse and argued that "if there is anything good in capitalism, it is that there is no Mother Earth there [my translation]. He was quite widely applauded by political actors who see no room for, or no need for, anything like Pachamama in "the revolution" and his critique became a plea in the debate on *pachamamismo*, a debate that thrives and divides not only *indianista* activists and intellectuals—on the one hand the *indianista* student organization MINKA, the constituents of which tend to see anything that is not directly related to the seizure of power as a culturalist disturbance and, conversely, the equally *indianista* Escuela de Pensamiento Pacha who posit "ancestral knowledge" as the very fundament of political action, but alternatively for Marxist thinkers, the abovementioned Stefanoni who see no revolutionary potential whatsoever in a "cataract of words in Aymara," and, oppositely, J. J. Bautista and Rafael Bautista who claim to have discovered another Marx by taking their analytical point of departure in the realities of indigenous peoples. Rafael Bautista recently argued:

> The economists . . . call their own madness "rationality," and they call
> us crazy. . . . We who say that we must retain development and
> progress, they call us crazy . . . they call us . . . *pachamamistas*.[6]

However valid the criticism of *pachamamismo* may be when directed at
the contradictions in governmental politics and discourse and the essentialist staging of indigeneity and "ancestral spirituality," if everyone
would comply with the idea that coloniality/modernity can only be criticized from within its own ontological assumptions and that any criticism
based on knowledges produced from within other ontological and epistemological frameworks—from within *damnés* realities—is by definition il-
legitimate New Age rubbish or culturalist (mis)representations of reality,
we would end up in a situation of grotesquely reactionary proportions; a
situation in which a critical debate about the colonial, capitalist world-
system is reduced to an exclusive fuss of modernity on modernity's own
terms. Fortunately, there are those who do not comply, neither with hegemonic academia on a global level, nor with those who try to impose a
modern/colonial conceptual straightjacket on critical thinking in Bolivian
academia. Fortunately, there are those who disobey.

CONFRONTING THE COLONIALITY OF REALITY: ONTOLOGICAL DISOBEDIENCE

While, as discussed above, there are attempts at confronting the coloniality of reality from within one of its very strongholds—the university—,
be that by founding an other university (such as UTA) or by introducing
other knowledges, realities, and actors into established higher education,
there are also many critical actors working outside of the dominant academic institutions, creating their own spaces for critical knowledge production. One such initiative is the Laboratorio del Pensamiento Indio, a
group of *indianista* students and intellectuals in El Alto who, among other
things, publish critical texts (see for instance Mamani, Choque, and Del-
gado on "rebel memories") and participate in public debate. Another
initiative is the aforementioned Escuela de Pensamiento Pacha, the members of which meet in their small and cold El Alto premises to sketch out
the political and philosophical strategies for the indianization of society
and being. Sometimes, however, they meet elsewhere, as for instance in
the kitchen of my small adobe house on the slopes of La Paz, to discuss
"knowledge," "truth," and "reality." One such evening, poring over a
bag of coca leafs, Pachakuti said:

> Our grandfathers were not researchers, but they were knowledgeable.
> It's *pacha*[7] that teaches us everything. . . . According to Western logic,
> man makes theory. And the dominated tries to liberate themselves in
> the logic of the dominant. But these are only arguments between hu-

mans; there is nothing of *pacha* there. . . . To overcome all this, we cannot use the same logic.

Indigenous ontologies and *damnés* realities may indeed be used as a folklorist smokescreen to cover up the contradictions and incoherencies of governmental politics and discourse. However, in Escuela de Pensamiento Pacha something else is going on. A radical criticism of modernity/coloniality is being articulated from a relational ontology; epistemological and ontological disobedience is practiced, defying the dominant notion that there is no "revolutionary potential" in indigenous ontologies. They are confronting the coloniality of reality from within the entrails of modernity, but also from its margins and from beyond its tentacles. They are carving out spaces for the decolonization of reality through other ways of knowing and being, and spaces for the reemergence— within the zone of being—of *damnés* realities through the cracks and fissures of dominant reality. This is "the affirmation of another world," neither a position "of pure negation" nor of radical epistemic relativism. At the most, they put "Truth," with a capital "T," within quotation marks and thereby question powerful actors' claims to absolute truth. Reality is not "de-realized" by such an act, it is rather "re-realized" from within other relational fields, from other ontological premises, and from other ontological loci of enunciation.

De Sousa Santos, Arriscado Nunes, and Meneses have convincingly argued that "there is no global social justice without global cognitive justice." While "cognitive justice" has been rewardingly discussed in terms of "espistemic justice" and the recognition of the plurality of knowledge, I would argue that cognitive justice is not only about epistemic justice, but also about ontological justice. Or in other words, epistemic justice, in order to be anything but a disembedded, logocentric project of modern academia, ought to be anchored in ontological justice, since epistemic justice is inconceivable within the coloniality of reality. Moreover, drawing on de Sousa Santos' "sociology of absences and emergences," I would argue that "reality" cannot be reduced to that which powerful actors in a world of grotesque power asymmetries allow to exist; also that which is not allowed to exist is there, as potentially emergent present realities. These are realities that are regenerated through ontological disobedience and in which the criteria to validate knowledge stretch beyond the insular, closed system of academia. These are realities, the *damnés* realities, not without Europe, but rather, in Blaser's terms, realities in spite of Europe; realities with the potential to resist coloniality/ modernity and generate alternatives. Or in the words of a *feminista-indianista* activist in her forties:

> Resistance and alternatives have always come from the indigenous peoples and our worlds. It hasn't come from Europe. Look at the Zapa-

tistas! If it wasn't for these other worlds, we would have destroyed the planet completely by now!

Nevertheless, ontological disobedience does not imply the revindication of a hermetically sealed precolonial indigenous world; rather, ontological disobedience is a *ch'ixi* practice in a *ch'ixi* reality. If you consult an Aymara dictionary you will find that *"ch'ixi"* means "gray" or "spotted." When put to theoretical use by Silvia Rivera, however, this seemingly dull concept reveals intriguing dynamics by which elements from different cultural and cosmological contexts coexist in one and the same lifeworld or in one and the same practice. They do not completely fuse or meld; to the human eye they may seem one greyish blend, but they exist side by side as though they were tiny spots of black and white. In this sense, in current Bolivian society the disembedding and decontextualizing forces of modernity are present alongside the embedding and contextualizing relational forces and ideas of "community." When I speak of reality as *ch'ixi* or of a *ch'ixi* ontology, it is to draw attention to the miscellaneous nature(s) of reality and the coexistence without complete fusion of elements from different realities in one and the same practice. The *damné* reality reivindicated by Escuela de Pensamiento Pacha and the dominant reality generated and reproduced in hegemonic academia are neither two discrete realities that people move between, nor a complete hybrid fusion; they are rather elements that are simultaneously present in people's practices, experiences, and lifeworlds, overlapping and interconnected in a myriad of power-infused ways.

However interesting indigenous knowledges and lifeworlds may be to the anthropologist, the framing of the issue in terms of "ontologies," as in "multiple realities," may obstruct the theorizing of power and global inequalities. "Rather than immersing ourselves in alternative ontologies and denying the reality of 'a common world,'" Hornborg therefore argues, "anthropologists would do well to contemplate [global] material inequalities."

While sympathizing with Hornborg's appeal to anthropologists to abandon intradisciplinary navel-gazing and instead put our analytical tools to work in order to make global power asymmetries critically manifest and while sharing his concern for the poor prospects for theorizing power if we follow Latour in arguing that there is no such thing as "society" or "capitalism," I cannot help asking if there is *necessarily* a contradiction here. Do we *necessarily* need to abandon the project of immersing ourselves in other ontologies in order to contemplate global inequalities? And more fundamentally, do we need to accept and reproduce the coloniality of reality in order to address the concerns of political economy? I think not. I would rather argue that Hornborg's and others' badly needed critical attention to power asymmetries as expressed for instance in unequal ecological exchange within the capitalist world-system may be fruitfully combined with a critical attention to the ontological power asymmetries, that is, the coloniality of reality, underpinning such unequal material flows, since the former are a condition for and a justification and naturalization of the latter, and the latter are a material expression of the former. The coloniality of reality goes hand in hand with the commodification of reality and the emergence and reproduction of consumer society since modernity, coloniality, and capitalism produce certain subjectivities and a certain dominant reality within which certain subjectivities unfold. A fundamental part of the ontological disobedience—as practiced by Escuela de Pensamiento Pacha, UTA, and others—is to produce other realities within which other subjectivities are allowed to unfold together with other social organizations of production and consumption.

Hornborg is most likely right in arguing that "appeals to the virtues of animism [or 'indigenous ontologies'] are not likely to turn the tables on capitalism." Apolitical ontological rumination is probably not what the world needs the most at the moment. Nevertheless, it is questionable if a radical critique of the world-system necessarily must be articulated according to the ontological premises underpinning the mechanisms of that very world-system. This is why I propose to ontologize (i.e., sensitize to the coloniality of reality)—and thereby decolonize, political economy, and simultaneously politicize (i.e., sensitize to material inequalities)—and thereby decolonize—the so-called ontological turn (a project already initiated by Blaser and de la Cadena, among others). This parallel movement of ontologizing politics and politicizing ontology may engender the critical tools necessary for the production of knowledges that *simultaneously* challenge ontological/epistemological and political/economic power asymmetries, that is, addressing the coloniality of reality and knowledge and the concerns of political economy as interconnected and overlapping dimensions of global injustice. However, without disobedience of different kinds—ontological and epistemological, political and pedagogical, within and beyond academia, within and beyond Bolivia—such a combined project has gloomy prospects.

NOTES

1. I mention René and Freddy Acarapi's names here, not in order to disclose the identity of any such thing as "my informants," but in order to emphasize my great intellectual debt to them. Carlos Yujra is another knowledgeable friend, *amawt'a* and writer, without the collaboration and support of whom I would have been able to write very little of value.

2. First published in 2010 in the Bolivian newspaper *Página 7*, and later republished in *Tabula Rasa* 2011.

3. Jose J. De Carvalho and Juliana Flórez-Flórez, "The Meeting of Knowledges: A Project for the Decolonization of Universities in Latin America," *Postcolonial Studies* 17 (2014): 123.

4. Whether or not indigenous people are a majority of the Bolivian population seems to depend primarily on the phrasing of the questions about ethnic identity in the national census of population (see Kaijser 2014, 72).

5. For a more thorough ethnographic account of these epistemological and ontological premises, see Burman (2012).

6. Museo de Etnografía y Folklore, La Paz, July 9, 2015.

7. Depending on context, *"pacha"* may mean "time," "space," "season," "earth," or "cosmos."

BIBLIOGRAPHY

Autoridad Plurinacional de la Madre Tierra. *Política Plurinacional de Cambio Climático.* La Paz: Autoridad Plurinacional de la Madre Tierra, 2015.

Bautista, Juan J. *Dialéctica del fetichismo de la modernidad: Hacia una teoría crítica del fetichismo de la racionalidad moderna.* La Paz: Editorial Autodeterminación, 2015.

Bessire, Lucas, and David Bond. "Ontological Anthropology and the Deferral of Critique." *American Ethnologist* 41 (2014): 440–56.

Blaser, Mario. "Ontological Conflicts and the Stories of Peoples in Spite of Europe: Towards a Conversation on Political Ontology." *Current Anthropology* 54 (2013): 547–568.

Burman, Anders. "Now We Are Indígenas! Hegemony and Indigeneity in the BolivianAndes." *Latin American and Caribbean Ethnic Studies* 9 (2014): 247–271.

———. "Places to Think With, Books to Think About: Words, Experience and the Decolonization of Knowledge in the Bolivian Andes." *Human Architecture* 10 (2012): 101–120.

———. *Descolonización aymara: Ritualidad y política (2006–2010).* La Paz: Plural Editores, 2011.

———. "Chachawarmi: Silence and Rival Voices on Decolonization and Gender Politics in Andean Bolivia." *Journal of Latin American Studies* 43 (2011): 65–91.

Canessa, Andrew. "Conflict, Claim and Contradiction in the New 'Indigenous' State of Bolivia. *Critique of Anthropology.* 34 (2014): 153–173.

Carrithers, Michael, et al. "Ontology Is Just Another Word for Culture: Motion Tabled at the 2008 Meeting of the Group for Debates in Anthropological Theory, University of Manchester." *Critique of Anthropology.* 30 (2010): 152–200.

Correo del Sur. "Evo: En la consulta se pierde mucho tiempo." *Correo del Sur* (July 13, 2015).www.correodelsur.com/20150713/politica/evo-en-la-consulta-previa-se-pierde-mucho-tiempo.

De Carvalho, Jose J., and Juliana Flórez-Flórez. "The Meeting of Knowledges: A Project for the Decolonization of Universities in Latin America." *Postcolonial Studies* 17 (2014): 122–139.

de la Cadena, Marisol. *Earth Beings: Ecologies of Practice across Andean Worlds.* Durham: Duke University Press, 2015.

———. "The Politics of Modern Politics Meets Ethnographies of Excess Through Ontological Openings." Fieldsights—Theorizing the Contemporary, *Cultural Anthropology,* 2014. Online www.culanth.org/fieldsights/471-the-politics-of-modern-politics-meets-ethnographies-of-excess-through-ontological-openings.

———. "Indigenous Cosmopolitics in the Andes: Conceptual Reflections Beyond 'Politics.'" *Cultural Anthropology* 25 (2010): 334–370.

de Oliveira Andreotti, Vanessa, Sharon Stein, Cash Ahenakew, and Dallas Hunt. "Mapping Interpretations of Decolonization in the Context of Higher Education." *Decolonization: Indigeneity, Education & Society* 4 (2015): 21–40.

de Sousa Santos, Boaventura, Joao Arriscado Nunes, and Maria Paula Meneses. "Opening Up the Canon of Knowledge and Recognition of Difference." *Another Knowledge is Possible: Beyond Northern Epistemologies,* Boaventura de Sousa Santos, ed., xix–xii. London: Verso, 2007.

de Sousa Santos, Boaventura. "Public Sphere and Epistemologies of the South." *Africa Development* 37 (2012): 43–67.

———. *Epistemologías del sur*. Mexico: Siglo XXI, 2010.

Escobar, Arturo. "Worlds and Knowledges Otherwise: The Latin American Modernity/Coloniality Research Program." *Cultural Studies* 21(2007): 179–210.

Grosfoguel, Ramón. "The Structure of Knowledge in Westernized Universities Epistemic Racism/Sexism and the Four Genocides/Epistemicides of the Long 16th Century." *Human Architecture* 10 (2013): 73–90.

Hornborg, Alf. "The Political Economy of Technofetishism: Agency, Amazonian Ontologies, and Global Magic." *Hau: Journal of Ethnographic Theory* 5 (2015): 47–69.

Ingold, Tim. *The Perception of the Environment: Essays in Livelihood, Dwelling and Skill.* London and New York: Routledge, 2000.

Kaijser, Anna. *Who is Marching for Pachamama? An Intersectional Analysis of Environmental Struggles in Bolivia under the Government of Evo Morales.* Doctoral dissertation, Lund University, 2014.

Lazar, Sian. *El Alto, Rebel City: Self and Citizenship in Andean Bolivia.* Durham: Duke University Press, 2008.

Maldonado-Torres, Nelson. "On the Coloniality of Being: Contributions to the Development of a Concept." *Cultural Studies* 21 (2007): 240–270.

McNeish, John A. "Extraction, Protest and Indigeneity in Bolivia: The TIPNIS Conflict." *Latin American and Caribbean Ethnic Studies* 8 (2013): 221–242.

Mignolo, Walter. "Epistemic Disobedience, Independent Thought and De-Colonial Freedom." *Theory, Culture & Society* 26 (2009): 123.

———. *Local Histories/Global Designs: Coloniality, Subaltern Knowledges, and Border Thinking.* Princeton: Princeton University Press, 2000.

———. "I Am Where I Think: Epistemology and the Colonial Difference." *Journal of Latin American Cultural Studies: Travesia* 8 (1999): 235–245.

Ministerio de Educación. *Ley de educación "Avelino Siñani-Elizardo Pérez" No. 070.* La Paz: Ministerio de Educación, 2010.

Pérez, Elizardo. *Warisata: La escuela ayllu.* La Paz: Burillo. Reinaga, Fausto. 1978. *El Pensamiento amautico.* La Paz: PIB, 1963.

Restrepo, Paula. "Legitimation of Knowledge, Epistemic Justice and the Intercultural University: Towards an Epistemology of 'Living Well.'" *Postcolonial Studies* 17 (2014): 140–154.

Rivera, Silvia. *Mito y desarrollo en Bolivia: El giro colonial del gobierno del MAS.* La Paz: Piedra Rota, Plural Editores, 2014.

———. "Ch'ixinakax utxiwa: A Reflection on the Practices and Discourses of Decolonization." *The South Atlantic Quarterly* 111 (2012): 95–109.

Stefanoni, Pablo. "¿Adónde nos lleva el pachamamismo?" *Tabula Rasa* 15 (2011): 261–264.

Strathern, Marilyn. *Partial Connections.* Walnut Creek: Altamira, 2004.

Ticona, Esteban, ed. *Bolivia en el inicio del pachakuti: La larga lucha anticolonial de los pueblos aymara y quechua.* Madrid: Ediciones AKAL, 2011

Viveiros de Castro, Eduardo. "Who Is Afraid of the Ontological Wolf? Some Comments on an Ongoing Anthropological Debate." CUSAS Annual Marilyn Strathern Lecture, May 30, 2014.

———. "Cosmological Deixis and Amerindian Perspectivism." *Journal of the Royal Anthropological Institute* 4 (1998): 469–488.

Yampara, Simón. "Cosmovivencia Andina: Vivir y convivir en armonía integral— Suma Qamaña." *Bolivian Studies Journal* 18 (2011): 1–23.

Žižek, Slavoj. *¡Bienvenidos a tiempos interesantes!* La Paz: Vicepresidencia del Estado Plurinacional de Bolivia, 2011.

SEVEN

Delinking from Western Epistemology

En Route from University to Pluriversity
via Interculturality

Robert Aman

In 1992 Argentinian philosopher, Enrique Dussel, delivered his now renowned *Frankfurt lectures*. The place was carefully selected. In the heart of academic Europe, Dussel went on to launch a stern attack on the school of thought carrying the city's name. By questioning their understanding of the genealogy of modernity, it became obvious that the addressees in the lectures were not primarily third-world intellectuals, to whom his concern was evident enough, but scholars in and around Europe that are self-proclaimed custodians of the project of modernity and Enlightenment.[1]

> Modernity is, for many (for Jürgen Habermas or Charles Taylor) an essentially or exclusively European phenomenon. In these lectures, I will argue that modernity is, in fact, a European phenomenon but one constituted in a dialectical relation with a non-European alterity that is its ultimate content. Modernity appears when Europe affirms itself as the "center" of a World History that it inaugurates: the "periphery" that surrounds this center is consequently part of its self-definition. The occlusion of this periphery (and of the role of Spain and Portugal in the formation of the modern world system from the late fifteenth to the mid-seventeenth centuries) leads the major contemporary thinkers of the "center" into a Eurocentric fallacy in their understanding of modernity. If their understanding of the genealogy of modernity is thus partial and provincial, their attempts at a critique or defense of it are likewise unilateral and, in part, false.

Dussel thus immediately disputes the standard narrative of modernity: that it emerged in Europe to confront in the colonies the pre-modern, whether conceptualized as barbaric, primitive, or natural. For Dussel, modernity lies between these two positions; that is, in the hierarchy that links the colonizer to the colonized, grounded in the evaluative binary structures of Eurocentric thought, such as center/periphery, tradition/modernity, and primitive/civilized. In interconnecting modernity with Europe's offshore ventures, Dussel reminded his audience that they, too, were heirs of a colonial legacy. A full understanding of their scientific and cultural traditions, national cultures, and academic disciplines required awareness and knowledge of the imperial system that had set their culture of modernity in place. As such, it was therefore all the more extraordinary, Dussel continued, that a vast majority of European intellectuals carried on as though their focus areas were located outside and beyond the political, economic, and cultural connections that through colonial imperialism have an inextricably integrated character never seen before.

As we are witnessing an ever-increasing concern within various academic disciplines for discerning the intimacy between the political institutions of the "West" (understood as a region, or as the origin of modernity) and the history of imperialism, the works of Dussel—and, indeed, many others—does not only analyze epistemologies that evolved in tandem with imperial powers their works also opens up for an systematic understanding of the process by which academic institutions, schools of learning and groups of intellectuals have gained their insights and reputation at the expense of silencing and marginalization of other ways of knowing, understanding and believing. Succinctly put, the hierarchies instilled by imperialism disavowed colonized populations in different corners of the world from being capable of intellectual labor. Whether the site of production is in the West or elsewhere, then, the knowledge accredited with status as "scientific," "truthful" and "universal" are the ones created with the modern human and natural sciences; sciences deriving from the European Enlightenment and modernity.

Against the backdrop of the symptoms outlined above, this essay aims to make the claim that the decolonization of the modern university requires a move away—or with the vocabulary in use here: to delink—from its almost exclusive reliance on Eurocentric modes of reasoning. For all the difficulties involved in such a task, I will try to show that such a shift would imply an active engagement with what is articulated, thought, and envisioned outside of these frames. As I will argue, it is only by such commitment that it is possible to radically reform the university from relying on, as is the case with the modern Western ones, provincial epistemological traditions claiming universality for themselves to creating a space open to a horizontal dialogue between epistemes from different traditions—in short: from a *uni*versity to a *pluri*versity.

To give flesh to my argument on the ways in which different epistemological traditions are perpetuated through power and geographical
location, I will bring together two distinct paradigms of the very notion
of "interculturality": a concept whose global relevance reveals itself in
public policy, anti-discriminatory and anti-racist intervention, and international security. Projecting transcendence, a cross-cultural dimension,
interculturality appears to be based on the view that we have obligations
to others, a certain responsibility that stretches beyond those to whom we
share formal ties of a common passport, religious affiliation, or citizenship. According to its advocates, interculturality can provide the basis for
new democratic projects as it responds to diversity among learners on the
bases of socially ascribed or perceived differences, such as sex, ethnic
origin, language, religion, nationality, social origin, economic condition,
ability, and so on. This is because, as Nasar Meer and Tariq Modood
suggest, interculturality is allegedly able to reconcile universal values
and cultural specificities. Such universal language is not least reflected in
contemporary educational policies among supranational bodies. Instances of higher education are outlined as, to paraphrase UNESCO, fundamental pieces for construing interculturality and generating the skills
necessary for a citizen in a society characterized by intercultural dialogue: "Intercultural Education provides all learners with cultural
knowledge, attitudes and skills that enable them to contribute to respect,
understanding and solidarity among individuals, ethnic, social, cultural
and religious groups and nations."

Without denying the benevolent intentions invested in such approach,
my readings set out to underscore that there are reasons to be skeptical
toward all presumptions of flat substitutability between cultures, a kind
of asymmetrical interrelation that allows everything to be translated into
a universal idiom. Reliant on a theoretical backdrop that points out the
ways in which epistemological, historiographical, and political discourses are interwoven and work together to sustain an order that allows
European cultural patterns to universalize themselves, I will bring in
another understanding of interculturality with its roots in the particular
and with strong reverberations of the historical experience of colonialism.
In another part of the world, the very notion of *interculturalidad* — translation: interculturality — is a core component among indigenous social
movements in the Andean region of Latin America in their struggles for
public and political recognition. Attempting to break out of the prison of
colonial vocabulary — modernization, progress, salvation — *interculturalidad* relies on another logic, another rationality that in certain respects sets
it apart from interculturality. Neither can interculturality and *interculturalidad* be reduced to mere *faux amis* — words that sound the same across
languages but that have completely different significations — as the two
notions operate across an epistemic divide; a rift that will be conceptualized as a colonial difference. Having been represented as inferior, indige-

nous people in Latin America have not been in a position to present their own epistemic credentials, much less judge European ones, and as a result, *interculturalidad*, as will be seen, greatly emphasizes the historical and socio-political conditions under which it prevailed.

INTERCULTURALITY/*INTERCULTURALIDAD*

A late December day in 2005 marked a forceful emergence of indigenous people on the political scene as Evo Morales was elected Bolivia's—and indeed in Latin America in modern times—first president of indigenous origin. In his inaugural speech before the congress in La Paz, Morales declared that "the indigenous communities, which are the majority of the Bolivian population, have historically been marginalized, humiliated, despised, doomed to extinction." But "today," he continued, "begins the new year for the originary peoples of this world, a new life in which we search for equality and justice, a new millennium."

More than five centuries had elapsed since Europe cut the veins of the indigenous populations (*los pueblos indígenas*) open, by initiating the destruction of their empires, societies, and communities, demanding labor from their bodies and confessions to a foreign God. As part of the bloodletting, the indigenous populations were unavoidably drawn into the emergence of a new global division of commerce—from merchandise to human cargo—that saw both Latin America and Africa stripped of memories, exuberance, and manpower. By concentrating on the numbing ghastliness of colonialism, Morales' speech conveys that the *conquistadores* were not only armed with weapons; they also carried with them a sign system, a new master code, which excluded the indigenous populations from collective memory in the process of their inscription onto European maps.

Akin to Morales' attempt to reveal the geopolitical perspective from which history tends to be written, Eric Wolf uses "People without History," a metaphor that emphasizes the epistemic power differential that placed both continents and people outside of history before the advent of European eyes to testify to their existence. In this sense, to be part of history is a privilege of European modernity; excluding every society which does not use alphabetic writing or communicates in a vernacular other than the imperial languages of modern Europe. This is visible not only in the renaming—the baptism—of a landmass already known as "Abya Yala" as "America" after one of its European witnesses but also in the later addition of "Latin" to further emphasize its literal inscription into another sign system. "I learned to love this land," notes Colombian author William Ospina, "through the words of someone who did not love it."

Although Bolivia achieved independence in 1825, the republican ideals of equality and fraternity as embraced by revolutionary troops comprised of European descendants, continued to collide with the memories and experiences of the indigenous populations. Liberation from Spain, then, had marginal effect on the situation of the indigenous populations as newborn republics replicated the colonial structures in new terms and the very discourse of nationalist unity used for imperial decolonization continued to push the indigenous populations to the margins of society with the continuous enhancement of the colonial difference between modern European idioms (languages of science and knowledge) and those of the indigenous populations (languages of religion and culture).

Given this state of affairs, the Morales government emphasized the need to decolonize the educational system. The purpose was, on the one hand, to break down the racial structures imposed by colonialism and, on the other hand, to implement the knowledge systems, histories and languages of the indigenous communities as an integral part of the curricula to put an end to the privileging of European thought as a universal model. According to the first article of *Nueva ley de la Educación Boliviana* (The New Bolivian Education Act), education is now centered on the objectives of decolonization and multilingualism under the name of *interculturalidad*. It is intercultural "because it articulates a Multinational Educational System of the state based on the fortification and development of the wisdom, knowledge and belonging to our own languages of the indigenous nations," the article reads; it is intercultural "because it promotes interrelation and living together with equal opportunities with appreciation and mutual respect between the cultures of the Multinational State and the world."

On a rhetorical level *interculturalidad* gains its legitimacy by invoking the past as the reason for another future beyond the logics of modernity that have concealed histories, repressed subjectivities, subalternized knowledge systems, and silenced languages. "The best way to decolonize Bolivia," Morales stresses, "is to recover our culture and ways of living," which conveys an understanding of how Bolivia—as has any other part of the region with its diverse indigenous populations—has always been multicultural but represented as monocultural by the Spanish rulers and, later, the Creole elites. Subsequently, *interculturalidad* is intertwined with an act of restorative justice for the way in which the nation-state for centuries has turned the indigenous populations into its blind spot.

From here we can go on to establish, in more precise terms, that there are several translations of interculturality in play simultaneously. Although each is the other's equivalent in their respective language schemas, interculturality is not *interculturalidad*—just as Latin America is not Abya Yala. As I henceforth will distinguish between the translations of the notion, the emphasis on the medium of language makes the contradictions that separate the two—interculturality contra *interculturalidad*— yet more apparent: Where indigenous movements target the colonially imposed structure of society that has annulled and muted other languages and ways of being, the EU refers to interculturality as a political project that characterizes the founding of the union with its "rich cultural and linguistic diversity, which is inspiring and has inspired many countries across the world." In addition, the EU identifies conditions for interculturality in the cultural and linguistic heritage of the member states, claiming that this serves as a foundation from which "to develop active inter-cultural dialogue with all countries and all regions, taking advantage of for example Europe's language links with many countries." Thus one ascribes importance to local languages that became global through colonialism, while for the other, those very languages echo the imperial orders that *interculturalidad* is an attempt to overcome. In sum, the diverse peoples, geographies, and political histories invoked by interculturality are linked to *interculturalidad* via Europe's colonial past.

In what follows, I will focus specifically on the core meanings attached to *interculturalidad* in terms of retrieved languages, reinscribed histories, and the production of knowledge, beginning with an elaboration of the logic of domination as it is rooted in the modern/colonial world—here referred to as coloniality. Shortly thereafter, with reference points drawn from the work of Walter Mignolo and his notion of *delinking,* I introduce the theoretical backdrop that guides my analysis. Then, I offer a brief account of the empirical material by providing an overview of interviews conducted with students and teachers in local academic courses on *interculturalidad* in Bolivia, Ecuador, and Peru. In the fourth and main part of the essay, I develop an argument for *interculturalidad* to be understood as an act of resistance led by indigenous needs and principles of knowledge with the purpose to delink from Western epistemology—inside as well as outside formal educational settings.

DELINKING FROM EUROPEAN MODERNITY

According to the *Oxford English Dictionary*—the most diligently compiled index of English-language usage—modernity is "the quality or condition of being modern" with the additional definition of "a modern way of thinking." In constructing binary opposites, and in alluding to the Enlightenment, rationality, and science, what "modern thinking" tends to disavow is that "tradition" —or, "traditional thinking" —is in itself a creation of the discourse of modernity. Put differently, the dividing line between the modern and those who are not or have yet to become modern was drawn by the very discourse that defined modernity. According to Mignolo, tradition was a necessary creation, an invention essential to defining modernity as the location in time of the ideals to be attained by humanity and to situating it in the geopolitical space of Western Europe.

The indigenous populations provided the mirror in which Europe, as an identity and culture, could recognize itself as modern. Put differently, the dividing line between the modern and those who are not or have yet to become modern was marked out by the very discourse that defined modernity; its presence is essential to establishing modernity as the location in time of the ideals to be attained, and to situating it in the geopolitical space of Western Europe.[2] However, to say that modernity is an invention is not to say that there is a single interpretation of it. On the contrary, modernity has been conceptualized in numerous ways, full of robust waves of polemic and contradictions that target divergent political, intellectual and aesthetic practices. Without turning a deaf ear to modernity's many voices, in this essay I will rely on Arturo Escobar's definition of modernity as "the coherence and crystallization of forms (discourses, practices, structures, institutions) that have arisen over the last few hundred years out of certain cultural and ontological commitments of European societies." I will quote Escobar at length:

> With the modern ontology, certain constructs and practices, such as the primacy of humans over non-humans (separation of nature and culture) and of some humans over others (the colonial divide between us and them); the idea of the autonomous individual separated from community; the belief in objective knowledge, reason, and science as the only valid modes of knowing; and the cultural construction of "the economy" as an independent realm of social practice, with "the market" as a self-regulating entity outside of social relations—all of these ontological assumptions became prominent. The worlds and knowledges constructed on the basis of these ontological commitments became "a universe." This universe has acquired certain coherence in socio-natural forms such as capitalism, the state, the individual, industrial agriculture, and so forth.

The final sentences of this citation are fundamental to my discussion: they point at the ways in which a certain type of European modernity has been able to claim universality for itself and, in the process, to come across as natural and desirable far beyond the realm in which it originated. Based on such an understanding of modernity, Mignolo traces its development within the context of colonialism; modernity is seen as a result of Europe's colonial ambitions. To marry modernity with coloniality is thus to reveal that there is a darker side of modernity, a destructive logic hidden underneath keywords such as "salvation," "development," and "progress," or, to put it differently, coloniality. According to Mignolo, Eurocentrism can be defined in precisely those terms—a view of history in which modernity is there to supersede traditions and backwardness, whereby colonialism is—unfortunately or otherwise—a means to a better end. What such a perspective recognizes is the ways in which the colonial powers, supported by the control of knowledge, could impose a devaluation of non-Europeans who did not conform to the model and norm of modernity, produced as Other, an absolute negation, expelled from the borders of civilization, exercised through a matrix that positions certain groups within colonial and racialized hierarchies. "There cannot be modernity without coloniality," Mignolo asserts: "the two constitute each other, as coloniality demarcates the hierarchies at modernity's heart."

Through the expansion of capitalism and a racial matrix, the colonial powers could impose a devaluation of ways of knowing, representing and conceptualizing that did not fit parameters established by modern knowledge, science, and law. "Modernity," Mignolo continues, "was imagined as the house of epistemology"; and from the window of this "house" the colonized regions of the world—from Latin America to Africa, from India to the Caribbean—were rarely seen as possessing any attributes belonging to "human nature," and were never credited with the ability to produce anything besides primordial objects. From this perspective, then, the colonies appeared as an incomplete, damaged, and unfinished domain, and their histories were reduced to a series of setbacks in the development of human nature. "There is nothing comparable when it comes to the black man. He has no culture, no civilization, and no 'long historical past,'" as Frantz Fanon famously put it.

Working from the assumption that knowledge is colonized, the task ahead then is to decolonize it. Taking up Samir Amin's proposition that certain peripheries should "delink" themselves from the economic and political systems of the West, Mignolo extends the concept of "delinking" by adding epistemology to the project. Mignolo problematizes Amin's project by arguing that it could certainly bring about a polycentric world, but not an epistemic shift. Attempting to correct what he discerns as blindness to the colonial difference in Amin's argument, Mignolo argues that it is necessary to go around European history to another memory in order to reinscribe into contemporary debates categories of thought, social organizations, and economic conceptions that have been silenced by the progressive discourse of modernity.[3] From this angle, delinking is a passage to a decolonial alternative and it is dedicated to the constitution of other modes of modernization by bringing to the fore knowledge systems that have been colonized and delegitimized but that nonetheless enable us to move outside of the logics of modernity.

However, what Mignolo proposes, once the colonial identity is abolished, is not a return to some kind of "authentic" identity—the Quechua, the Maya, the Guaraní, and so on—as it existed before the arrival of Europeans, with its traditional modes of social organization and authority. Embedded in the project of delinking is rather an acknowledgment that it is possible to transcend or overcome modernity only by approaching it from the perspective of the colonial difference, for even if one sought to reconstruct, for instance, Aymara and Quechua frameworks of knowledge and categories of thought, this effort would have to pass through the very European categories that have denied them legitimacy. Thus, to delink is also to decenter; that is to say, to reveal that those categories that pass for universal or modern are in themselves particularities that undeniably reflect the specific cultures and knowledge systems which have shaped them, and the languages in which they are articulated. While this is a thread to be developed in the upcoming discussion, it must be made clear in closing that delinking refers to an epistemic shift that has yet to occur; it is therefore only possible to speak of it in a way that emphasizes what it *could be,* rather than what it *is.*

A COURSE IN THE ANDES

I draw upon material from a course on *interculturalidad* provided by an indigenous organization spread over the Andean region of Bolivia, Ecuador, and Peru. Founded in 1999 as a social movement with the aim of establishing indigenous educational models, the organization provides courses on *interculturalidad* to adult students. With each course spanning over a year, the students study part-time and are given academic credits on completion of the course. To ensure the informants' anonymity, the name of the pan-Andean organization will not be disclosed; however, the fact that four universities have agreed to impart academic legitimacy by acting as collaborators of the course in awarding credits to the students reveals not only that the organization is strongly positioned within the indigenous communities but also that the course in itself is deemed to conform to a certain standard. According to the syllabus, the aim of the course is to retrieve and construct knowledge in direct relation to Andean culture and identity in local languages and terminology based upon indigenous methodology. Both the heterogeneity encapsulated by the terms "Andean" and "indigenous" and the common experience of negated identities, ways of thinking and interpretations of the world are acknowledged. Interviews were conducted individually with the three teachers and eight of the students from the course, focusing specifically on definitions of *interculturalidad* and its practical significance. All interviews were tape-recorded and later transcribed verbatim. In the analyses, how and with whom the specific interviews were performed will be clarified.

Before proceeding a caveat is necessary: I have no intention of pushing for generalizations or offering a comprehensive account of approaches to *interculturalidad* among indigenous alliances in the Andes. In drawing on material that also potentially contains internal disparities (of class, ethnicity, gender), I want to make it abundantly clear that only a few threads of a much larger tapestry are accounted for here. Nor should

Morales' ascension to power, in the case of Bolivia, be read as a guarantee that *interculturalidad* for the government now means the same thing as for the grassroots movements that supported his campaign—not even a certainty that there is agreement on the meaning of *interculturalidad* within the MAS. On the contrary, Escobar claims that the Morales administration have failed to accomplish profound and satisfactory changes in line with the radical programs proposed by several social movements, which, he continues, highlights how *interculturalidad* as an attempt to transform the existing order is more likely to be struggled for from below than above. What, then, may be a sign that *interculturalidad* risks losing some of its subversive edge in the hands of the state also suggests that to speak of *interculturalidad* as a unified discourse may at times be as inaccurate as to claim a single interpretation of the word "multiculturalism."

Despite the lack of a harmonious definition of *interculturalidad* and the sometimes conflictive space between government and social movements, what unifies the diverse expressions and experiences existing among the indigenous populations in different parts of Latin America is the condition of being out of place in relation to European modernity—the awareness of coloniality. In terms of analytical approach, I have previously mentioned the way in which *interculturalidad* can be conceived as an attempt to delink, whereby particular attention is placed on articulations that run counter to a framework deemed to be Western. Engagement in such an interchange of experiences, memories and significations not only reaches toward the possibility of non-Eurocentric modes of thinking but also may contribute to an understanding of how any attempt to invoke a universal reach for interculturality, as in the case of the EU and UNESCO, risks reproducing coloniality through the European tendency to affirm its own singular outlook on the world, and to elevate that outlook to a universal law.

INDIGENOUS FACE, SPANISH VOICE, LOST IDENTITY

In the first instance, *interculturalidad*, as coded among indigenous alliances, has less to do with the condition of living in ethnically and culturally diverse societies, since that would presuppose the mutual recognition of diverse parties. Rather, the indigenous populations found themselves on the other side of the wall which separates the visible from the invisible part of the social space, officially excluded from the national borders now crossing the land they had cultivated before the arrival of Columbus. From this point of view, the deployment of *interculturalidad* as a watchword for indigenous movements in their political mobilization demanding to be fully recognized as citizens affiliates itself to a long sequence of previous acts of insurgence—from Túpac Katari's siege of La Paz in 1780 to the Katarista indigenous movement in the 1970s; from the

Chayanta uprising in 1927 to the "Water War" in the beginning of the millennium which erupted in response to the privatization of Cochabamba's public water service. While different acts of resistance and rebellions throughout Bolivian history have had varying degree of success in turning the indigenous populations into equal citizens, one noteworthy accomplishment during the 1990s was the official recognition of Aymara, Guaraní, Quechua, and other languages spoken before colonial domination. In the wake of the developments in Bolivia, the other Andean nations eventually followed, as Ecuador and Peru went on to revise their constitutions—the former in 1998, the latter in 2011—to acknowledge indigenous languages as part of the state alongside Spanish.

To further add to the terminological confusion, another consequence of the waves of unprecedented popular uprisings in Bolivia during the 1990s was the rewriting of educational policies in accordance with a new concept: *interculturalidad*. Nevertheless, when adopted by the government, *interculturalidad* came merely to signify bilingual education, and the dimension of decolonialization, which was profoundly emphasized by the indigenous movements in their articulations of the concept, was effectively erased. Although these governmental measures allowed for the organization of education in indigenous vernaculars around the country, in the eyes of the MAS it was purely a preventive political move: an appropriation of the notion of *interculturalidad* that aimed to appease the indigenous populations while disavowing the elements that might have posed a risk to the privileges of the ruling elites. Under these conditions, Spanish continued to be the *lingua franca* of the nation, as indigenous languages were merely transformed into yet another school subject—similar to the study of a foreign language. As is clear in this particular case, it is solely the indigenous populations that are expected to become bilingual—not the Creoles.

While these distorted versions of *interculturalidad* merely paid lip service to alterity, it is indeed evident by now that for many indigenous alliances the request for educational rights in indigenous vernaculars in the name of *interculturalidad* extends beyond language learning; this demand is a call for the inscription across subjects and curricula not only of languages but also of knowledge systems, values and beliefs that have been silenced within official discourses ever since the conquest. Thus, in reaction to state policy initiatives, indigenous alliances began to develop inhouse intercultural education, a concrete example of which is the course under scrutiny.

Interculturalidad, explains a middle-aged student whom I interviewed in Urubamba, a small town in the Peruvian highlands, allows different indigenous cultures to view and interpret the world through the lens of their own beliefs in their own languages. The importance of this maneuver of reconstruction appears to stem from the interference of coloniality in the initiatory pedagogy of school and society:

> On a general basis we have sometimes rejected our culture, we who
> come from indigenous cultures (*los que provenimos de culturas indígenas*).
> This is because of prejudices, of ignorance; we believe that we're inferi-
> or, we become ashamed of our culture (*tenemos vergüenza de nuesta
> cultura*), we become ashamed of our language, ashamed of our mother
> tongue. They have taught us this (*nos han enseñado eso*), that the Euro-
> pean culture (*la cultura europea*) is the superior one, that it's the most
> developed, supposedly. Education here clearly has an occidental for-
> mat wherein they teach us to value what is European (*a valorar lo euro-
> peo*) and not what is ours.

By diagnosing core symptoms of the effect of European influence on life
in the Andes, the interviewee describes a colonial difference in which
being indigenous is equated with lack, synonymous with inferiority in
relation to what is ascribed to Europe. Although she is recounting these
issues in a predominantly general manner, the student's articulation of
negative emotions in relation to being indigenous—an experience of
shame leading to gradual rejection—is significant. The process explained
is that of identification and disavowal, in which pretensions to be part of
the nation's univocal subject require the adoption of a perspective on life,
knowledge, and subjectivity (among other things) derived from modern
European models. In locating the dissemination of European texts in an
impersonal "they" related to the educational system, the student depicts
a two-stroke process: the schools bind pupils to a state written in and
from the language of the colonizers, which in turn, continues to exacer-
bate the colonial wound.

A recurring theme in the postcolonial works of José María Arguedas is
the idea that the instruments applied to conserve the power balance between Europe and its others are eventually idealized and appropriated
by its victims. In his novel *Deep Rivers*, set in the Peruvian highlands, a
schoolboy laconically justifies his lackluster effort to learn Quechua in
this way: "I am not in the habit of speaking Indian," before adding, "I am
thinking of living in Lima or abroad." A defensive strategy used to escape the agony of inadequacy, this character's words closely resemble
those spoken by the student above. Both quotations touch upon the way
in which speaking in an indigenous language emerges as a shameful sign
of failure and brutishness, while Spanish appears to be a symbol of development and supremacy. Symptoms of coloniality are not limited to the
language itself; colonialist vestiges are equally ingrained within languages. In the case of Spanish, imperialist attitudes have found a home in
the realm of the idiomatic negative imperative—*¡ No seas indio!* (*Don't be
Indian!*)—in everyday speech that encourages the recipient to stop acting
ignorantly and instead be civilized. Thus, to call someone an *indio* to their
face is as much of an insult in the Andean region as pretty much anywhere else in Latin America. Behind that term are centuries of discourses,
images and unequal power relations that are deeply racist. Against such

paradigm not constituted by modernity. The unlikelihood of being able to do so illustrates not only the way that certain local knowledge systems have acquired global reach, in contrast to others that remain local, but also a permanent dependency on an imperial legacy. Again, this is not to disregard the contribution of European thought: the footnotes of most scholarly writings, including this one, are ample testimony to our indebtedness to that intellectual history. Rather, it is to acknowledge the joint constitution of the world as both modern and colonial, in which one was the prerequisite of the other, and which has enabled Europe to transform its own local histories into a global pattern—the ideas of enlightenment, civilization, and modernity as the goal and norm of all humanity. Continuously lingering on this theme, a course teacher presented *interculturalidad* as a strategy for combatting

> a modernity of industrial capitalism (*una modernidad del capitalismo industrial*) that has been responsible for the conformity of one way of being, of living, of thinking in the world (*una forma de ser, de vivir, de pensar en el mundo*), one way to be in the world, which it has installed as the only possibility. Then, this view of development makes progress the final stage of human evolution (*el último escalon de la evolución humana*), at which we all are obliged to arrive; an utterly colonial benchmark.

In describing the relentless symptoms of coloniality, the teacher's words speak to the deprivation of agency and recognition in an order dominated by European patterns. With the industrial revolution in its pocket, the key to modernity is a particular understanding of development and progress in which subjects can only be spoken for or spoken to through a narrative of transition that always privileges the "modern"—Europe. As explained by the interviewee, all forms of being, knowing, and advancing not invoked by modernity are translated in terms of absence, lack, and incompleteness. When Fredric Jameson asserts that "it is easier to imagine the end of the world than to imagine the end of capitalism," he implicitly underscores how delinking from modernity—circumventing the capitalism with which it is interrelated—is deemed almost essential by indigenous populations, although it may be impossible to envisage from a Western viewpoint.[5] The universal tendencies that modernity and capitalism have achieved together, however, become provincial when another rationale is added to the mix. A student interviewed in Cochabamba describes a logic of resistance to the dominant paradigm of capitalism in relation to the land:

> In the big world (*el mundo mayor*) the land is valued as a piece of merchandize (*objeto de mercancía*). In the Andean world it isn't, rather we care for it with respect, as something that gives us life (*como algo que nos da vida*), that is part of . . . like a person, more (*como una persona más*).

The ellipsis in the quotation above indicates the locus from which the interviewee speaks, part of a general movement of resistance which attempts to reclaim the land. The planetary metaphor underlines a subjugated position by contrasting "Andean" and "Big"—an inclination that bears traces of the dictum *the West and the Rest*—which draws sharp boundaries between the agents and the silenced in a hierarchy both of ontology (European versus indigenous) and epistemology (science versus beliefs) determined by geopolitical location. Adhering conscientiously to this reasoning means that the adoption of the noun "Andean" rather than "Bolivian" can be read on the one hand as an act of resistance to the territorial demarcations that are a hallmark of the modern state, by signaling a broader affinity to a land overlapped by violently imposed frontiers. On the other hand, evading the term "Bolivian" can also be a viewed as a subtle critique of the Bolivian state's failure to invoke the indigenous populations as part of the national body. Certainly, the comparative framework applied in the quotation indicates the privileged space I occupy as part of *el mundo mayor* (since the need to define the Andean world in terms of its differences from this other world only arises because of my presence), carrying with me an academic language that tends to translate otherness as the inhabitation of a marginal position.

Equally important is the way in which the interviewee opposes the split between nature and culture—that is, the structure of modernity—through attempts to ascribe agency to the land. She articulates a view of the land that equates it with a human subject, in contrast to the dominant paradigm of modernity, which, in providing legitimacy to the capitalist logic of exploitation, regards nature as lifeless and mechanistic. In eschewing the binaries alleged to be central to modernity, the quotation highlights the way in which the common Western opposition between nature and humanity lacks a signifier; *Madre Tierra* cannot be conquered and dominated or exploited for the sake of monetary profit. Humans, living systems, nature and—in Western eyes—lifeless objects are not distinguished, but are rather all conceived as part of a network of living interactions.

"It's my territory that gives me my identity," a student informs me as we stroll in the small garden of her workplace, a short ride from Cuzco. Delving further into this reasoning, she underlines the importance of *interculturalidad* as a return to one's identity and to respecting Mother Earth (*la Pacha*) because "she is our mother (*ella es nuestra madre*) who provides us with our food (*nuestros alimentos*). We also respect our water without contaminating it because the water is life, it has life (*el agua es vida, tiene vida*)." Surrounded by a dramatic landscape, she points her finger at snow-capped mountain peaks and continues: "We also respect our Apus that surround us and protect us (*nos rodean y nos protegen*)."

Notable here is the repeated emphasis on points of identification that were equally apparent in the previous section on the struggle over language that stems from the indispensable interrelation of ways of life and the territory. A claim for the existence of life in the waters and protection from los Apus—symbolically, *Apu* is an honorific for a person in Quechua—signals not only interaction with the landscape and dependency on it but also, as mentioned, a demand for a profound understanding of human and nature as inseparable, always locked in an intricate dance, and in an intersubjective relationship of co-realization and fertilization. By contrast, Western epistemic traditions are, among other things, characterized for claiming detachment of the known from the knower. Consequently, they rely on a separation between mind and world, or between reason and nature, as an ontological a priori. As such, the knowing subject is thus able to know the world without being attached to it, that is, the knowing subject is able to produce knowledge that is supposed to be universal and independent of context.

Within the logic of the cosmovision explained by the interviewee, life becomes circular rather than linear; modernity's firm emphasis on development and progress lacks a proper equivalent. This is not to suggest, however, the absence of methods of reasoning or the use of specific technologies but to underline, drawing on the utterances above, the way that European modernity invariably is revealed to be provincial and context-bound when light is cast on loopholes in the universalist tendencies of its rhetoric. From the perspective that life is circular, modernity must be formulated around the establishment of a relationship with the territory—a firm shift away from the view of nature as another conquered object. Just as Waman Puma and Hegel come from different circumstances, meaning that their respective theories are produced in languages that are in turn part of multiple singular histories, a sole modernity can never claim universal validity in a single language.

CONCLUSION

In taking two sides of the contemporary educational paradigm of interculturality by way of example, what I have here pinpointed is a certain tendency to overlook the fact that when concepts relying on Western epistemology is exported to places whose experiences do not correspond, or correspond only partially, to the framework of knowledge within which the notion is produced, the other side of modernity reveals itself; that is, coloniality, which has historically hidden, silenced, and forced itself upon non-European cultures. Those non-European locations that have been classified in imperial epistemology as non-places, the places of the barbarians, the inferiors, the primitives who had to learn to think through modern European imperial vernaculars.

Despite the aforementioned differences in meaning and sometimes even colliding points of view, *interculturalidad* reveals that there cannot

be a singular modernity irrespective of time, space, environment, or social conditions. As no particular kind of modernity or singular type of
epistemology can account for all possible interventions in the world, the
forms of modernity will have to vary between different countries depending on specific circumstances and social practices. In comparison to
interculturality, to speak of *interculturalidad* is thus to emphasize the colonial difference; a difference that is also a source of critical knowledge as it
simultaneously makes visible coexisting paradigms of thought that have
been silenced and disavowed. More precisely, to delink means to produce, transform, and disseminate knowledge that is not dependent on
the epistemology of European modernity—that is, the norms and the
problems of the West—but that, on the contrary, responds to the need of
the colonial difference. In short, the notion of interculturality overlooks
the relation of power, while the concept of *interculturalidad* is explicitly
based on colonial power differentials.

   Although we live in a time in which criticizing the West comes close
to almost self-flagellation, incisive critiques of the violence of modernity
is, however, necessary for deepening our comprehension of its seemingly
endless ability to reformulate and reconstitute itself in the face of vigorous and varied resistance. Nonetheless, the point is not that European
modernity is unreasonable in itself, or that those grand narratives of citizenship, rights, and nation-state produced within this discourse are
merely culturally specific. The key issue is rather that these narratives
have been able to come across as natural and desirable far beyond the
realm where they originated. Put differently, the problem—because there
is a problem indeed—with this tradition is that it has become hegemonic.
To disregard the fact that modernity is a product of a particular place, a
particular time, and particular people, also entails a denial of those social,
historical, and geographical circumstances that produced modernity,
which implies a denial of the possibility that universal ideas can be real-
ized in other times, by other people, in other places.

   What I have attempted to do in this essay by way of *interculturalidad* is
to approach the pedagogical task of engaging with modernity's shadow;
to push for the necessity to think seriously about La Paz, Puno, and
Otavalo—or Port-au-Prince, Dakar, and Rabat, for that matter—not only
New York, Oxford, or Paris as possible sites of knowledge. Hence, pluriversity is a process of knowledge production that is open to epistemic
diversity; a dialogical dynamic between different cultures that are set on
equal standing, an intercultural dialogue in which intercultural is understood as inter-epistemic. After all, as Aníbal Quijano states, "epistemic
decolonization is necessary to make possible and move toward a truly
intercultural communication; to an exchange of experiences and significations as the foundation of another rationality that legitimately could
claim some universality."

NOTES

1. See Enrique Dussel, "Eurocentrism and Modernity (Introduction to the Frankfurt Lectures)," *boundary 2* (1993): 65–76.
2. See Walter Mignolo, *The Idea of Latin America* (Oxford: Blackwell Publishing, 2005).
3. See Walter Mignolo, "Delinking: The Rhetoric of Modernity, the Logic of Coloniality and the Grammar of De-Coloniality," *Cultural Studies*, 21 (2007): 449–514.
4. See Gayatri Spivak, "Subaltern Studies: Deconstructing Historiography," In: R. Guha & G. C. Spivak,(eds.), *Selected Subaltern Studies* (Oxford: Oxford University Press, 1988).
5. See Fredrick Jameson, "Future City," *New Left Review* 21 (2003): 65–79.

BIBLIOGRAPHY

Alcoff, Linda. "Mignolo's Epistemology of Coloniality." *CR: The New Centennial Review*, 7 (2007): 79–101.

Aman, Robert. "Why Interculturalidad Is Not Interculturality: Paradoxes in Translation Between Indigenous Movements and Supranational Bodies." *Cultural Studies* 29 (2015): 205–228.

———. *Impossible Interculturality? Education and the Colonial Difference in a Multicultural World*. Linköping: Linköping University Press, 2014.

———. "The EU and the Recycling of Colonialism: Formation of Europeans Through Intercultural Dialogue" *Educational Philosophy and Theory*, 44 (2012): 1010–1023.

———. Esclavitud en América Latina: Visión histórica representada en libros escolares suecos y colombianos, *Teré: Revista de filosofía y socio política de la educación*, 5 (2009): 31–39.

Amin, Samir. *Delinking: Towards A Polycentric World*. London: Zed, 1990.

Arguedas, José María. *Deep Rivers*. Austin: University of Texas Press, 1987.

Burman, Anders. "Places to Think With, Books to Think About: Words, Experience and the Decolonization of Knowledge in the Bolivian Andes." *Human Architecture* 10 (2012): 101–119.

Chakrabarty, Dipesh. *Provincializing Europe: Postcolonial Thought and Historical Difference*. Princeton: Princeton University Press, 2000.

Chatterjee, Partha. *A Possible India: Essays in Political Criticism*. Delhi: Oxford University Press, 1997.

Danius, Sara, and Stefan Jonsson. "An Interview with Gayatri Chakravorty Spivak." *boundary 2* (1993): 24–50.

Dewey, Patricia. "Transnational Cultural Policymaking in the European Union." *The Journal of Arts Management, Law, and Society* 38 (2008): 99–118.

Dussel, Enrique. "Eurocentrism and Modernity (Introduction to the Frankfurt Lectures)." *boundary 2* (1993): 65–76.

Escobar, Arturo. "Latin America at a Crossroads." *Cultural Studies* 24 (2010): 1–65.

European Commission. *Communication from the Commission: A European Agenda for culture in a globalizing world*. Brussels: EC, 2007.

Fanon, Frantz. *Black Skin/White Masks*. New York: Grove Press, 2008; 1952.Jameson, F. "Future City." *New Left Review* 21 (2003): 65–79.

Mbembe, Achille. *On the Postcolony*. Berkeley: University of California Press, 2001.

Meer, Nasar, and Tariq Modood. "How Does Interculturalism Contrast with Multiculturalism?" *Journal of Intercultural Studies* 33 (2012): 175–196.

Mignolo, Walter. "Epistemic Disobedience, Independent Thought and De-colonial Freedom." *Theory, Culture, Society* 26 (2009): 1–23.

———. "Delinking: The Rhetoric of Modernity, the Logic of Coloniality and the Grammar of De-Coloniality." *Cultural Studies*, 21 (2007): 449–514.

———. *The Idea of Latin America.* Oxford: Blackwell Publishing, 2005.

———. "The Geo-politics of Knowledge and the Colonial Difference." *The South Atlantic Quarterly* 101 (2002b): 57–96.

———. "The Enduring Enchantment (or the Epistemic Privilege of Modernity and Where to Go from Here)." *The South Atlantic Quarterly* 101 (2002a): 927–954.

———. *Local Histories/Global Designs: Coloniality, Subaltern Knowledges, and Border Thinking.* Princeton: Princeton University Press, 1999.

Mignolo, Walter, and Freya Schiwy. "Double Translation: Transculturation and the Colonial Difference." In: Tullio Maranhao and Bernhard, Streck. eds. *Translation and Ethnography: The Anthropological Challenge of Intercultural Understanding* Tucson: University of Arizona Press, 2003.

Quijano, Anibal. "Colonialidad y modernidad/racionalidad." In H. Bonilla, ed., *Los conquistados. 1492 y la población indígena de las Américas.* Quito: Tercer Mundo Editores, 1989.

Spivak, Gayatri. "Subaltern Studies: Deconstructing Historiography." In: Ranajit, Guha & Gayatri Spivak, eds., *Selected Subaltern Studies.* Oxford: Oxford University Press, 1988.

UNESCO. *Guidelines on Intercultural Education.* Paris: UNESCO, 2006.

Vergès, Françoise. *Monsters and Revolutionaries: Colonial Family Romance and Metissage.* Durham: Duke University Press, 1999.

Walsh, Catherine. *Interculturalidad, Estado, Sociedad: Luchas (de)coloniales de nuestra época.* Quito: Universidad Andina Simón Bolívar/Abya-Yala, 2009.

Webber, Jeffery. *Red October: Left-Indigenous Struggles in Modern Bolivia.* Chicago: Haymarket, 2012.

Wolf, Eric. *Europe and the People without History.* Los Angeles: University of California Press, 1982.

EIGHT

Decolonizing Humanities

The Presence of the Humanitas
and the Absence of the Anthropos

Tendayi Sithole

In the humanities, the term "human" exists in relation to the world, and the study of the human is what broadly encompasses the humanities. The silent humanities' scandal remains to be the ontological position which still includes the *anthropos* and the *humanitas*. It is important to make the distinction in human sciences regarding the conception of being which involves the ontological question of who is human and who is not. This can be understood in the distinction between the *humanitas* (civilized, modern, intelligent, virtuous, etc.) and the *anthropos* (barbaric, primitive, uncivilized, idle, oversexed, etc.). The ontological difference is funda-mental to explain the ways in which the study of the human is ontologi-cally imprinted. This intervention proposes to critique the humanities from the darker side of modernity, and from the locus of enunciation of the *anthropos*. It is essential to challenge epistemic violence, and to open vistas for ecologies of knowledges as opposed to knowledge.

The ontological scandal facing the humanities is the problematic ab-sence of the *anthropos* as those who are racialized, dehumanized, and violated against to make a case for epistemic justice. Here, the concern is to understand the politico-ethico-ontological fundamental questions in the humanities which house various disciplines, and to urge the human sciences to take seriously the category considered the full embodiment of being. This is because the humanities have been and continue to be the epistemic practice of the *humanitas*—that is, the study of the human by the human to understand the human condition and its relation to the social and the world at large. However, it is through the *anthropos* as the category of absence that engagement with humanities will be made through decoloniality as the matter of critique. In other words, the effort to rethink humanities is trapped within modernity/coloniality. What is advocated here is the advancing of the subjectivity of that which is criminalized to understand how the humanities still remain the domain of the *humanitas* and not the *anthropos*.

THE *HUMANITAS* AND *ANTHROPOS* IN THE HUMANITIES

Though this distinction often is not clearly pronounced in the human sciences, it is essential to clarify that not everybody is the figure of the human and, in that vein, the *humanitas* is the human while the *anthropos* is not.[1] Of course, what is the human is what takes center stage in the humanities, and this only signifies the *humanitas*. The key point is to understand the human sciences from the ontological absence of the *anthropos*. The figure of the *anthropos* is the one excluded from the world, and, of course, the world of the *humanitas*. The world is the thought of the *humanitas* and the one which is articulated in these terms. If the human sciences operate in such a world, they are susceptible to perpetuating the very tendencies of such a world where epistemic injustice prevails.

The *humanitas* and the *anthropos* do not coexist in the humanities. Only the *humanitas* exists while the *anthropos* are erased as the canon is the exclusive domain of the *humanitas*. The *anthropos* are on the receiving end of the ontological erasure, meaning the presentation of the humanities has nothing to do with the *anthropos*. Therefore, the collapse of the *anthropos* into *humanitas* is the desperate creation of a monolithic existential zone. In other words, there seems to be the propagation of the idea that the human condition being studied is universal—that is, the socio-historical, existential experience of Euro-North America is the same as the world at large. Also, the humanities are in such a state of denial by the very acts of erasure, therefore, there is no need to rethink but to unthink human sciences. To unthink here means the subject who has been doing the thinking and the rethinking is not only the singular subject under the monolithic of truth from the *humanitas*, but the *anthropos* as the enunciator of the lived experience. The monolithic truth of the *humanitas* rests on the fallacy that reason is the sole domain of the Euro-North America episteme. To unthink also means taking seriously the distinction between the *humanitas* and the *anthropos* and putting it in the human sciences to recognize the fact that there is not only one category of being through which the world should be seen.

The *anthropos* as the category of thought is problematic because it has been defined, represented, thought about, acted upon, and even distorted. The *anthropos* has to define the terms of engagement from its locus of enunciation; what is key is asking fundamental ethico-politico-ontological questions. The categories of the ethical, political, and ontological are key because what befalls the *anthropos* in the human sciences is presented from the viewpoint of the *humanitas*, the very negation of what is ethical, political and ontological. The condition of erasure is the one that befalls the *anthropos*. And to articulate the *anthropos* from its existential condition is to unmask the difference masked as sameness by the *humanitas*, and to eliminate the tendency of making the *anthropos* see the world from the viewpoint of the *humanitas*.

It is in the humanities that the *anthropos* are made to believe that they are subjects and their being is a given. If their being is a given, it means that they do not have to search for the value and essence of being, let alone look at their material conditions. The positionality of the *humanitas* in the human sciences is not sincere but one that borders on deceit, hypocrisy, and bad faith which is the denial of truth and responsibility. This can be understood from the basis where the *anthropos* are made to believe that they are the *humanitas*, but at the same time reminded that they are not human enough, if not at all. Why is it that the *anthropos* are made to believe to be something that they are not, and what purpose does this serve in the humanities?

It is in the humanities where the term *anthropos* is reflected, represented, and even constructed as the subject of deficiency. This even goes to the extent of rendering the *anthropos* the erased subject. To be erased is to assume existential absence and the question of being cannot be a given since the *anthropos* cannot be human by virtue of their erasure. Therefore, it is not essential for the *anthropos* to entertain what they are not. The question of being human should not be a given but something worthy of pursuit. Additionally, this question should be determined by the *anthropos* and not the *humanitas*.

THE HAUNTING PRESENCE OF DISCIPLINARITY

The state of the discipline within the humanities assumes presence and it will not diminish any time soon, not even as far as articulating the discipline is concerned. Therefore, the discipline is still with us and will not go away. So, the conventional view is that the presence of the discipline must remain intact for to construct and articulate knowledge. Disciplinarity constitutes epistemological rigidity and certainty which is fundamental to the foundational canon(s) and constitutive to the discipline.[2] It is in the annals of the discipline that those which fall outside the representational scope of Euro-American episteme should be relegated to the margins of barbarity or, worst-case scenario, face epistemicide. Smith argues the discipline can be redeemed when the strategy concerning knowledge construction is the object of analysis which is the foregrounding of reinvention of the discipline.[3] The discipline is knowledge and there cannot be knowledge proper outside the presence of the discipline and, to some extent, there cannot be knowledge in its valid form without creating specialized knowledge. The purpose being solely that such specialization is tantamount as the ammunition to make the discipline able to solve problems that come with modernity.

It is essential to confine the discipline as the constitutive repository of knowledge within the content of modernity since both are critical in shaping modernity and also providing solutions to problems within modernity. As such, it is clear that the discipline, the important center in constructing specialized knowledge, is key to solving problems brought about by modernity, or which modernity seeks to challenge, and is making the world in its political, social, cultural, and economic sense. Such construction of the world tries to create particular kinds of subjectivities which deepen the understanding of complex nuances around which the discipline functions. According to Farred, the discipline stands on the act of erasure: by being expansive, it actually leaves many things unsaid.[4] The discipline confers knowledge practices and the ways in which knowledge is made about the *anthropos*.

Certainty, purity, difference, precision, accuracy, validity, and universalism, to name just a few, reveal the very foundations of the discipline. Therefore, the discipline is through its frames, methods and modes of inquiry "the surest mark of 'erased' knowledge."[5] The construction of the world based on knowledge is the collapse and erasure of other *knowledges*. These types of knowledge, which are produced through the confines of the discipline, both normalize and pathologize different kinds of behavior and identities.[6] The organization of *knowledges* has been that of knowledge, where the Euro-North American epistemic practices coalesce and bring everything into its center to form knowledge. As Gordon notes, "notions of knowledge were so many that *knowledges* would be a more appropriate designation."[7]

The haunting presence of the discipline is testimony to the fact that the configuration of knowledge has been singular in nature where *knowledges* do not exist. According to Gordon, the modes of producing language evidently are enlisted as things in the service of colonization, thus leading to epistemic colonization. As Ndlovu-Gatsheni diagnoses, epistemological colonization is the invasion and destruction of African imaginaries that contribute to the decapitation of African subjectivities making it impossible to engage in any form of political imagination shaping genealogies, mission, horizons and futures of African subjectivities.[8] Epistemic colonization occurred and is sustained by means of epistemic violence masked in Euro-North American epistemology. This is the deliberate, non-existence of singularity to make way for modernity uninterrupted, and the discipline has been the master in making singular knowledge and not allowing *knowledges*.

Though the discipline is seen in that light in modernity—solving problems to understand the complexities of modernity—what is not clear is what purpose does this serve in relation to the discipline being the auxiliary of the colonial project, and which today in the era of emancipation where the Euro-American is still othering the "Other." The "Other" is the subject at the margins of the *humanitas*, specifically the *anthropos*. Why is it accepted that the discipline is the embodiment of knowledge? Or put in another way, why is knowledge thought of within the confines of the discipline? These questions highlight the linkages between the discipline and knowledge, and symbolize a unified, inseparable entity and that which reifies the presence of knowledge instead of knowledges. The state of inseparability will mean that which is to be called knowledge and that which cannot emerge for the discipline should be considered as knowledge and knowledge as discipline. However, knowledge is not prison to the discipline, even within the context of the university and its pedagogic practices. It is projected as such and affirmed by its positionality as something separate within the confines of modernity.

At another level, the university which houses the discipline in the form of departments, the latter discharging the knowledge through construction, reflection, validity, and critique with the end-goal of producing graduates is the knowledge in specialized form. As Smith notes, one discipline cannot answer a complex variety of questions pertinent to the existential conditions of the *anthropos*.[9] What makes the discipline exist and persist in its tradition, even in the time of its crisis, is the demand for consistency, which collapses into maximum consistency to be consistent.[10] This consistency is the one in which the discipline's haunting presence is entrenched because, as a defensive position, it is able to produce its own regime of truth and parade it in the form of absolutism. This absolutism produces the epistemic order of worldly things where the acts and practices of selfhood within the confines of knowledge and disciplinarity conveniently what make the Euro-American empire the center.

DECOLONIALITY AGAINST THE SCANDAL OF MODERNITY

What humanities in this current state of affairs has to deal with serious questions of existence of the *anthropos*? The foundational and constitutive nature of the humanities is the one is still haunted by coloniality. If modernity is salvation, why does it create subjection? It is the task of decoloniality to reveal the deception embedded in the project of modernity which the human sciences in various disciplines try to rehabilitate. Modernity creates chains that shackle the *anthropos*, and there is a problem in a world with its postcolonial condition to reappropriate and reproduce the colonial structural tendencies embedded in modernity. For Walsh, there is a need for new communities of thought which are embedded in the structural positionality of the *anthropos*.[11] In other words, decoloniality informs the continuous struggles which claim and practice their affinity with the *anthropos*, with its existential conditions as a lens. It is a form of political project which attempts to raise the possibility of new and other worlds. What Walsh emphasizes is a form of thought and existence which is decolonial in orientation.

Coloniality does not mean colonialism, but the continued legacy of colonialism in the absence of the colonial administration. Decoloniality constitutes a different agenda which places itself in the darker side of modernity and exposes what modernity hides.[12] Decoloniality is rooted deeply in genealogies of understanding which examine coloniality as long-standing patterns of power that emerged as a result of colonialism, and define social, economic, and cultural conditions in absence of the colonial administration.[13] Therefore, coloniality is the survival, metamorphosis, continuity, and maintenance of subjection, making it necessary for decoloniality to be grounded in histories and lived experiences of the anthropos. Essentially, decoloniality tries to break away from coloniality which approves subjection. For this to be possible, decoloniality is informed by praxis of a different kind that confronts the hidden deceptions of modernity.

It is imperative for Mignolo to define decoloniality as "critical thoughts emerging in the colonies and ex-colonies."[14] Decoloniality makes visible the underside of modernity as it is the metacriticism in the humanities. It means that it criticizes theories, paradigms, and approaches that are also critical of modernity, but which are within the bounds of modernity like post-structuralism, post-modernism and post-colonialism. This is the thought that responds and critiques modernity in its mutating form—that is, coloniality as it hides its locus of enunciation by claiming to be objective, totalizing, and universal. As a particular kind of critical thought, Mignolo insists decoloniality unpacks critical theory and its genealogy of thought, and opposes the fundamentalist position of comparing, measuring, evaluating, and judging human experiences. Decoloniality is not a theoretical dead-end but the "search for other possible knowledges and worlds."[15]

The humanities are not only in crisis but they are haunted by the calls for decolonization. This is an indictment where now the *anthropos* as the figure of the subject erased claims re-existence in the humanities, and really exposes the scandal of humanity as having nothing to do with those humans who are dehumanized. Such re-existence is not the *anthropos* being projected as the *humanitas*, but the *anthropos* is the *anthropos*. To re-exist means the presence of the anthropos in the human sciences is not the extension or clone of the *humanitas*. This is alienation at its best since the *anthropos* is rendered outside to that which is human. So, for the *anthropos* to be human would mean to take the present moment of existence seriously, and something which the human sciences need to focus on—the darker side of modernity.[16]

It is in this era that modernity is in serious question, and questions arise, not from within modernity, but from within its darker side. To unthink human sciences from the darker side of modernity and to put the *anthropos* as the master signifier is the essential starting point. Indeed, one cannot deny the fact there are a numerous ways through which modernity is defended in the human sciences, and attempts are made to rehabilitate it. There is nothing wrong with this; however, there is something wrong if this is the perspective the *anthropos* are asked to take. It is the task of the *humanitas* to defend modernity and it is the task of the *anthropos* to unmask what modernity hides. To be at the darker side of modernity is to be the *anthropos*. This is the side where modernity in the human sciences is questioned as a scandal and not something that should be rehabilitated since this has nothing to do with ending dehumanization.

The scandal of modernity should be understood from the colonial encounter to the multiplicity and complexity of coloniality. What coloniality hides is the decadence of modernity and enough effort is made in the humanities to present modernity as if it was a good affair and a fair deal for the *anthropos*. Here, modernity creates the impression that it is the totalizing experience of being. So, what is the concern is what Mignolo refers to as the "hidden agenda of modernity" and is the very thing that causes modernity to be read from its darker side. The *anthropos* need to unmask the hidden agenda of modernity to see how coloniality operates.

In its broader discursive terrain, modernity constitutes two faces—the one face which civilizes the *anthropos* to be in the existential domain of the *humanitas*, and the other of subjection which makes explicit the *anthropos* cannot be the *humanitas*. These two faces of modernity operate in tandem, and this strengthens the relevance of decolonial epistemic to confirm it is deeply entrenched in the extension of modernity called coloniality. The latter is the concept the captures the ugly face of modernity to understand the whole industrial complex of subjection in the post-colony. The *humanitas* are the subject of modernity and, as such, they are located at its departure. The humanities are located in modernity and the kind of knowledge practices. The humanities from the vantage point of the *humanitas* project a totalizing narrative but it is essential to point out and reiterate that the *anthropos* are not the *humanitas*. Modernity is exclusively a Euro-North American expansionist project of claiming to redeem the *anthropos* by erasing it. This appeal is the greatest deception because it turns most of the *anthropos* savagery to being, leading the appeal to attain the status of irrefutable truth. Ultimately, it is the *anthropos* who suffer from the ontological crisis which is created and sustained by modernity in the colonies. This is epistemic violence which is devastating and overlasting.[17] It is the violence that finds its own justifications where those whom it violates are rendered non-existent, and they cannot make a claim about being violated.

EPISTEMIC DISOBEDIENCE AGAINST EPISTEMIC VIOLENCE

Epistemic violence excludes, marginalizes, demonizes, and even eliminates forms of episteme that differ from modernity.[18] This is a form of violence which is indirect and non-physical but has devastating effects in that it erases the subjectivity and the existence of the *anthropos*. It is a form of violence that affirms the existence of the *humanitas* only as a subject. So, under the operation of epistemic violence, the *athropos* are the *Other* and also under the gaze of the *humanitas* as the master signifier. That is to say, the *humanitas* define, interpret, and represent the *anthropos* as that which assumes the positionality of the *Other*. What Teo brings to the fore is that epistemic violence can be understood through the negative consequences it has for the *anthropos*.[19] The basis defining, interpreting and representing the *Other* is done outside the existence of the *Other*. As Teo argues, epistemic violence takes place through framing the knowledge of the *Other* and through practices that internalize the *Other*.

Epistemological violence has been and continues to be committed to some degree under the name of human sciences, but it is justified as not violence but as the epistemic practice of the discipline. To identify epistemic violence in human sciences in general, and in the discipline in particular, is an act that calls for quick reaction from the *humanitas* which often connotes the idea that it is an unfounded claim. This is the very act of refusing to take responsibility and to be stuck in the comfort zone of denialism. This position is expected because the *humanitas* do not see themselves as violent in their epistemic practice. Since there is the absence of the *anthropos* as the enunciator, there is no need to be ethical to the *Other* in the ontological and epistemological sense.

What is interesting in the human sciences is the concept of the "empirical" which suggest the totality of truth, something which is often immune from criticism. The empirical is absolute through the scientific merit of validity and reliability. Therefore, the empirical cannot be subject to indictment and is ethically omnipotent. It is the concept of the empirical which does not refer to the positionality of the *anthropos* as the enunciator. There is no way that what is empirical could be seen as epistemic violence and a weapon used by the *humanitas* against the *anthropos*. It also seems that the situation should be determined by the *humanitas* and not by the anthropos who are affected by the epistemic practices of the *humanitas*. What is essential to point out is that the potential for harm should be determined by the *anthropos* themselves. In the face of epistemological violence, the criticism of the *athropos*, through their ontological absence, is seen as meaningless because it has no scientific merit. It is convenient to reject any form of criticism from the *anthropos,* consequently, there should be no expression of criticism.

The epistemological hegemony in human sciences offers little if nothing at all for the *anthropos* as enunciators. To affirm the presence of the *anthropos* is to be where one thinks—what is called the locus of enunciation. The epistemological hegemony of the Euro-North American knowledge practices has epistemic violence as the basis of its epistemicide—eliminating other knowledges and assuming the singularity of knowledge. It is important for discourses on and about the state of humanities to revisit the silences and epistemological violence. The epistemicide resulted in the global expansionism of Euro-North American knowledge and the displacement of other knowledges. This is something that humanities need to reflect on because it is still a past and present historical scandal. To displace other knowledges and to commit epistemicide on them clearly means there is an indictment in the humanities. These knowledge claims are a constitutive part of the culture that denied existence, and they are claims informed by existential questions. It is necessary to state that decoloniality enables the foundation to understand, interrogate, and challenge the decolonization of the humanities. To decolonize the humanities is not to rehabilitate, but to judge humanities from the epistemic practices and the positionality of the *anthropos.*

The solution to disentangle from epistemic violence by the *humanitas* is epistemic disobedience of the *anthropos* through increased criticism in the face criminalization by the *humanitas.* The politics of the *anthropos* should be informed in the human sciences by epistemic disobedience to pursue epistemic justice. This means the antagonism against past injustices is an initiative which should be understood in political and strategic terms.[20] As Mignolo stated, "for this simple reason, the task of decolonial thinking and the enactment of the de-colonial option in the twenty-first century starts from epistemic de-linking: from acts of epistemic disobedience."[21] He continued, "Delinking from webs of imperial knowledge is to form the black subject who is not caught within the "racial matrix of modern/colonized world."[22] Political agency arises as a matter of response and destruction to this racial nature of modern and colonial world. The epistemic delinking and epistemic disobedience are the nature of the emerging politics of the *anthropos.* The decolonial option takes root in this form. As Walsh states, delinking aims to recover and reconsider knowledges distorted and lost during the colonial encounter and process.[23] This calls for the need to redefine and resist the imposition of modernity through its imposed superior civilization and the superiority of social institutions.

"By presenting itself as an option, decolonial critique opens up a way of thinking that delinks from the chronologies of new epistemologies or new paradigms."[24] Delinking as Mignolo articulates, does not mean accepting the conditions imposed upon the oppressed self thereby opening options of delinking to chart decolonial horizons. For this to occur, the critique of modernity should be outside modernity. As Mignolo insists, for delinking to be possible, there should be epistemic disobedience. Modernity constitutes epistemological canonism which totalizes the regime of truth and then projects itself as the sole truth. Epistemological canonism cannot be questioned due to the myth and deception of modernity as universality. The idea of the universal is exorcized from the human sciences since it represents epistemic violence *par excellence*.

THE *ANTHROPOS* AS JUDGES

For the *anthropos* to assume the role of a judge in the human sciences, it must have the capacity to judge, and this requirement rests both on epistemology and ontology. The *anthropos* has been judged by the *humanitas* and, as such, has been judged to the point of being treated as an outlaw. For Maldonado-Torres, the capacity to judge is the ethico-political act of a decolonial gift which affirms the very existence of the *anthropos*.[25] The political gift in the context of decoloniality does not take place in the continual sense of being offered. It is a paradox that the political gift is taken even before it can be offered. As Maldonado-Torres notes, the *anthropos* as dispossessed subjects cannot give, and subjects who do not regard other subjects as not being subjects cannot give anything to those subjects. This paradox is at the heart of epistemology and ontology which, as they stand, are informed by the colonial logic of gift and dispossession as a means of subjectivity. So, what does it mean for those who are dispossessed to assume the capacity of judge? As a partial answer, this means those who are banned from being judges are those who actively engage in affirming their existence in their own terms. In doing this, they will engage in what Gordon calls "teleological suspension."[26]

Teleological suspension is about the law of the damned (*anthropos* at the margins of the human sciences cut off ontological content through subjection). It is the law of will to live freely and at the epistemic level, to fight for freedom from epistemic violence. The law of the *anthropos* as judges is the continued resistance, the insurrection thought criminalized in most of the discipline where power is given to those whom the discipline was supposed to discipline. The law of the *anthropos* is the law of demands, and these demands are not only socio-political but largely ontological demands, which are insatiable as they assume a character of that which cannot be satisfied. The satisfaction will only happen when everything begins again—that is, the end of the Euro-North American discipline and knowledge as the only thought, but that which coexists with others.

When teleological suspension calls for theodicy, a crisis of theory and method, epistemic liberation is a necessary condition to pursue. The politics of possibility evolve through the search of liberation and the exorcism of the colonial virus. The ethics of liberation are at the center of epistemology and ontology; however, human sciences do not dwell on these from the positionality of the anthropos. Mignolo asserts that the *anthropos* as a judge is situated where "critical thoughts emerging in the colonies and ex-colonies" are foregrounded.[27] Mignolo states decoloniality as a particular kind of critical thought unpacks critical theory and its genealogy of thought, and opposes fundamentalist position of comparing, measuring, evaluating, and judging human experiences.

Therefore, it is necessary, as Gordon notes, for the *anthropos* to engage the radical anti-colonial critique by means of teleological suspension.[28] For this suspension to occur, Gordon demands there must be differentiality between reason and rationality to truly account for the epistemic conditions of social life. The discipline is more consistent and embedded in rationality rather than in reason because it is rationality which resists teleological suspension. Such resistance is to be expected since teleological suspension means the end of rationality. However, as Gordon notes, there is a need to be suspicious of reason as reason, since its articulation and justifications leads to rationality and common sense. It is within common sense that the rigidity of the discipline is reified, and whatever challenges it is easily dismissed.

What makes theodicy able to survive even in its crisis mode is what Smith refers to as "authoritative judgment."[29] This has been the task within the epistemic circles confined to the Euro-North American center as the custodians of knowledge. Therefore, judgment is said to rest with those who have the capacity to judge and, as such, not those who are judged. The subject position of being judge means acts in the form of rewards and punishment, and from the standpoint of knowledge as opposed to *knowledges*. Those who are judged have no say; what is external to them is that which has the capacity to judge. The problem here is that *knowledges* have no merit, and the judgment against them is made from the standpoint of knowledge. According to Smith, the lived experiences of those who are judged do not matter as the reference points of judgment. Then it means judgment itself is theodicy. Teleological suspension, therefore, points out the decadence at the level of the Euro-American theory and method, and calls for the suspension of both method and theory, and pushes for the proliferation of other methods and theories at its margins, outside the center of the empire. The opposition to meta-theory and absolutist methodologies prevents the reduction of phenomena to universal application.

TOWARD DE-COLONIAL TURN

De-colonial turn refers to a process and undertaking of "producing a radical and alternative knowledge."[30] De-colonial turn is located on border thinking and delinking. This means they are not part of modernity and they are not criticisms of modernity within modernity, but outside it. Modernity is reformed and in this model, it has the capacity to arrest criticism since criticism will be within it. This is prevalent in the era where epistemic privilege of the Euro-North American centric canon continues to be a theoretical apparatus. Decoloniality is a "pluriversal epistemology of the future; an epistemology that delinks from the tyranny of abstract universals."[31] Looking at the world should be rounded in localized experiences of the *anthropos*. It is the epistemological breaking ground which should not be mediated. Instead, it should be the one informed by the lived experiences of the emerging subjects who open up the new vistas of knowledge and the modes of understanding the world around them outside of the totalizing project of modernity. According to Walsh, "Western thinking must be confronted and a different thought constructed and positioned from 'other' histories and subjectivities."[32]

Decoloniality as a genealogy, trajectory, and horizon in the human sciences is necessary to be imagined and engaged, creating a path leading to decolonization. Decolonization is the action that tries to undo the complex colonial matrices of power. Exploitation, domination, colonialism, and genocide are among those requiring another form of politics to counter the epistemic practices in the human sciences. This means politics which are outside the mainstream informed by the experiences of the *anthropos* and informed by resisting tradition as they challenge the subjection of coloniality, part of the violence that rewards, disciplines and punishes.

Anti-politics are the anti-hegemonic politics of struggle against epistemic violence that is unethical. They are politics of the critical discourse which form political intervention since politics are informed by modern discourse. The starting point of this discourse is that the empire through the colonial encounter is the very cause of the colonial condition. Decoloniality rather than postcoloniality is the heart of delinking. Maldonado-Torres explains:

> Decolonization itself, the whole discourses around it, is a gift itself, an invitation to engage in dialogue. For decolonization, concepts need to be conceived as invitations to dialogue and not as impositions. They are expressions of the availability of the subject to engage in dialogue and the desire for exchange. Decolonization in this respect aspires to break with monologic modernity.[33]

Decolonial turn is a particular manifestation of scepticism toward coloniality which seeks to reintroduce the new conception of the world to bring accounting to historical and contemporary injustices.[34] At the center of decolonial turn is the subjectivity of the *anthropos*, a subjectivity which is combative in nature. For Maldonado-Torres, the roots of decolonial turn are critical responses to racism and colonization articulated by racialized and colonized subjects:

> The decolonial turn highlights the epistemic relevance of the enslaved and colonized subjectivities into the realm of thought at previously unknown institutional levels. It introduces questions about the effects of colonization in modern subjectivities and modern forms of life as well as contributions of racialized and colonized subjectivities to the production of knowledge and critical thinking.[35]

As Walsh points out, the absence of colonial experience does not allow any articulation of such an experience.[36] This also includes the impossibility of being located in any epistemic location of colonial difference. Such a form of agency and articulation of thought is ignored and, at best, suppressed since it is not a critique of coloniality within coloniality, but a critique of coloniality outside coloniality. Decolonial turn advocates new ethics of humanity and recourse which are directed toward the bankruptcy and hypocrisy of the empire which is scandalized by a tendency of being unethical par-excellence and negating the humanity of the *anthropos* . Decolonial turn is about constant search for humanity, and in this instance, the humanity of the *anthropos*. Phenomenologically, it is about offering a new philosophical basis of confronting coloniality and searching for truth to realise liberation.[37] This attacks the very basis of the crisis of modern Euro-American imperial condition. Decolonial turn is informed by the principled stance of dismantling social injustices, a pushing for radical transformation, and the construction of the new society where there will be the self in the *anthropos*.

According to Maldonado-Torres, "de-colonial turn involves interventions at the level of power, knowledge, and being through varied actions of decolonization."[38] Decolonial turn ensures that the experience of the *anthropos*—of being enslaved, colonized and oppressed—is combated by injecting subjectivity infused with consciousness through critical thinking and subject formation. For this to be possible, there must be a clear and renewed subject position to assert the construction of meaning of the world. Quijano argues that decolonial turn is the struggle against exploitation and dehumanization.[39] It is a destruction of coloniality of power, knowledge, and being. It is not a matter of putting an end to modernity, but rendering it impotent after its destruction in the face of the oppressed world. According to Walsh, the aim of decolonial turn is . . . "to build new critical communities of thought, interpretation and intervention."[40]

Decolonial turn opposes the paradigm of war that is a constitutive part of modernity; it is the paradigm which has made the social formation of the world.[41] According to this perspective, modernity is the scandal of war, death, and dehumanization hiding behind redemptive salva-tionistic tendencies. Political and epistemic intervention, as Maldonado-Torres argues, should come from the condemned of the earth. Decolonial turn exposes the darker side of modernity, and also brings into being decoloniality. Decolonial turn introduces a forms of delinking, which Maldonado-Torres regards as a radical dislocation of Europe and its roots.[42] As Mignolo states, decoloniality as it originates from the third world, is a necessary thought to rethink, recreate, and reconstitute the ontology and the existential condition of the *anthropos*.[43]

TOWARD ECOLOGIES OF KNOWLEDGES

Decoloniality argues for the existence of other *knowledges*. This is the very idea is based on of challenging knowledge in its singularity with its claim of universal applicability. What is being advocated are the ecologies of knowledges landing to a pluriversalized idea of worlds. Savransky coins the term "onto-epistemological pluralism" to account for knowledges in their role and making being cast in a new light.[44] These new ways of knowing are knowledges created by those who are being excluded in the realm of the singularity of knowledge. As Savransky notes, "onto-episte-mological pluralism" opposes Euro-North American epistemological ex-clusion and epistemicides by pursuing the modes of knowing and repre-sentation so the epistemological demands of those who are oppressed come to life. What is brought to the fore is what has been caught by the tentacles of subjection. It is the emerging opposition forces affirming themselves to create other worlds and ecologies of knowledges rather than seeking to be integrated into the world and its universal knowledge.

The emergence of such knowledges destroys the very structure of subjection and its mode of containment. Ecologies of knowledges rebel against the idea of knowledge as its basis of reason. Ecologies of knowl-edges seek to firmly attach knowledges to ontological positions.[45] This takes seriously the fact that knowledges emerge from the materiality of ontological conditions and positions. This forms part of the views about and of the world, as opposed to world views since the latter suggests the singularity of the world with knowledge as the master signifier rather than knowledges of worlds. They dwell on the shift of geography of reason which locates the *anthropos* from where the *anthropos* thinks in contrast to where the *humanitas* thinks. This shift is necessary as thought emerges from where the body as the lived experience assumes its loca-tion. This allows articulating the shift of geography of reason and grounds it from the theory emerging from the lived experience of the *anthropos*. The geography of reason affirms the location of terrain has shifted, and the most recent systematic mutations might suggest new directions or the situated politics of knowledge.[46] Ecologies of knowledges affirm differentiality of knowledges. The mere fact that they are in their plurality means they are different. This opposes the totalizing tendency of Euro-North American episteme which posits sameness while its articulation engages epistemicides.

The conception of the world is where many worlds fit and where the emergence of subjugated histories and knowledges emerge. Ecologies of knowledges are troublesome where epistemology and ontology come together. Ecologies of knowledges suppose the ethico-politico act of thinking Africa—its knowledge and experience seen from the vantage point of insurrection. Ecologies of knowledges denote situate knowledges. These are *knowledges* situated at the existential conditions of African subjects. As such, ecologies of *knowledges* give leeway to lives which have been liquidated by subjection. Their illegitimacy as not being knowledges from the Euro-North American episteme loci of judgment is the master code under contention.

Ecologies of knowledges are not thought from the zero-point position and linear thinking, but from the very positionality of the subject's location.[47] According to Santos, there exist signs of exhaustion in the crisis of knowledge.[48] Euro-North American knowledge propagates itself as "the locus which formulates collective goals valid for everyone."[49] According to Rodriguez, ecologies of knowledges contest the idea that knowledge resides with Euro-North American subjects who are modern and complex as opposed to primitive and inferior other.[50] This perpetuated the idea of hierarchizing, racializing, and dehumanizing those who are said not to be the producers of knowledge. This idea justifies the colonization of *knowledges* into knowledge and *humanitas* determining what qualifies as knowledge and what does not is bad faith. So, the purpose of knowledge is to discipline over the mind and body. In other words, inventing the other to serve the interests of the Euro-North American empire.[51]

Ecologies of knowledges call into question "the rationality of the cannons of conquerors and the preaching of missionaries."[52] They object to epistemologies of ignorance which are propagated by the very act of epistemicides. As Santos states, "colonialist ignorance consists in refusing to recognize the other as an equal and converting the other into an object."[53] The process of domination and disfiguring went along with epistemic ignorance (which is deliberate ignorance) to eliminate resistant forces against that which it imposes. Ecologies of knowledges are armed with what Santos calls "a new critical gaze" which means the new ways of knowing and seeing from the locus of enunciation of those who are at the receiving end of subjection. For Santos, this new critical gaze gives new tools to an archeological task of excavating, and searching for subjugated and marginalized knowledges, and constructing new epistemes informed by liberation. Taking this form, Connery argues that this interrogation requires new foci and new urgency in these times of differential crisis.[54] Connery suggests that ecologies of knowledges should open up parameters favorable to political and epistemological imagination. For Mignolo, the decolonial option is the singular connector of myriad struggles informed by decoloniality.[55] This struggle is informed by the commitment to obliterate the ontological distinction between the *humanitas* and the *anthropos*. For this to occur, it is imperative to highlight decoloniality as the creation of many other worlds and knowledges.

CONCLUSION: ANOTHER WORLD IS POSSIBLE

Another world is possible. This possibility is bolstered by the fact that there is no nihilism in the *anthropos* by the political advocacy of decolonizing futures. This means another world where many other worlds fit is possible. It is what the humanities should confront as the reality since the role political advocacy plays is to bring to an end the monolithic "I" of the *humanitas* through coalition with the "we" of the *anthropos*. The "we" is there are no politics of erasure from the positionality of the *anthropos*, but the affirmation of the re-existence of the *anthropos* as subjects. It is up to the human science to take on the decolonial task. But, naturally, it is the task of the *anthropos* since they are the ones who are erased from epistemic practices. Unthinking human sciences is the act of re-existence of the *anthropos* as the enunciator and its subjectivity taking center stage.

The larger aim of this intervention has been to eliminate the pretense inherent in coloniality/modernity which seems firmly entrenched in the human sciences. What is essential in human sciences is to begin opening up silent episteme and unthought thinking—that is, the politics of knowledge infused with the emergence of the *anthropos*. The goal is to eliminate differences and obscure them as sameness while affirming and making clear the differences as the distinction between the *humanitas* and the *anthropos*. The *humanitas* cannot continue to control the *anthropos* in the human sciences. The *anthropos* should validate their presence by unmasking the deception, trickery, and crisis of modernity, and advocate for human sciences not to be the hegemonic constructs of the *humanitas*. The advocacy is to decolonize and encourage new ways of thinking, doing, sensing, and knowing. Human science needs to be decolonized through the *anthropos* assuming their locus of enunciation and to move forward. What is clear is that another world is possible where many worlds and knowledges exist, and that is the pluriversal world.

NOTES

1. See Walter Mignolo, *The Darker Side of Western Modernity: Global Futures, Decolonial Options* (Durham, NC & London, UK: Duke University Press, 2011), 82.

2. See Martin Savransky, "Worlds in the Making: Social Sciences and the Ontopolitics of Knowledge" *Postcolonial Studies*, 15 no.3 (2012): 351–368.

3. See Mark Smith, *Culture: Reinventing the Social Sciences* (Buckingham, UK & Philadelphia: Open University Press, 2000), 3.

4. See Grant Farred, "Science Does Not Think: The No-Thought of the Discipline." *The South Atlantic Quarterly*, 110 no.1 (2011): 57–74.

5. See Grant Farred, "Science Does Not Think: The No-Thought of the Discipline." *The South Atlantic Quarterly*, 110 no.1 (2011): 60.

6. See Mark Smith, *Culture: Reinventing the Social Sciences* (Buckingham, UK & Philadelphia: Open University Press, 2000), 115.

7. See Lewis Gordon, "Shifting the Geography of Reason in an Age of Disciplinary Decadence" *Transmodernity*, 1 no.2 (2011): 95–103; 95.

8. See Sabelo Ndlovu-Gatsheni, "Colonial Matrix of Power and the African Intellectual/ Epistemological Crisis" Unpublished Paper (2011) 9.

9. See Mark Smith, *Culture: Reinventing the Social Sciences* (Buckingham, UK & Philadelphia: Open University Press, 2000), 2.

10. See Lewis Gordon, "Shifting the Geography of Reason in an Age of Disciplinary Decadence" *Transmodernity*, 1 no.2 (2011): 97.

11. See Catherine Walsh, "Shifting the Geopolitics of Critical Knowledges: Decolonial Thought and Cultural Studies 'Others' in the Andes" *Cultural Studies*, 21 no.2–3 (2007): 233.

12. See Walter Mignolo, "Introduction: Coloniality of Power and De-colonial Thinking" *Cultural Studies*, 21 no.2–3 (2007): 155–167.

13. See Nelson Maldonado-Torres, *Against War: Views from the Underside of Modernity* (Durham and London: Duke University Press, 2008), 218.

14. See Walter Mignolo, "Introduction: Coloniality of Power and De-colonial Thinking" *Cultural Studies*, 21 no.2–3 (2007): 155.

15. See Catherine Walsh, "Shifting the Geopolitics of Critical Knowledges: Decolonial Thought and Cultural Studies 'Others' in the Andes." *Cultural Studies*, 21 no.2–3 (2007): 234.

16. See Walter Mignolo, *The Darker Side of Western Modernity: Global Futures, Decolonial Options* (Durham, NC & London, UK: Duke University Press, 2011), 90.

17. See Anibal Quijano, "Coloniality of Power, Eurocentrism, and Social Classification" in *Coloniality at large: Latin American and the postcolonial debate* (Darhum and London: Duke University Press, 2008), 181–224.

18. See Ramón Grosfoguel, "The Epistemic Decolonial Turn: Beyond Political-Economy Paradigms" *Cultural Studies*, 21 no. 2–3 (2007): 213.

19. See Thomas Teo, "What Is Epistemological Violence in Empirical Social Sciences?" *Social and Personality Psychology Compass*, 4 no. 5 (2010): 295–303.

20. See Catherine Walsh, "Shifting the Geopolitics of Critical Knowledges: Decolonial Thought and Cultural Studies 'Others' in the Andes" *Cultural Studies*, 21 no.2–3 (2007): 234. 231.

21. See Walter Mignolo, "Epistemic Disobedience, Independent Thought and Decolonial Freedom" *Theory, Culture and Society*, 26 no. 7–8 (2009): 15.

22. See Walter Mignolo, "Epistemic Disobedience, Independent Thought and Decolonial Freedom" *Theory, Culture and Society*, 26 no. 7–8 (2009): 17.

23. See Catherine Walsh, "Shifting the Geopolitics of Critical Knowledges: Decolonial Thought and Cultural Studies 'Others' in the Andes" *Cultural Studies*, 21 no. 2–3 (2007): 232.

24. See Walter Mignolo, "Geopolitics of Sensing and Knowing: On (De)coloniality, Border Thinking and Epistemic Disobedience" *Postcolonial Studies*, 14 no. 3 (2011): 273–274.

25. See Nelson Maldonado-Torres, "Cesaire's Gift and the Decolonial Turn" *Radical Philosophy Review*, 9 no. 2 (2006): 111–138.

26. See Lewis Gordon, "Shifting the Geography of Reason in an Age of Disciplinary Decadence" *Transmodernity*, 1 no.2 (2011): 99.

27. See Walter Mignolo, "Introduction: Coloniality of Power and De-colonial Thinking" *Cultural Studies*, 21 no.2–3 (2007): 155.

28. See Lewis Gordon, "Shifting the Geography of Reason in an Age of Disciplinary Decadence" *Transmodernity*, 1 no.2 (2011): 99.

29. See Mark Smith, *Culture: Reinventing the Social Sciences* (Buckingham, UK & Philadelphia: Open University Press, 2000), 15.

30. See Ramón Grosfoguel, "The Epistemic Decolonial Turn: Beyond Political-Economy Paradigms" *Cultural Studies*, 21 no. 2–3 (2007): 211.

31. See Walter Mignolo, "Introduction: Coloniality of Power and De-colonial Thinking" *Cultural Studies*, 21 no.2–3 (2007): 159.

32. See Catherine Walsh, "Shifting the Geopolitics of Critical Knowledges: Decolonial Thought and Cultural Studies 'Others' in the Andes" *Cultural Studies*, 21 no. 2–3 (2007): 266.

33. See Nelson Maldonado-Torres, "On the Coloniality of Being: Contributions to the Development of a Concept" *Cultural Studies*, 21 no. 2–3 (2007): 261.

34. See Nelson Maldonado-Torres, *Against War: Views from the Underside of Modernity* (Durham and London: Duke University Press, 2008), 193.

35. See Nelson Maldonado-Torres, *Against War: Views from the Underside of Modernity* (Durham and London: Duke University Press, 2008), 8.

36. See Catherine Walsh, "Shifting the Geopolitics of Critical Knowledges: Decolonial Thought and Cultural Studies 'Others' in the Andes" *Cultural Studies*, 21 no. 2–3 (2007): 227.

37. See Nelson Maldonado-Torres, *Against War: Views from the Underside of Modernity* (Durham and London: Duke University Press, 2008), 35.

38. See Nelson Maldonado-Torres, "On the Coloniality of Being: Contributions to the Development of a Concept" *Cultural Studies*, 21 no. 2–3 (2007): 262.

39. See Anibal Quijano, "Coloniality of Power, Eurocentrism, and Social Classification" in *Coloniality at large: Latin American and the postcolonial debate* (Darhum and London: Duke University Press, 2008), 182.

40. See Catherine Walsh, "Shifting the Geopolitics of Critical Knowledges: Decolonial Thought and Cultural Studies 'Others' in the Andes" *Cultural Studies*, 21 no. 2–3 (2007): 233.

41. See Nelson Maldonado-Torres, "On the Coloniality of Being: Contributions to the Development of a Concept" *Cultural Studies*, 21 no. 2–3 (2007): 260.

42. See Nelson Maldonado-Torres, "Cesaire's Gift and the Decolonial Turn" *Radical Philosophy Review*, 9 no. 2 (2006): 137.

43. See Walter Mignolo, "Geopolitics of Sensing and Knowing: On (De)coloniality, Border Thinking and Epistemic Disobedience" *Postcolonial Studies*, 14 no. 3 (2011): 274.

44. See Martin Savransky, "Worlds in the Making: Social Sciences and the Ontopolitics of Knowledge" *Postcolonial Studies*, 15 no. 3 (2012): 353.

45. See Encarnación Rodríguez, "Decolonizing Postcolonial Rhetoric" in *Decolonizing European Sociology: Transdisciplinary Approaches* (Surrey and Burlington: Ashgate, 2010), 49–67.

46. See Christopher Connery, "Reflections on the Politics and Locations of Knowledge Making in a Time of Crisis," *Concentric*, 38 no. 2 (2012): 47.

47. See Walter Mignolo, "Geopolitics of Sensing and Knowing: On (De)coloniality, Border Thinking and Epistemic Disobedience" *Postcolonial Studies*, 14 no. 3 (2011): 275.

48. See Boaventura de Sousa Santos, "From the Postmodern to the Postcolonial – and Beyond Both." in *Decolonizing European Sociology: Transdisciplinary Approaches* (Surrey and Burlington: Ashgate, 2010), 225–242.

49. See Santiago Castro-Gomez, "The Social Sciences, Epistemic Violence, and the Problem of the Invention of the Other," *Nepantla*, 3 no. 2 (2002): 269–285.

50. See Encarnación Rodriguez, "Decolonizing Postcolonial Rhetoric" in *Decolonizing European Sociology: Transdisciplinary Approaches* (Surrey and Burlington: Ashgate, 2010), 53.

51. See Santiago Castro-Gomez, "The Social Sciences, Epistemic Violence, and the Problem of the Invention of the Other," *Nepantla*, 3 no. 2 (2002): 271.

52. See Encarnación Rodriguez, "Decolonizing Postcolonial Rhetoric" in *Decolonizing European Sociology: Transdisciplinary Approaches* (Surrey and Burlington: Ashgate, 2010), 49–67.

53. See Boaventura de Sousa Santos, "From the Postmodern to the Postcolonial – and Beyond Both." in *Decolonizing European Sociology: Transdisciplinary Approaches* (Surrey and Burlington: Ashgate, 2010), 230.

54. See Christopher Connery, "Reflections on the Politics and Locations of Knowledge Making in a Time of Crisis," *Concentric*, 38 no. 2 (2012): 47.

55. See Walter Mignolo, "Geopolitics of Sensing and Knowing: On (De)coloniality, Border Thinking and Epistemic Disobedience" *Postcolonial Studies*, 14 no. 3 (2011): 282.

BIBLIOGRAPHY

Castro-Gomez, Santiago. "The Social Sciences, Epistemic Violence, and the Problem of the Invention of the Other." *Nepantla*, 3 no.2 (2002): 269–285.

Connery, Christopher. "Reflections on the Politics and Locations of Knowledge Making in a Time of Crisis." *Concentric*, 38 no. 2 (2012): 45–63.

de Sousa Santos, Boaventura. "From the Postmodern to the Postcolonial – and Beyond Both." In Encarnación Rodríguez, Manuela Boatcâ & Sergio Costa (eds.). *Decolonizing European Sociology: Transdisciplinary Approaches*. Surrey and Burlington: Ashgate, 2010.

Farred, Grant. "Science Does Not Think: The No-Thought of the Discipline." *The South Atlantic Quarterly*, 110 no. 1 (2011): 57–74.

Gordon, Lewis. "Shifting the Geography of Reason in an Age of Disciplinary Decadence." *Transmodernity*, 1 no. 2 (2011): 95–103.

Grosfoguel, Ramón. "The Epistemic Decolonial Turn: Beyond Political-Economy Paradigms." *Cultural Studies*, 21 no. 2–3 (2007): 211–223.

Maldonado-Torres, Nelson. *Against War: Views from the Underside of Modernity*. Durham and London: Duke University Press, 2008.

———. "On the Coloniality of Being: Contributions to the Development of a Concept." *Cultural Studies*, 21 no. 2–3 (2007): 240–270.

———. "Cesaire's Gift and the Decolonial Turn." *Radical Philosophy Review*, 9 no. 2, (2006): 111–138.

Mignolo, Walter. *The Darker Side of Western Modernity: Global Futures, Decolonial Options*. Durham, NC & London, UK: Duke University Press. 2011.

———. "Geopolitics of Sensing and Knowing: On (De)coloniality, Border Thinking and Epistemic Disobedience." *Postcolonial Studies*, 14 no. 3 (2011): 273–283.

———. "Epistemic Disobedience, Independent Thought and Decolonial Freedom." *Theory, Culture and Society*, 26 no. 7–8 (2009): 159–181.

———. "Introduction: Coloniality of Power and De-colonial Thinking." *Cultural Studies*, 21 no. 2–3 (2007): 155–167.

Ndlovu-Gatsheni, Sabelo. "Colonial Matrix of Power and the African Intellectual/Epistemological Crisis." Unpublished Paper (2011).

Quijano, Anibal. "Coloniality of Power, Eurocentrism, and Social Classification." In Mabel Moraña, Enrique Dussel, and Carlos Jáuregui (eds). *Coloniality at large: Latin American and the postcolonial debate*. Durham and London: Duke University Press, 2008.

Rodriguez, Encarnación. "Decolonizing Postcolonial Rhetoric." In E. G. Rodríguez, M. Boatcâ & S. Costa (eds.). *Decolonizing European Sociology: Transdisciplinary Approaches*. Surrey and Burlington: Ashgate, 2010.

Savransky, Martin. "Worlds in the Making: Social Sciences and the Ontopolitics of Knowledge." *Postcolonial Studies*, 15 no. 3 (2012): 351–368.

Smith, Mark. *Culture: Reinventing the Social Sciences*. Buckingham, UK & Philadelphia: Open University Press, 2000, 3.

Teo, Thomas. "What Is Epistemological Violence in Empirical Social Sciences?" *Social and Personality Psychology Compass,* 4 no. 5 (2010): 295–303.

Walsh, Catherine. "Shifting the Geopolitics of Critical Knowledges: Decolonial Thought and Cultural Studies 'Others' in the Andes" *Cultural Studies,* 21 no. 2–3 (2007): 224–239, 233.

Part III

Decolonizing Pedagogy
and Human Rights

NINE

Philosopher-Teachers and That Little Thing Called Hasty Decolonization

Nassim Noroozi

Of the many compulsory textbooks to read in order to obtain your degree in Persian literature is a work called *Kashf-al-Asrar* (*The Unveiling of Mysteries*). This is how a book that we were obliged to read became an everlastingly favorite and formative work in my discernment of pedagogies of resistance and liberation. The work I am panegyrizing about is, in the first glance, a twenty-four volume exegesis of the Quran. This work is not a regular explanation and annotation of the Quran, however, and although there has been two conferences in Iran in the past three decades honoring the linguistic-hermeneutical contributions of its author, the scholarship that spans the pedagogical intents behind the creation of Meybodi's oeuvre has been but sparse.

There is a threefold structure to this book that makes it a source inspiring enough for writing a chapter on pedagogies of resistance and decolonial educational philosophies. Each of these sections is called *turns*. The first turn are composed of a few verses of the Quran along with a masterfully succinct translation of those verses into Persian. The second turns are conventional exoteric commentaries and traditionalist explanations of the Quranic verses. This turn is mostly in Arabic, which is a language a regular Iranian would barely understand. Second turns are mainly functional and filled with legal and societal annotations and accounts for those verses. Then come the last turns, in which Arabic is rarely used. Third turns are kept for the esoteric exegeses originally written by Ansari, a grand teacher and orator of the eleventh century.

The first turn is artistically insightful mostly because you understand what the Arabic verses are saying. The second turn is as conventional and as laborious a commentary can be. Oftentimes there can be around dozens of Arabic accounts of one verse; it takes time to read this turn and it makes the reader sink into a cumbersome and phlegmatic rendition of the verses. In the third turn you are recurrently presented with "surprisingly free and allegorical interpretations of the verses" combined with "passages of dramatic storytelling" that are more often than not, completely opposite to what the first and second turns have painfully established throughout the book.[1] Keeler, a scholar in this field, calls Meybodi's book a didactic prose.[2] She does mean it linguistically, but I nonetheless want to look at his threefold turns as an instructive source that can inspire ethical turns for decolonial pedagogies.

Here is an example of how the three turns undertake a controversial verse on the prohibition of drinking in Islam and how it aims to weaken the potential violence that can be interpreted from it. "They ask you about wine and gambling. Say, "In them is great sin and [yet, some] benefit for people. But their sin is greater than their benefit. . . . Thus Allah makes clear to you the verses [of revelation] that you might give thought."[3]

Meybodi's first turn is comprised of translating the verses into Farsi, an act of inviting in a language other than Arabic that was oftentimes excluded because it was not Arabic. In the second turn, he discusses the legal and punitive measures of drinking alcohol under religious commandment. In this conversation drinking is rendered a sin. Therefore, "whether one drinks a sip or gets drunk from any fermented drinks there must be lashing as a retributive measure."[4] The turn stipulates and categorizes punishments and the number of lashes corresponding to age and social status. The last turn however is reserved for a different undertaking in explicating the verses, one other than expanding on the sin itself. The turn begins by delineating the different types of drinkers: Meybodi writes (through Al-Ansari's commentary) how some humans are drinkers of the "wine of comprehension," and some drink and get drunk from the "goblet of softheartedness." The exegetic turns—on the sin of drinking wine—is then followed by a story of how a "disheveled lovelorn" enters a winery, gives a coin to the taverner and asks for some wine. The taverner utters that he has no more wine left. The lovelorn says, "I am already a disheveled man in (caught in turbulences of my thoughts). I can't bear the truth of wine (or actual wine) at this point. Supply me with just a drop and you will see how intoxicated I will get from its smell. You'll see what a euphoric exaltation I will make in this world with the fragrance of that one drop."[5] The turn is then filled with poetry to further admire such exaltations.

Meybodi thus takes three epistemological turns: one with a direct translation (inviting in the language—the knowledge—that was pushed out for centuries), another one with an anticipated rational and legal account of the verses, and a third one with an esoteric commentary that is beyond the rationality of the previous turns, in that it invites in the *whats* and *whos* that were excluded, damned, and consequently crowded out from the previous turns (both of which read: alcohol is forbidden therefore whoever drinks it is a sinner).[6]

What is constructively lacking in these three turns is a final synthesis. There is a *rigorous absence* of a conclusion after the third turn even though this turn is the last one. The want of a final "therefore," a "hence" in favor of any turns stops you from settling on a definitive conclusion. Yes, in drinking wine there is a sin, yes drinkers-sinners need to be lashed, and yes, lovelorn people drink and the world becomes an exalted wondrous place because of their drinking. There is not a linear arrow that one finds in an if-then decisive logic, or it is that the linear logic does not have epistemological *supremacy* over a non-linear one such as the third turn. Instead, the three turns aim to give the readers' system of knowing the most difficult thing one can give: *time*, as opposed to writing turns dedicated to eventually *shaping* the ideas with another substitutive idea, logic, or theory.

Here, it seems as if the pedagogical objective of the three turns is not introducing another idea as valuable, but a giving of time. A time to the reader to take its own epistemological turns after having read the three turns, as well as time-space to the other outlawed beings—the disheveled lovelorn—to exist. As if the turns aim to *slowly* disable the arrow of binary logic and meanings ("drinkers are sinners, not believers").

This, what I shall call *pedagogy of time*, therefore, has an aim beyond instilling one liberatory "knowledge" as the ultimately favored one. Rather, its aim is to disrupt what regulates students-readers' economy of knowledge, and in doing so it commits itself to confront accelerated time to confront politics of speed in thinking.[7] The idea of politics of speed is not just a recent conceptual trademark exclusive to neoliberal times and capitalism.[8] It can also found or be founded on oversimplification; a sense of *epistemic hurriedness* in order to reach a predefined conclusion in favor of one structure of thought.[9] In Meybodi's pedagogy of time, for example, having solely one turn (like, say, a direct translation, or a section on legal explanations of the verses, or even Al-Ansari's commentary) could have been considered as not pledging to confront politics of speed. But the fact that there are three turns, each painstakingly put together in order to make epistemic hurriedness difficult testifies to Meybodi's pledge to confront such politics.

This is the commitment of pedagogy of time: one that while its fundamental struggle is to disrupt what regulates students' economies of knowledge (I will expand on this shortly), it does not appoint conclusive endpoints for this struggle. It also does not aim for oversimplified and epistemically hurried theoretical reflections. This is an important commitment. In times when decolonial pedagogies have been examined and critiqued for having been too often "fixated on a simplistic decolonization of Western knowledge and practices," too often favoring resorts to a "quick reclaiming the indigenous practices as superior to Western ones" as opposed to "fostering analytical arguments," and when there is a call by indigenous pedagogues to "encourage openness to further inquiry in and through complex and contested knowledge terrains," decolonial philosophies of education can prosper from a pedagogy that aims for an otherwise regulating of economies of knowledge in the classroom, one that confronts politics of speed.[10]

Perhaps the critics of epistemic hurriedness in decolonial pedagogies would agree on the goal of decolonial philosophies not being to assimilate into a decolonial structure of knowledge but to provide the space and time that Euro-centric philosophies took away from us in the first place when labeling non-European world-views as primitive and not worthy of pedagogical sustenance and evolvement.[11] After all, Enrique Dussel's astute reflection on how Europeans resorted to violence by relying on their linear rationality (in answering the question "Are the Amerindians human beings?" that is, Are they Europeans, and therefore rational animals?) pinpoints that it was a simplified accelerated logic against radical otherness that—among other things—cushioned colonization in the first place.[12]

As such, in this chapter I will reflect on how a pedagogy of time strives for a different regulation of the students' economy of knowledge by the following commitments: it has a different pace and different (epistemic) moves in depicting the points it wants to make, and it tackles the primary and well-established meanings specifically in order to free a multitude of secondary ones. Such commitments, specifically the slow disabling of the primary meanings in favor of freeing "a plethora of secondary ones" is what make this pedagogy an ethico-decolonial engagement.[13]

However, in order to do so, I will have to regrettably leave Meybodi's work at this juncture to better explore the pedagogy of time specifically in (post-)colonial times. What can help is a move to a case of pedagogy that simulates the Meybodian turns, yet engages with colonization by some means. I propose one of Jacque Derrida's lectures for this matter. This is a strategic move and does not mean that one can find in Derrida— nor in European post-structuralism—a more complex and sophisticated pedagogy per se. Critiques of relying on post-structuralism and postmodernism for investigating colonization, and the consequential need to therefore *decolonize* postcolonial studies that draw from such work, put my argument into relief.[14] The fact that Meybodi opens the stage for this chapter calls for the need for other thoughts to become strategic tools in decolonial struggles, to help rethink critical thought or critical knowledges from other spaces and places, and to move the attention from "intra-modern" discussions of modernity to other terrains and works that European theorists—Derrida included—"could not have ever imagined."[15] However, because pedagogy of time takes seriously the present and the modern, and since we are living in a modern/(post)colonial time, the need to make reference to a work that aims to disrupt the regulation of colonial economies of knowledge seems more germane.

To illustrate Derrida's commitment to pedagogy of time, I will examine one lecture in a series of his lessons published under the title "The Beast and the Sovereign" (vol. II). This is Derrida's first lecture, in which he shares his pensive investigations on the politics of concepts such as boredom, sovereignty and solitude. He does so through reflecting on Defoe's *Robinson Crusoe*, which is about an ambitious British man who turns down becoming a lawyer and takes off to the sea instead, experiencing successful and failed voyages such as ending up shipwrecked on an island. I will try to imagine how Derrida—qua teacher—planned his lessons and his pedagogy so as to disrupt the students' conventional regulation of economy of knowledge, although it naturally is difficult to distinctly compartmentalize the commitments of this pedagogy of time in separate segments. Just like Derrida pursues to read Heidegger and Defoe in his course as faithfully yet as *freely* as possible and does his best to keep to his heading of the course, I will try to interpret Derrida's pedagogy as faithfully but nonetheless as freely as possible keep to my heading which is trajectory of a decolonial pedagogy of time.[16]

TURNS, WINDS, AND PEBBLES:
AN OTHERWISE THAN LOGICAL PEDAGOGY

Pedagogy of time pledges itself to carry out different epistemic moves to present its points. Similar to Meybodi's gripping non-linear epistemological *turns*, Derrida refrains from advancing his points in the classroom in a stringently logical way. His pedagogy aims to question the ethics of logo-centricity, and he therefore commits himself to make points in rigorous otherwise-than-logocentric ways: he mentions he wants to "try out a few sentences . . . like warm-up notes for one's voice or vocal chords" (3), he asks us to imagine as if we have found a stone on a shore, and wants us to look at an imaginary statement ingrained on that stone, he opens his lecture with seemingly unrelated and grandiloquent ways to address serious issues: "What is an island?":

> If you hear [*entendez*] this sentence, or these sentences come to you borne by the wind or an echo: "Qu'est-ce qu'une île? Qu'est une île," if you hear them in French, if you hear them without reading them, you think you understand them, but you are not sure.[17]

He then makes even more preclusive moves so as to deliberately stop students from instantaneously getting to the point, which is him planning to offer a scrupulous critique of Defoe's novel and through that a critique of modernity. In answering the question what an island is, he says; "An "il" [*Une "il"*] can designate that insular thing one calls an island . . . , the island of beauty, Treasure Island. . . . Or *The Island of Despair*, as Robinson Crusoe nicknames it on the very opening page of his journal."[18]

He asks us to abandon and isolate the question, leaving it "floating in the air that is carrying it." Sure we have heard it, "but we have to yet read it." In order to read it, Derrida asks us to continue "to stroll on the shore where we have just set foot" in order to make us "stumble" on another sentence; "The beasts are not alone"; "let's act as though the seminar were now starting this way, on an island, in an island, starting with this sententious aphorism."[19] For Derrida, these warm-up notes are serious. They have the "authority and cutting edge of an aphorism, that is, a sentence that is . . . a judgment in the form *S is P*, subject + predicate," but they are presented in different ways, they are "inscribed in stone, given over, entrusted to a stone found on the beach, on an island where we would have just come ashore."[20] He wants to make sure we know for now at least that "they are not proceeded or followed by other sentences," logics, or theories.[21] They are there not to condone any one other theory or structural analysis of the world as absolute, although the lecture is founded on the theories and analyses—chief among them Marx's interpretation—that aim to critique Robinson Crusoe.

He later abandons these questions "on the high seas" only to come back to it later, "we'll see where they come ashore."[22] It seems like he has forsaken the questions, because he moves to read other people's ideas about Robinson Crusoe, yet he is slowly trying to distort the rather positively connoted idea of being alone on an island through Joyce and Woolf, and through them bring in a history and a politics to this celebratory feeling. He reads how Joyce treasured the representation of a "national type of a rational that an English man is" (Joyce, quoted in Derrida 2011, 15), and how this prefigured: an "imperialist and colonialist sovereignty" for Britain, "the first herald of the British empire" and "the great island setting off to conquer other islands, smaller islands (like Ireland) but above all is—lands bigger than it, like Africa, New Zealand or Australia."[23] He thus brings ashore an otherwise representation of the novel in the classroom by disputing the notion of a venturesome European individual (Robinson Crusoe) seeking to be a sovereign on an island he has landed on, knows nothing about its inhabitants, and reduces them to beasts and savages.

These petrified sentences are non-logocentric *preludial* attempts to disrupting the regulation of students' economy of knowledge. As if he tries to interfere with logo-centric ways of knowing to shed light on how students' knowledges can be Euro-logo-centric and how this type can have a reputation to be geopolitically violent, thereby attempting to show how knowledges are subject to ethical questions. These different epistemic moves bespeak of specific pedagogical intentions, like bringing the history (especially the political history) of the concepts, to an audience who perhaps wishes to see concepts (loneliness, individualism, adventures on islands) or works of art (Robinson Crusoe) or rationalities (as admired in Joyce) as uninvolved with any imperial prefigurations of the current world order.

The importance of such moves is further underscored when one remembers that this is a philosophy class in Europe, with Europeans as Derrida's students, and perhaps students who are not necessarily upset at Robinson Crusoe, nor angry at colonization; perchance students who are, at the end of the day, the beneficiaries of colonial imperialism and Euro-centric modalities; people who might regard the novel as a source of inspiration for adventurousness and capturing the unknown (my feeling when I read Robinson Crusoe as a kid). Once one regards Derrida's moves as pedagogical ventures to disrupt the Euro-logo-centric regulation of economies of knowledge, such odd measures might appear to be less based on apathy and more stemmed from an ethical, "otherwise than logo-centric" engagement with potential violence of certain modes of knowledge.

WITHSTANDING POLITICS OF SPEED

To present its central concerns, pedagogy of time as an ethico-decolonial undertaking is committed to a different pace. It does not dispatch a series of points, essentially because the objective is to disrupt what methodically determines students' regulation of economy of knowledge and experience. This commitment to a different unhurried pace is mostly in order to give time to generate space for the "what"s and "who"s that were excluded or relegated (and thus been subjected to epistemic violence) in works of philosophy or art. Similar to Meybodi's, who in a slow pace provides the space for the wondrous drunk lovelorn to exist in an interpretation of a text in which he was originally considered as an outlaw, Derrida also unhurriedly invites in concepts and people who have been refused admittance in texts.

This purposeful un-hurriedness, the slow inviting in of other meanings for students is a conscious move in Derrida's pedagogy. One example of these unhurried moves is the way Derrida handles the investigation of Robinson Crusoe's novel. The question is similar to other philosophers' questions like Marx and Delueze, but the ways he provides the answers are markedly different. Derrida embarks on the same thinking journey Deleuze did before him. Deleuze had asked the same question

Derrida is asking: "What is the meaning of the fiction 'Robinson'?" and Deleuze's answer is to a great extent similar to Derrida's: "A world without others."[24] Derrida's concern though is that the answer is accelerated.

It is not that the answer is completely wrong (although he substantially critiques it), but that the answer is hasty, direct, and fast, perhaps not epistemically *unhurried* enough for disrupting what regulates the economy of students' knowledge in favor of providing space for an otherwise thought, one which excluded concepts to have the chance to appear as pivotal. Derrida knows this.[25] He mentions "Deleuze's answer comes fast."[26] Deleuze's *phenomenology* of associating Robinson Crusoe's adventure only to perversionism and sadism seems hasty, Derrida's *pedagogy* tries to avoid that, "Deleuze hurries to add that this perversion is not constitutional but linked to an adventure, to a story that can be both the story of a neurosis and the proximity of a psychosis."[27] Derrida cautions us of an accelerated closure: "Conclusion: "We must imagine Robinson to be perverse; the only Robinsonade is perversion itself."[28] By cautioning against Deleuze's hurried attempts to answer the question, Derrida aims to provide a space through his pedagogy for more questions to be created. Questions whose final answers are not determined by Derrida, although definitely multiplied by him.

He thus aims to regress to the stage before Deleuze's conclusions on Robinson Crusoe, and finds an excuse through Delueze:

> These are the last words of this chapter, the last sentence that, by associating the adjective "only" to "Robinsonade" ("the only Robinsonade is perversion itself"), leaves open the possibility of not reducing the book *Robinson Crusoe* to a Robinsonade, nor even to Robinson Crusoe himself, in his insular solitude, isolated from his history, his past, his future, the process of his socialization, his relation to many others, including slaves and animals.[29]

Derrida thus aims to tackle the epistemic hurriedness and oversimplification he sees in the reading of Deleuze. Pedagogy of time does not aim for rapid introductions of another structure of beliefs or rigid conclusions. Derrida's pedagogy is aiming for the slow unfolding of the political and colonial aspects of Robinson Crusoe's novel. Deleuze does go not beyond perversionism, "But," Derrida reads, "that will be *our* story."[30]

FOR DRUNKS AND SAVAGES:
PEDAGOGY OF DISABLING PRIMARY MEANINGS

I see one essential commitment of pedagogy of time as being un-strengthening well-established meanings to free—but not decisively assign—a plethora of secondary ones. Derrida's lecture is devoted to disabling these primary meanings. He does so through two movements: by peering into commentaries on *Robinson Crusoe* made by established figures, and by dissecting well-rooted key meanings in the novel. The figures whose comments on Defoe Derrida dwells on are James Joyce, Virginia Woolf and Rousseau. Defoe's work is invariably accolated as authentic and creative by all three.

In the first turn in Derrida's classroom, the primary meanings that are investigated are the ways *Robinson Crusoe* have been judged and evaluated "in our modernity."[31] One example is Joyce's admiration for Defoe's work in *Robinson Crusoe*. Derrida rereads Joyce, and through this reading explores the epistemological underpinnings that have been influential in shaping the present identity of Europe. Thus, Derrida who mentions at the beginning of the class that he wants to try out a few sentences "like warm-up notes," initiates a "theologico-political" and Marxist critique of *Robinson Crusoe* and its approbation in history of modern European thought, in the hope to address the violence embedded in this appraisal for modernity.[32]

Derrida examines how in Joyce's eyes, Defoe has saved the English nation from Shakespearean "pitiable characters of boorish peasants," "half-lunatics and half-fools," "gravediggers," "Venetian Jews," and "princes of Denmark."[33] For Joyce, it is Defoe who abstains from adapting foreign works and instead, "infuses a truly national spirit into the creatures with his pen."[34] Derrida sees the spectral presence of words such as "foreign works," "English," and "truly national spirit" in Joyce's panegyric on Defoe as indicative of the fact that *Robinson Crusoe* is not just an apolitically naive artistic contribution. He breaks down how Joyce despises the gravediggers and half-lunatics, yet revels in a "national type of a rational animal" that Crusoe is; how he loves in Robinson Crusoe the embodiment of the Anglo-Saxon spirit, the manly independence, the unconscious cruelty, the sexual apathy, the well-balanced religiousness, and the calculating taciturnity, and eventually, the true symbol of the British conquest and the ideal prototype of the British colonist.[35]

Derrida's discussion on Joyce canvasses ways in which *Robinson Crusoe*'s celebrated rationality is filled with violence against others, invading others and building empires off others' lands; as if Derrida wants to enervate these accolades to invite in dark sides of Crusoe's quest which was aided by much revered European rationality; what seems to deem—as the lecture unhurriedly unfolds it for us—others who are radically different as beasts and savages. For Derrida, Joyce's delight in Robinson Crusoe's rationality has subtexts. What is delineated in Joyce's admiration is "the prefiguration of an imperialist, colonialist sovereignty, the first herald of the British Empire," and as discussed earlier, it is about "the great island setting off to conquer otters islands, smaller islands (like Ireland) but above all islands bigger than it, like Africa, New Zealand, or Australia."[36]

While Joyce believes "whoever rereads this simple, moving book in the light of subsequent history cannot help but fall under its prophetic spell," Derrida tackles the historico-geographical harms of this enchant-ment.[37] In this light, through a rereading of Joyce's ideas on *Robinson Crusoe*, Derrida tackles the primary meanings and takes an interrogative turn to the epistemological *status quo*. Prior to designing this lesson Derri-da might have cogitated on how to generate, through his pedagogy, the notion of guilt in a classroom at the heart of Europe, in order to disrupt the regulation of the economy of knowledge through incorporating dark sides of the established knowledge all in an epistemically unhurried manner. Once one reads that Robinson's isolation on an island is not a geographically abstract concept it seems like the novel is no longer the same an innocent book, the product of a pure imagination of a creative artist; it is now a geopolitically, imperially guilty artifact.

The other figure that is persistently present in Derrida's classroom is Rousseau, whose two texts—*Emile* and *Discourse on the Origins of Inequality*—Derrida refers to time and again. Derrida is interested to in-vestigate Rousseau's infatuation with *Robinson Crusoe* in *Emile*. Although Rousseau hates books "because they teach us to talk about what we do not know," he nonetheless favors *Robinson Crusoe* teaching us about the unknown. Indeed, it is the only book that Rousseau wants to see Emile's head turned by, for him to be constantly occupied within his castle, the only book he wants Emile's imagination to be enlivened by:

> that he think himself to be Robinson; that he see himself clothed in animal skins, wearing a large bonnet, carrying a big saber, the whole grotesque outfit of the character. . . . I want him to worry about the measures to be taken, if this or that were to be lacking, to examine the conduct of his hero, to seek to see if he has omitted anything, whether there was not something better he could have done. . . . What is more, let us hasten to set him up on this island, while he limits his happiness to it.[38]

Him ascribing to the novel such a revered and principal role in Emile's education makes one associate how educating for modernity can entail, among other things, shaping Crusoe-like characters, Crusoe-like ways of knowing: an "individual" who wants to be a sovereign on an island where he has accidentally set foot on, a place whose history and people he is not familiar with, a man who believes his rationality justifies him being the sovereign on that land.

After having discussed the Rousseauian passions for Emile, one—the student in Derrida's class—has a feeling that Derrida is insinuating a spectral presence of Rousseau in our times; as if we are living in an actualized Rousseauian dream, an actualized Rousseauian education. At the risk of overreaching, as if we are living a world whose borders, as well as its education are shaped and sustained by the imperial ambitions of rational, modernly educated beings who deem other beings that are radically different as savages and beasts.

Derrida's probing into Rousseau's aspirations for Emile make us ponder that we—or Europeans sitting in a classroom in France—have inherited a dream filled with a colonial baggage and without us knowing its violence. Through a pedagogy committed to creating genealogical returns to how our knowledges are shaped Derrida adds layers of historical and political complexity to Rousseau's wish for Emile. Just like he said that we would keep turning over and over a polished stone and the enigmatic sentence about the beasts not being alone "in order to find the beginning, the end, its hidden meaning, perhaps the signature," he turns over Rousseau's admiration for *Robinson Crusoe* to reflect on the beginnings and the signatures of *structures* that have shaped our knowledge, as well as the hidden corners of our—and his students'—epistemologies.[39] Doing so to invite in ethical concerns about the violence embedded in our knowledge and to generate thoughts on how non-Rousseauian dreams would have looked like; also to make us imagine how many were sabotaged and ignored because his dream was considered the dream.

CONCEPTS THAT WANTED TO BE JUST CONCEPTS

The second way Derrida commits to freeing of secondary and excluded meanings in the classroom is through addressing concepts that have a positive presence in quotidian European thought. Derrida tries to crowd in certain semantic undertones that he realizes were crowded out in well-established texts in order to make students ponder on the political subtexts of those thoughts. One such attempt can be seen when he looks at Robinson Crusoe's ostensibly adventure-laden and ambitious concept of loneliness, which is also the central theme of the first class.

The lecture starts with the sentence "I am alone," in an attempt to impart Robinson Crusoe's fear of being the only one "human being" on an island; "either that I should be devoured by wild Beasts, murder'd by Savages, or starv'd to Death for Want of Food."[40] Derrida's next pedagogical move is to invert the sentence "I am alone" to "the beasts are not alone" in order to invite in other meanings and other feelings into the classroom. As if Derrida wanted to, through his lecture, make students identify with the feared beasts and the savages, instead of feeling for Crusoe's loneliness. The beasts are not alone; Robinson Crusoe is now there on an island. It is because Robinson Crusoe is seeking sovereignty that the beasts and the savages are not alone anymore. The beasts and savages do not have the existential privilege—or right—to be left alone anymore. Also because they have been reduced to beasts and savages and not to radically different others: "The reference . . . to human "Savages" or "wild Creatures," the reduction of the narrator to a state of savage nature, almost that of a beast, since he has no house, clothes of weapon."[41]

The dark side of Robinson Crusoe's trajectory for solitude is thus examined at in Derrida's class under seeking mastery and the prefiguration of an imperialist sovereignty. Derrida sees the undertone of male sovereignty as "indissociable" from Robinsonian solitude. Rousseau might have taught the book in his classroom in France as an example of the originary contributions to art and imagination. In Derrida's class, when aiming for disabling primary meanings,

> The book is a long discussion between Robinson and so many beasts. And the theater of that discussion is, indissociably, a theater of solitary sovereignty, of the assertion of mastery (of self, over slaves, over savages and over beasts, without speaking—because the point is precisely not to talk about them— ... of women.[42]

Once other concepts are crowded in to the discussion through the distinct unhurried move of inverting the sentence "I am alone" to "the beasts are not alone," Derrida's students' feeling and knowing are likely to be inverted. One might put aside identifying with Crusoe's anxiety of being alone amongst savages and beasts, and become worried instead for other-than-Robinsons on that island, those who Robinson Crusoe calls beasts and savages. One might feel uneasily fearful for others that were not in their own eyes beasts and savages but are now beasts and savages due to the fact that Robinson Crusoe does not get their logics of being in this world, their rationality for being the way they are.

Derrida furthers the quest of freeing secondary meanings and un-bestializing others by addressing another concept, the idea of an ambitious dream. Rousseau is back here again in Derrida's class with his other *wish* which Derrida sees as being inspired by Robinson Crusoe's building a life on another island and seeking to be a sovereign there:

> I would have wished to be born in a country where the sovereign and the people could have but one and the same interest, so that all the movements of the machine could tend only to the common good; which being impossible, unless the people and the sovereign are one and the same person.[43]

Derrida tackles the actual worldly consequences of this dream of having wished to have been born somewhere else. This time Derrida's pedagogy aims for analyzing the geo-historical consequences of this Crusoe-inspired Rousseauian dream. He sees in Rousseau's *I would have wished* not just a dream happening in a "failed origin, rather than one of lost origin"; it is again, a geopolitically ambitious dream, as if he instills in students how Rousseau aims to take a "giant stride" to find a new origin for his dream on other people's lands. Derrida further brings in another idea here: "the absence of a responsibility" in this tense and mood. "What "I" can ever conjugate the verb "to be born" in this tense and in this mood: I would have wished?"[44] Perhaps one whose existence is contingent upon conquering:

> Unless *only* an "I" can do so, say it and think it, however empty and impossible this saying and thinking may seem to remain, this "I" that says and thinks in this way, and signs an "I would have wished to be born."[45]

Derrida expands on how this is a political and pre-political wish, a rather intentional "historical configuration" and "an epochal ensemble" that had its roots in the economic ambitions of Europe. He invites in Marx's critique that writes how philosophico-political fictions like these are "aesthetic superstructures at once significant, symptomatic and dependent on what they signify."[46] It so happens that Rousseau's written wish was also symptomatic of "an anticipation of [European] bourgeois society which had been preparing itself since the sixteenth century and which in the eighteenth century was taking giant strides towards maturity."[47]

This is reminiscent of Dussel's idea. Similar to Derrida who writes that this dream is not a spontaneous creation of ingenious imagination, Dussel notes that the creation of *philosophical ontology* did not happen in an abstract space. "It arose from a previous experience of domination over other persons, of cultural oppression over other worlds. Before the ego cogito there is an ego conquiro; 'I conquer' is the practical foundation of 'I think.'"[48] He reminds us that the global north has imposed itself on the south for more than five centuries through—among other political, economic, and imperial factors—leaning on the very linear rationality of "I think therefore I am." While Dussel tackles the geopolitical aftermath of "I think therefore I am" by arguing it was originally "I conquer therefore I am," Derrida seems to be canvassing the historico-political *before* of Rousseau's sentence by questioning the translucence of "I wish I would have been born."

The next meaning Derrida wishes to approach is the temporal violence of Crusoe-inspired Rousseauean dream. This dream is not an ephemeral moment of art. There is a "bildung," "a constructed world" in Rousseau's wish. This is a Rousseau that "recognizes himself in Robinson Crusoe, recognizes in him a brother."[49] The wish, as a pre-political dream, seemed to have not only shaped the world but it has endured as a marvelous fascination. This is something that scares Derrida: this world or this epoch of the world that goes well beyond the period of the eighteenth century, "in that the fascination exercised by *Robinson Crusoe* will survive for a long time; a fascination exercised not only on Joyce or Woolf but on every child and adult the world over."[50]

People are going to read *Robinson Crusoe,* and have read it, and not only this having read has shaped the present, Derrida is implying it, but it will continue to shape both pasts and presents: a European dream from the past that has molded (colonized) the past and the present of non-

Europeans, and has suspended the future from being a prospering one. Hence, Derrida's worry about the violence of perpetuating a fascination built on dichotomous savages-humans, humans-beasts logics. These making of disabling turns that Derrida concerns himself with hopes to flow in a different present into the classroom, one that might be able to breathe itself out of a historically colonial canon by precisely looking at the coloniality embedded in heroes of modern European thought.

Similar to Meybodi enervating a potentially violent logic (drinking is harmful and whoever drinks is a sinner and is therefore to be lashed) through staging epistemically unhurried and non-logocentric turns, Derrida's pedagogy of time disables the primary theses and frees secondary meanings through a radical ushering in of other concepts that were perhaps supposed to remain outside of the conversations on Robinson Crusoe's novel in the classroom.

Pedagogy of time is thus committed to an "ultra-political" regulating of students' economies of knowledges: in the sense that it is committed to addressing the violence of texts, meanings, and knowings, but it does not have its definitive endpoint answers normatively assigned, meaning "already designated to a specific political theory."[51] As Derrida shows, his pedagogy is founded on a Marxist, anti-Colonial, and Post-Modern bedrock. It undertakes capitalism, colonialism, and darks sides of modernity. Yet it consciously and painstakingly abstains from resorting to oversimplified dialectical assimilations into any other structure that declares to have explained the roots of all of problems by reducing it to one cause. Pedagogy of time gives time to historical decolonial becoming as opposed to snatching away time in favor of fixated conclusions.

This is why pedagogy of time, with its deliberate epistemic un-hurriedness and in its withholding from assimilation in a theory already-created-by-others, can find itself closer to what Fanon had in mind as an authentic configuration for resistance. In his book *Black Skins, White Masks*, he objects to Sartre rushing him to opt for a Marxist solution to fight racism, something he needed not to know.[52] Fanon needed to not know the endpoints of his resistance, and he especially did not need his theoretical and dialectical threshold in "becoming" to be suggested or enforced by someone else. Even though the colonial injustices "ignited fervor," he did not trust it nor did he want truths about colonial injustices "to be hurled in men's faces."[53] For Fanon, historical becomings entailed needing to lose yourself completely in what has caused harm violence, colonialism, or for him specifically, negritude. You need to forget what you never knew.[54] As if hurrying to a theoretically circumscribed solution belongs to those philosopher-pedagogues "who heat the iron *in order* to shape it at once"[55] (emphasis added).

Perhaps pedagogy of time in its undertaking of creating an ultra-political regulation of economy of knowledge would be something Fanon would condone: it tends to give time as opposed "to snatch it away."[56]

After all, a pedagogy like this is committed "to warm(ing) man's body and leav(ing) him" as opposed to "heating it and shaping at once," ultimately nudging them to wear a trampoline of resistance made and already created by others.[57]

Derrida's slow unhurried moves to disable primary meanings and Meybodi's pedagogy of three turns with no rigidly determined conclusions can regulate the economy of knowledge or resistance the way Fanon would have wanted, and it might be what we ought to demand in times when there is a need for radically slow Fanonian decolonial pedagogies; ones that warm up humans' thoughts and yet let them retain the fire through self-combustion, those that endow students with epistemological turns to make possible digging into our flesh to find meanings; pedagogies of giving time.[58]

NOTES

1. See Annabel Keeler, "Meybodi, Abu'l-Fażl Rašid-al-Din" in *Irannica* (Encyclopædia Iranica, 2009), 11.

2. See Annabel Keeler, "Meybodi, Abu'l-Fażl Rašid-al-Din," in *Irannica* (Encyclopædia Iranica, 2009), 11.

3. See Koran 2: 219, Sahih International, Muhsin Khan, Pickthall, Yusuf Ali, Shakir, Or Dr. Ghali, accessed June 2015, www.saheehinternational.com/?page_id=20.

4. See Abu'l-Fażl Rašid-ala-Din Meybodi, *Kašf al-asrār wa 'oddat al-abrār (Unveiling of mysteries and provision of the righteous)*, (AmirKabir Publication, 1965), 304.

5. See See Abu'l-Fażl Rašid-ala-Din Meybodi, *Kašf al-asrār wa 'oddat al-abrār (Unveiling of mysteries and provision of the righteous)*, (AmirKabir Publication, 1965), 307–308.

6. On the third turn Keeler writes, "It seems, however, that once the rational faculty is safely at bay, and the exegete is in the state of receiving inspiration rather than applying reason, the shackles of literalism may be allowed to fall away, and it is noteworthy that the esoteric sections of Meybodi's commentary actually include some surprisingly free metaphorical and allegorical interpretations of the Quranic verses. See Keeler, "Meybodi, Abu'l-Fażl Rašid-al-Din," 12.

7. I use the phrase "regulating the economy of knowledge" from Derrida. On page 20 of *Given Time* he discusses how the notion of gift as no return phenomenon as we commonly assume is impossible, to reflect on the potentialities of this impossibility. "The gift *itself* . . . should never be confused with the presence of its phenomenon. Perhaps there is nomination, language, thought, desire, or intention only there where there is this movement still for thinking, desiring, naming that which gives itself neither to be known, experienced, nor lived—in the sense in which presence, existence, determination, regulate the economy of knowing, experiencing, and living. In this sense one can think, desire, and say only the impossible according to the measureless measure . . . of the impossible." See Jacques Derrida, *Given Time: I. Counterfeit Money* Vol. 1 (Chicago: University of Chicago Press, 1992), 29. What I mean by what regulate the economy of knowledge in this chapter is not what Derrida develops however. I use the phrase to reflect on the factors that are decisive and centroidal in shaping students' knowledges; elements like—inter alia—theory, cultural, geography, school curricula, having experienced culture as an inherited actuality, epistemologies, ignorance and logo-centricity. On Derrida's complicated discussion about this economy of knowledge Carlson writes: "Contrary to common misreadings, Derrida does not claim that the gift is simply or straightforwardly impossible, or that "there is no gift," but rather that "of there is a gift" (and Derrida consistently approaches the gift in

the hypothetical), the gift would mark a figure of *the* impossible—which implies a distinction between "that about which one simply cannot speak" and, by contrast, "that about which one can no longer speak, but which one can no longer silence." *The* impossible here articulates a double bind: it engenders thought, language and desire surrounding that which thought, language and desire can never grasp "as such." Indeed, the very *possibility* of thought, language, and desire would require their relation to this figure of the impossible, since their full and actual conversion into "philosophy, science, and the order of presence" would annul them *as possible*. Like the impossible possibility of death in Heidegger, the impossible in Derrida even *remains* to be thought, spoken and desired: "Perhaps there is naming, language, thought, desire, or intention only there where there is movement still for thinking, desiring, naming that which gives itself neither to be known, experienced, or lived—in the sense in which presence, existence, determination regulate the economy of knowing, experiencing and living." *The* impossible in Derrida (the naming of God, death, justice, the coming of the Messiah, etc.) maintains the irreducible openness of futurity; it always remains to come, and hence remains, in its not yet, always possible. See Thomas Carlson, "4 Postemetaphysical Theology" *The Cambridge Companion to Postmodern Theology* (2003): 74.

8. See Simon Glezos, *The Politics of Speed: Capitalism, the State and War in an Accelerating World* (New York: Routledge: 2013).

9. See the discussion on "epistemic totality" in Noroozi, Nassim "Counteracting Epistemic Totality and Weakening Mental Rigidities: The Anti-totalitarian Nature of Wonderment" *Philosophy of Education Society Yearbook* (Urbana: 2015).

10. See Martin Nakata, Victoria Nakata, Sarah Keech, and Rueben Bolt, et. Al "Decolonial Goals and Pedagogies for Indigenous Studies" *Decolonization: Indigeneity, Education and Society* 1 no.1 (2012): 120.

11. For the violence incurred by applying European models of education see the Truth and Reconciliation Commission report on Residential Schools: "They came for the children: Canada, Aboriginal peoples and Residential Schools" (Truth and Reconciliation Commission of Canada: 2012). www.trc.ca/websites/trcinstitution/index.php? p=580.

12. See Enrique Dussel, *Philosophy of Liberation* (Maryknoll: Orbis Books, 1985), 3.

13. On freeing the plethora of secondary meanings Ian Almond writes, "[difference] at once confuses and makes things simpler. It breaks down complexities, undoes complications, dismantles structures into their various components. At the same time it makes a text difficult to read, disabling its primary sense in order to free a plethora of secondary ones, robbing the text of its semantic rudder so that it can no longer be said to sail in any particular direction." See Ian Almond, *Sufism and Deconstruction: A Comparative Study of Derrida and Ibn'Arabi* (New York: Routledge, 2004), 46–47.

14. See Ramón Grosfoguel "The Epistemic Decolonial Turn: Beyond Political Economy Paradigms," *Cultural Studies* vol. 21 no. 2–3 (2007): 211–223.

15. See Catherine Walsh, "'Other' Knowledges, 'Other' Critiques: Reflections on the Politics and Practices of Philosophy and Decoloniality in the 'Other' America" *Transmodernity* (2012): 12–26. Also see Arturo Escobar, "Worlds and Knowledge Otherwise: The Latin American Modernity/Coloniality Research Program" *Cultural Studies* 21, no. 2–3 (2007): 179–210.

16. See Jacques Derrida, *The Beast and the Sovereign* vol. 2 (Chicago: University of Chicago Press, 2011), 13.

17. See Jacques Derrida, *The Beast and the Sovereign* vol. 2 (Chicago: University of Chicago Press, 2011), 3.

18. See Jacques Derrida, *The Beast and the Sovereign* vol. 2 (Chicago: University of Chicago Press, 2011), 3.

19. See Jacques Derrida, *The Beast and the Sovereign* vol. 2 (Chicago: University of Chicago Press, 2011), 5.

20. See Jacques Derrida, *The Beast and the Sovereign* vol. 2 (Chicago: University of Chicago Press, 2011), 5.

21. See Jacques Derrida, *The Beast and the Sovereign* vol. 2 (Chicago: University of Chicago Press, 2011), 5.

22. See Jacques Derrida, *The Beast and the Sovereign* vol. 2 (Chicago: University of Chicago Press, 2011), 2.

23. See Jacques Derrida, *The Beast and the Sovereign* vol. 2 (Chicago: University of Chicago Press, 2011), 15–16.

24. See Jacques Derrida, *The Beast and the Sovereign* vol. 2 (Chicago: University of Chicago Press, 2011), 26.

25. To read Derrida's critique on Deleuze's thoughts on *Robinson Crusoe*, see *The Beast and The Sovereign* vol. 2, pages 26–27.

26. See Jacques Derrida, *The Beast and the Sovereign* vol. 2 (Chicago: University of Chicago Press, 2011), 26.

27. See Jacques Derrida, *The Beast and the Sovereign* vol. 2 (Chicago: University of Chicago Press, 2011), 27.

28. See Jacques Derrida, *The Beast and the Sovereign* See Jacques Derrida, *The Beast and the Sovereign* vol. 2 (Chicago: University of Chicago Press, 2011), 13.27. Derrida takes the word *Robinsonade* from Marx who uses it when describing fictions that are sympomatic of their age in his book *Introduction to the Critique of Political Economy*. "A socio-economical and metaphysico-ideological structure that corresponds "to an anticipation of [European] bourgeois society which had been preparing itself since the sixteenth century and which in the eighteenth century was taking giant strides towards maturity." Derrida writes, "You'll find the most visible and even spectacular expression of Marx's audacity, e interesting temerity that pushes him to recognize in this an epochal structure, a great socio-economico-ideological phase that he calls, precisely, a 'Robinsonade' and that he describes, naming in passing." See Jacques Derrida, *The Beast and the Sovereign* vol. 2 (Chicago: University of Chicago Press, 2011), 24.

29. See Jacques Derrida, *The Beast and the Sovereign* vol. 2 (Chicago: University of Chicago Press, 2011), 27.

30. See Jacques Derrida, *The Beast and the Sovereign* vol. 2 (Chicago: University of Chicago Press, 2011), 27.

31. See Jacques Derrida, *The Beast and the Sovereign* vol. 2 (Chicago: University of Chicago Press, 2011), 14.

32. See Jacques Derrida, *The Beast and the Sovereign* vol. 2 (Chicago: University of Chicago Press, 2011), 15.

33. See Jacques Derrida, *The Beast and the Sovereign* vol. 2 (Chicago: University of Chicago Press, 2011), 15.

34. See Jacques Derrida, *The Beast and the Sovereign* vol. 2 (Chicago: University of Chicago Press, 2011), 15.

35. See Jacques Derrida, *The Beast and the Sovereign* vol. 2 (Chicago: University of Chicago Press, 2011), 16.

36. See Jacques Derrida, *The Beast and the Sovereign* vol. 2 (Chicago: University of Chicago Press, 2011), 16.

37. See Jacques Derrida, *The Beast and the Sovereign* vol. 2 (Chicago: University of Chicago Press, 2011), 16.

38. See Rousseau, quoted in Jacques Derrida, *The Beast and the Sovereign* vol. 2 (Chicago: University of Chicago Press, 2011), 20.

39. See Jacques Derrida, *The Beast and the Sovereign* vol. 2 (Chicago: University of Chicago Press, 2011), 5.

40. See Defoe quoted in Jacques Derrida, *The Beast and the Sovereign* vol. 2 (Chicago: University of Chicago Press, 2011), 4.

41. See Jacques Derrida, *The Beast and the Sovereign* vol. 2 (Chicago: University of Chicago Press, 2011), 4.

42. See Jacques Derrida, *The Beast and the Sovereign* vol. 2 (Chicago: University of Chicago Press, 2011), 28.

43. See Jacques Derrida, *The Beast and the Sovereign* vol. 2 (Chicago: University of Chicago Press, 2011), 22–23.

44. See Jacques Derrida, *The Beast and the Sovereign* vol. 2 (Chicago: University of Chicago Press, 2011), 23.

45. See Jacques Derrida, *The Beast and the Sovereign* vol. 2 (Chicago: University of Chicago Press, 2011), 23.

46. See Jacques Derrida, *The Beast and the Sovereign* vol. 2 (Chicago: University of Chicago Press, 2011), 25.

47. See Marx quoted in Jacques Derrida, *The Beast and the Sovereign* vol. 2 (Chicago: University of Chicago Press, 2011), 25.

48. See Jacques Derrida, *The Beast and the Sovereign* vol. 2 (Chicago: University of Chicago Press, 2011), 3.

49. See Jacques Derrida, *The Beast and the Sovereign* vol. 2 (Chicago: University of Chicago Press, 2011), 24.

50. See Jacques Derrida, *The Beast and the Sovereign* vol. 2 (Chicago: University of Chicago Press, 2011), 24.

51. See Jacques Derrida, *The Beast and the Sovereign* vol. 2 (Chicago: University of Chicago Press, 2011), 21.

52. Bernasconi investigates Sartre's attempt to create a dialectic on Fanon's resistance against racism and why this attempt troubles Fanon: while Fanon was trying to contemplate on the negritude movement and to search for a way of negotiating his identity in a racist society, Sartre goes on to locate it "within a dialectic as a passing phase between white supremacy and "the realization of the human in a race-less society." See Robert Bernasconi, "On Needing Not to Know and Forgetting What One Never Knew: The Epistemology of Ignorance in Fanon's Critique of Sartre" in *Race and Epistemologies of Ignorance* (Albany: SUNY Press, 2007): 233. Sartre thus offers a dialectical theory of liberation: white racism as the thesis and Black anti-racism as antithetical to white racism in the hope of creating a race-less society.

53. See Frantz Fanon, *Black Skin, White Masks* (Pluto Press, 2008), 2.

54. See Robert Bernasconi, "On Needing Not to Know and Forgetting What One Never Knew: The Epistemology of Ignorance in Fanon's Critique of Sartre," 233.

55. See Frantz Fanon, *Black Skin, White Masks* (Pluto Press, 2008), 2

56. See Frantz Fanon, *Black Skin, White Masks* (Pluto Press, 2008), 101.

57. See Frantz Fanon, *Black Skin, White Masks* (Pluto Press, 2008), 2.

58. "Fervor is the weapon of choice of the impotent. Of those who heat the iron in order to shape it at once. I should prefer to warm man's body and leave him. We might reach this result: mankind retaining this fire through self-combustion. Mankind set free of the trampoline that is the resistance of others, and digging into its own flesh to find a meaning." See Frantz Fanon, *Black Skin, White Masks* (Pluto Press, 2008), 2–3.

BIBLIOGRAPHY

Almond, Ian. *Sufism and Deconstruction: A Comparative Study of Derrida and Ibn'Arabi.* New York: Routledge, 2004.

Bernasconi, Robert. "On Needing Not to Know and Forgetting What One Never Knew: The Epistemology of Ignorance in Fanon's Critique of Sartre." In Shannon Sullivan and Nancy Tuana (eds.), *Race and Epistemologies of Ignorance.* Albany: SUNY Press, 2007.

Carlson, Thomas. "4 Postmetaphysical Theology." In Kevin Vanhoozer (ed.) *The Cambridge Companion to Postmodern Theology.* New York: Cambridge University Press, 2003.

Critchley, Simon. *The Ethics of Deconstruction: Derrida and Levinas.* Edinburgh: Edinburgh University Press, 2014.

Derrida, Jacques. *The Beast and the Sovereign.* vol. 2. Chicago: University of Chicago Press, 2011.

———. *Given Time: I. Counterfeit Money.* vol. 1. Chicago: University of Chicago Press, 1992.

Dussel, Enrique. *Philosophy of Liberation*. MaryKnoll: Orbis Books, 1985.

Escobar, Arturo. "Worlds and Knowledge Otherwise: The Latin American Modernity/ Coloniality Research Program." *Cultural Studies* 21, no. 2–3 (2007): 179–210.

Fanon, Frantz. *Black Skin, White Masks*. London: Pluto Press, 2008.

Glezos, Simon. *The Politics of Speed: Capitalism, the State and War in an Accelerating World*. New York: Routledge: 2013.

Grosfoguel, Ramón. "The Epistemic Decolonial Turn: Beyond Political Economy Paradigms." *Cultural Studies* vol. 21 no. 2–3 (2007): 211–223.

Koran 2: 219, Sahih International, Muhsin Khan, Pickthall, Yusuf Ali, Shakir, Or Dr. Ghali, accessed June 2015, www.saheehinternational.com/?page_id=20.

Keeler, Annabel. "Meybodi, Abu'l-Faẓl Rašid-al-Din." *Irannica*. Encyclopædia Iranica, 2009.

Meybodi, Abu'l-Faẓl Rašid-ala-Din. *Kašf al-asrār wa ʿoddat al-abrār (Unveiling of mysteries and provision of the righteous)*, AmirKabir Publication, 1965.

Noroozi, Nassim. "Counteracting Epistemic Totality and Weakening Mental Rigidities: The Anti-totalitarian Nature of Wonderment." *Philosophy of Education Society Yearbook*. Urbana: 2015.

Nakata, Martin, Victoria Nakata, Sarah Keech, and Reuben Bolt. "Decolonial Goals and Pedagogies for Indigenous Studies." *Decolonization: Indigeneity, Education & Society* 1, no. 1 (2012).

Walsh, Catherine. "'Other' Knowledges, 'Other' Critiques: Reflections on the Politics and Practices of Philosophy and Decoloniality in the 'Other' America." *Transmodernity* (2012): 12–26.

TEN

Decolonizing Human Rights

Implications for Human Rights Pedagogy, Scholarship,
and Advocacy in Westernized Universities and Schools

Camilo Pérez-Bustillo

This chapter explores conceptual and substantive aspects of the challenges posed by decolonial thinking to human rights pedagogy, scholarship, and advocacy in Westernized universities and schools, and on the need to reconceive the epistemology, history, theory, and practice of human rights in order to undertake the complex task of "decolonizing" these dimensions. The approach taken to these issues here is based on my teaching and engagement as a human rights scholar and advocate in both the United States and Latin America, and as to the global implications of issues as to migrant rights and the rights of indigenous peoples.

In the United States, Western Europe, and Latin America international law and human rights are typically taught and conceived of as if they were of uniquely Western, and even more specifically European (or even Anglo-American) origin, within the context of modernity, the Enlightenment, and their universalist pretensions. From this perspective, the task for non-Western societies is to westernize themselves through processes of economic, political, social, and cultural "development" to a degree sufficient to enable the flourishing of the kinds of rights ostensibly enjoyed in Western contexts.

This is in essence the "hegemonic" version of human rights history and theory, which has been increasingly challenged in the academy and in the streets from "counter-hegemonic" perspectives grounded in the Global South, both beyond and within the Global North (e.g., immigrant communities and movements and those of other marginalized groups such as people of African descent, women, those identified as LGBTQ, etc.). Such alternative approaches instead emphasize the extent to which hegemonic Western conceptualizations and practices of human rights in fact pose key obstacles to the full recognition of these rights, which reflect the costs and impacts of the historical and contemporary crimes of the West (such as conquest, African slavery, genocide, colonialism, imperialism, and neo-colonialism), which are understood as constitutive of the emergence and spread of the capitalist mode of production and thus of modernity itself. From this perspective there are alternative routes to fuller conceptions and practices of human rights, which are capable of transcending their limitations and distortions in the context of Western hegemony. Such approaches are often described—or dismissed—as "utopian." This reflects the intertwined, contested relationship between human rights, hegemony, and utopia, which provides a guiding thread for this chapter. Such contradictions are heightened whenever hegemonic powers such as the United States seek to justify their interventions elsewhere as part of an overall civilizational project "in defense of human rights" accompanied with the kinds of moral, political, and/or religious claims of universality associated with American exceptionalism. Initiatives of this kind also tend to stigmatize and criminalize resistance to this overall project and its components as necessarily of a terrorist character, or as uniquely grounded in competing global communities and visions such as that of Islam.

What would it look like if the history, conceptualization, and practice of human rights were taught and approached differently in Westernized contexts? This task is especially urgent in settings such as Latin America, Africa, and Asia where colonial legacies continue to permeate contemporary societies, and in other contexts such as the United States and Western Europe where the increasing presence of communities rooted in the Global South challenges long held assumptions as to identity, diversity, and inclusion.

LATIN AMERICA AND UTOPIAN VISIONS OF HUMAN RIGHTS

There is a longstanding tradition that connects the pursuit of utopian visions in Latin America with the defense of human rights. This is reflected in recurrent processes of resistance and rebellion by the region's indigenous peoples, people of African descent, and other excluded sectors against colonialism, slavery, racism, and related forms of domination, including their contemporary equivalents in the context of neoliberal capitalist globalization. Efforts to rethink the epistemology, origins, history, and limits of hegemonic paradigms and practices of human rights, with emphasis on the transformative potential of counter-hegemonic alternatives, "from below" are key expressions of this utopian impulse today.[1]

This chapter's approach is deeply indebted to convergent aspects of the critiques of modernity and coloniality developed by Walter Mignolo, Aníbal Quijano, Enrique Dussel, and their colleagues in what some refer to as the Modernity/(de)Coloniality project, with its emphasis on the "constitutive and complementary character" of modernity and coloniality. It also builds upon counter-hegemonic reconceptualizations of international law and of the relationship between law and globalization, which include an emphasis on situating contemporary struggles for human rights in relationship to the defense of the "commons" and/or "communality," which are closely related in turn to Raúl Zibechi's insistence upon the "territoriality of resistance" in Latin America today.[2]

All of this lays the basis for the emphasis here on cases related to struggles for recognition of the rights of indigenous peoples and migrants in Latin America and among Latinos in the United States, which necessarily involve a rethinking of hegemonic notions regarding the nation-state, human rights, citizenship, democracy, and participation. This is especially so when such concepts are approached critically from the perspective of migrants, refugees, and displaced persons, many of them of indigenous origin, in contexts such as Chiapas and Guerrero in Mexico and the Northern Cauca region in Colombia, and the streets of New York. These processes of human mobility and migration must be understood ultimately as the "harvest of empire."[3]

Migrants, refugees, and displaced persons are approached here from an integral perspective encompassed within the conceptual framework of "peoples in movement."[4] My emphasis is on the convergent causes of processes of forced migration and displacement (including the impact of neoliberal policies, free trade, and other forms of state violence and state criminality; the securitization, militarization, and externalization of migration policies and borders plus the intensified criminalization and commodification of migrants; and environmental devastation and climate change), on a global scale, and their regional impact in the Latin American context.

The assumption for purposes of this chapter is that most contemporary migration in the US-Latin American context is in fact forced, to the extent that it is attributable to structural and systemic causes such as those highlighted above, whose combined effect is the denial of the right to a dignified life. This also means that processes of migration, refuge, and displacement are much more inter-related than is generally recognized.

Mexico and Colombia are key cases from this perspective, since each is traditionally associated with apparently distinct patterns of migration (Mexico) or displacement (Colombia), which in practice are much more convergent than they might appear at first blush, in terms of both their causes and consequences. This includes an emphasis on exploring how processes of large scale international migration in the US-Mexico context (35 million people of Mexican descent or origin in the United States, US Census Bureau 2013, the largest single immigrant diaspora in the world) are intertwined with more hidden, longstanding processes of internal migration which are characteristic of the country's poorest and most marginalized indigenous communities, within the context of regions such as Guerrero and Chiapas. Similarly in the Colombian context, it is has been massive forced displacement (5.7 million people, IDMC 2015; Colombia is second only to Syria on the overall list) which is most widely recognized, but the connections between such processes and issues of refuge and migration are often overlooked or under-emphasized.

This chapters focuses greater attention than is common in hegemonic frameworks, on indigenous peoples and communities as increasingly central protagonists of migration processes in settings such as Mexico, Central America, and the Andean region (especially Ecuador), and on indigenous peoples and communities of African descent in Colombia as victims of the most widespread and concentrated forms of forced displacement. This in turn often leads to their pursuit of refuge or migration elsewhere as the next stage in the struggle for survival and dignity of those who have been displaced. Meanwhile in contexts such as Guerrero and Chiapas in Mexico, forced displacement due to structural factors, which includes the so-called "drug war," also sets the stage for the intensification of processes of international migration.

Also highlighted here are issues related to the rights of indigenous peoples and to contexts involving processes of forced migration and displacement, and to the increasing convergence between these domains- issues related to indigenous peoples who are migrants and/or have been forcibly displaced or are resisting such displacement- because of the extent to which such subjects and dimensions of rights are marginalized within the framework of hegemonic, state-centered approaches, as we suggest further below. The emphasis here instead is on such issues from the perspective of social movements grounded in the peoples and communities affected, "from below," and to the extent possible, "from within."

The emphasis here is on the shared characteristics of the protagonists of such processes as transnational collective subjects of actions in defense of their rights. Key examples of this emergence of migrants as global actors include the immigrant rights movement in the United States and its increasingly complex links with movements in defense of migrants and migrant rights in countries of transit and origin throughout Latin America, and the equivalents of such movements in the Euro-Mediterranean (African and Middle Eastern) context, and in that of Australia and its Pacific neighbors.[5]

This chapter is specifically grounded in Enrique Dussel's exploration of the philosophy, theology, ethics, and politics of liberation, "from the perspective of the victims" of contemporary systems of exploitation and domination, which is applied here to the highly contested terrain of human rights in Latin America, and in related contexts such as that of the immigrant rights movement in the United States. Of central concern here is the relationship between this approach and social movements such as Mexico's Zapatistas, and their impact in shaping related struggles for dignity and autonomy among the country's indigenous peoples such as the *Policia Comunitaria* ("Community Police") of Guerrero's Montaña (or Highlands) region and the *Sociedad Civil de Las Abejas* ("The Bees") in Chiapas (survivors and family of the victims of the Acteal Massacre in December 1997), and their "equivalents" in similar contexts in Colombia, Ecuador, Bolivia, and Chile (particularly among the Mapuche indigenous people).[6]

Key referents here include the Minga indigenous movement and the *Guardia Indígena* (Indigenous Guardians) of the Northern Cauca region in Colombia, and indigenous movements in defense of water, life, and dignity elsewhere in the region, who exemplify the utopian dimensions of contemporary expressions of resistance and rebellion against the ravages of neoliberal policies, mega-projects, and environmental devastation.[7] This includes efforts such as those of the Zapatistas, the *Policía Comunitaria* (PC) in Guerrero, *Las Abejas* of Acteal, and Colombia's *Guardia Indígena* to construct alternative visions and projects of community autonomy and popular justice.

Inspiration is drawn, for example, from Dussel's emphasis on the extent to which the ideological hegemony of the West (modernity, the Enlightenment, liberalism, neoliberalism, etc.) is grounded in its material domination of the world through the colonialist and imperialist imposition of capitalism as a world system, beginning in the Americas. This is reflected in the appropriation of the human rights paradigm in service to the supposed imperatives of the market and the capitalist state, and thus of "domination" rather than "liberation."

From this perspective processes of "liberating philosophy," and as to the liberation or decolonization of "human rights," are inherent, interrelated components of broader struggles to liberate humanity from the systems of domination which hegemonic epistemologies and theoretical frameworks have helped produce, sustain, serve and legitimize.[8] As Dussel has argued, "it seems as if a Philosophy of Liberation must take the liberation of philosophy itself as its point of departure" (restated as such in his introduction to *Ethics of Liberation*, 2013):

> Throughout history, at least since the Greeks, philosophy has frequently been bound to the engines of power and ethnocentrism. Nevertheless it is true that there have always been philosophic counter-

discourses of greater or lesser critical density, and it is with this counter-hegemonic tradition that I would identify my own work.[9]

The emphasis here, in the same spirit, is on highlighting the contributions of counter-hegemonic traditions of human rights in Latin America and some of their key contemporary expressions. Drawing, in sum, on key concepts developed by Mignolo, Quijano, and Dussel, among others, one of the guiding questions for purposes of this chapter, is: what might a non-Western, "trans-capitalist, trans-liberal, trans-modern," "pluriversal," intercultural version of human rights actually look like in practice?[10] My argument here is that some of the most creative answers- and many further questions- are embedded in the experiences of the sectors that are highlighted here (indigenous peoples, migrants, and their convergence).

Normally such questions are explored from a perspective centered around nation-states as the relevant framework for analysis. Such aspects are key in Latin America given recent transformations at the constitutional level in contexts such as Venezuela, Ecuador, and Bolivia which have led to their "refoundation" as "plurinational" and "pluricultural" states, or in Colombia, which have resulted in the formal recognition of human rights way beyond the traditional bounds of liberal Modernist orthodoxy. Nonetheless decidedly mixed results in contexts such as Colombia and increasingly in Ecuador and Bolivia, and uncertainties in Venezuela in the wake of the death of Hugo Chávez, highlight the need to look more deeply beyond the level of phenomena within the framework of the formal configurations of state power.

Mexico and Colombia are especially complex, explosive, and thus propitious, cases within the broader Latin American landscape, if, as we argue, international human rights standards should be taken seriously, given the sheer gravity and volume of human rights violations in both countries. They are also especially compelling cases because of the extent to which US policy is central in enabling and promoting large-scale state crimes in both settings, together with the increasingly prominent role of paramilitary forces in both settings, whose origins and trajectory are permeated by impunity and state complicity.

Thirty years ago it was Colombia, together with the Central American region which were the epicenters of regional crisis. Today that burden has shifted to Mexico. But Mexico's current human rights crisis, the worst in its recent history, is itself the product of the importation from Colombia of the "drug war" model that has devastated the land of Gabriel García Márquez.

POVERTY, SOCIAL MOVEMENTS OF THE POOR, HUMAN RIGHTS, AND GLOBAL JUSTICE

This chapter also highlights the relationship between my overall approach and the broader issues of "global justice," including the epistemological challenges of developing alternative paradigms of human rights suggested by Dussel, Sousa Santos, Mignolo, and Baxi, among others. My emphasis here on connecting issues of global justice and "unjustice" to the need to approach contemporary global poverty and inequality not "only" as a profound challenge to global ethics, development studies, and the philosophy of law and as a "massive and systemic" violation of human rights that must be addressed within the framework of economic and social rights, the right to development, and "international poverty law" but also as a "serious crime" under international law.[11]

In such contexts hegemonic versions of human rights in fact clearly emerge as key obstacles to the realization of rights in practice, as the emancipatory origins of such rights are swallowed up by the regulatory imperatives of liberal and neoliberal governmentality.[12] The function of human rights then becomes in fact to make "human suffering invisible."[13] Much of this is present in the World Bank's intensive deployment of liberal and neoliberal discourse as to governance, the "rule of law," participation, and human rights within the context of its purported commitment to the prevention, reduction, and eradication of poverty, while at the same time promoting policies which deepen actual poverty and inequality in Latin America and throughout the Global South, and increasingly in Europe (Greece, Spain, Italy, Portugal, Ireland, etc.) and the United States, in the wake of the 2008 global crisis.

The centrality of poverty and of counter-hegemonic social movements of the poor in our approach is also reflected in an understanding of cases such as the Zapatistas and the CRAC-*Policía Comunitaria* in Guerrero, as well as migrant rights movements, as movements rooted in the poorest and most excluded sectors, and as movements of the "poor" in a more epistemological sense (e.g., poverty as a material and discursive space from which rebellion and resistance is constructed). This approach builds in part on Amartya Sen's understanding of poverty as a lack of control over one's own circumstances and thus, from the perspective of international law and international human rights norms, as a violation of an individual and collective right to self-determination, which includes the deprivation of the conditions necessary to enable a person or community to have an equal (non-discriminatory) opportunity to "live a life worthy of a human being," understood, in sum, as a "right to a dignified life," as the Zapatistas have repeatedly affirmed since their public emergence in January 1994.[14]

UTOPIAN VISIONS

What is meant by what is "utopian" in such contexts? Saramago himself had little patience for what he considered to be outmoded and empty notions of utopia or hope in the face of the generalized injustices he identified with globalized capitalism of the 1990s.[15] From Saramago's perspective, utopia and hope only made sense if they were understood as projects in construction.[16] Along these lines, our reading of Dussel is that it is liberation which makes "hope" or "utopia," concrete and possible; the relevant landscape suggested by the experiences which are our referents in this chapter lies somewhere in between Bloch's *Principle of Hope* and Dussel's *Principle of Liberation*, at a step beyond Saramago's abandonment of both utopia and hope.[17] A better way of putting this might be: the experiences which are our principal referents here suggest that the approaches of both Bloch and Dussel have meaning only to the extent that they contribute to understanding and underlining the significance and resonance of such cases and their implications.

As one of the Zapatista delegates who marched to Mexico City in 1997, 1999, and 2001 during their principal campaigns for the constitutional recognition of indigenous rights once explained to us in a brief exchange: "autonomy is the space where citizenship is constructed." This is what Bloch's conceptualization of "hope" and Dussel's of "liberation" mean, at least in part, in practice, in the context of the Zapatista movement and that of similar experiences elsewhere, in Latin America and beyond.

This seems to be roughly convergent with what Wallerstein argues in terms of his conceptualization of "utopistics":

> "Utopistics is the serious assessment of historical alternatives, the exercise of our judgement as to the substantive rationality of alternative possible historical systems. It is the sober, rational, and realistic evaluation of human social systems, the constraints on what they can be, and the zones open to human creativity. Not the face of the perfect (and inevitable) future, but the face of an alternative, credibly better, and historically possible (but far from certain) future."[18]

Franz Hinkelammert adds another layer to our thinking about utopia in the context of the experiences highlighted in this chapter. In his view, which helps inspire our efforts here, "the analysis of reality has to be undertaken from the perspective of that which is not, and not from that of what is. Only in this way can truth be revealed" which we take to imply that it is critique which is constitutive of what is utopian, a dimension which remains at best implicit in Wallerstein's approach.[19] It is worth noting, along similar lines, that the thought of Bartolomé de Las Casas (whose contributions to Latin American utopian visions as to human rights we discuss below) may have had a direct impact on Thomas

More's original formulation of the concept of utopia according to painstaking research undertaken by Victor N. Baptiste.[20] It has long been argued that More's Utopia was clearly influenced by the "discovery" of the Americas as an expansion of the literal horizons of possible worlds within the framework of sixteenth-century European epistemology.

As summarized by Gutiérrez, Baptiste's argument is that Las Casas' influence on More was even more direct, based on a line by line comparison of the original Latin versions of the manuscripts of Las Casas' *Memorial* and More's *Utopia*, which were both published in 1516. Las Casas' text outlines his vision of an imaginary colonial settlement with Spaniards and indigenous peoples living together in mutual freedom and reciprocity, including inter-marriage, within a framework of peaceful, not forced, evangelization. Baptiste speculates that it is very likely that Erasmus would have sent the draft of Las Casas' text to More in 1515, and that this explains multiple similarities in the two texts. In Baptiste's view, in sum, More's *Utopia* is grounded in Las Casas' experiences in the Caribbean and the proposals he derived from them directed at a more "humanistic" form of colonization (long before he arrived at a much more radical perspective later). Regardless of whether the relevant influences on More were direct or indirect, it is clear that our understanding of "utopia," in More's work and beyond, has both a Latin American origin and implies Latin America as an essential, central, point of reference.

HISTORY OF UTOPIAN VISIONS OF HUMAN RIGHTS IN CONTEMPORARY LATIN AMERICA

Dussel, Mignolo, Quijano, and Hinkelammert have elaborated detailed arguments illustrating the central role of the European conquest of the Americas in the configuration of both modernity and its inherently colonial and racialized character ("coloniality"), which in turn lay the foundation for the consolidation of Eurocentrism and *"Occidentalismo"* as their most crucial epistemological, ideological and cultural expressions, and for the emergence of capitalism as a global system. This framework provides a basis for both an alternative theory to that of hegemonic "macronarratives" as to the origin of modernity (in the fifteenth and sixteenth centuries, in Latin America, with the European Conquest, and not in the eighteenth and nineteenth centuries, in Western Europe, with the Enlightenment and the Industrial Revolution), and as to the origins and contemporary dimensions of human rights.

The traditional Eurocentrist historical narrative as to the origins of human rights begins with Magna Carta in Medieval Britain in 1215, but then leaps directly to Grotius' publication of his book *The Laws of War and Peace in 1625* (a key forerunner of modern conceptions of international law and of what is encompassed today by international humanitarian law, the Geneva Conventions, the concept of war crimes, and so on, as elaborated philosophically later by Kant), and picks up the thread with the Treaty of Westphalia in 1648 (origin of the modern international system of "nation-states"), the "Glorious Revolution" in 1688, and then with the "American" (United States) and French Revolutions in 1776 and 1789. The European Conquest of the Americas between 1492 and 1619 is of course completely absent from this chronology, as is the Haitian Revolution between 1791 and 1804 and the Latin American independence struggles against Spain between 1810 and 1830, and their origins in indigenous and campesino rebellions in the Andean region in the early 1780s.

An even more truncated version is quite common, which begins with the US Declaration of Independence and Bill of Rights, and the French Declaration of the Rights of Man and Citizen, and focuses primarily on developments since the creation of the UN in 1945 and the adoption of the Universal Declaration of Human Rights in 1948. Much of the rest prior to 1776 is essentially categorized as source material (e.g., concepts such as the rule of law, due process, habeas corpus, freedom of speech, conscience, and religion, etc.) for what flowered later in the US and French contexts. Somewhere in between lie more detailed accounts such as that of Jonathan Israel in his trilogy regarding the roots and development of what he describes as the "radical" and "democratic" currents of the Enlightenment.[21]

The European Conquest of the Americas provides a very different point of departure, which is grounded in the history of the construction of the "colonial difference" explored with varying emphases by Quijano, Mignolo, and Dussel. This context includes a hegemonic, albeit relatively "humanist" current exemplified by Francisco de Vitoria and his successors within the "Salamanca School" (which lay the foundations for the work of Grotius), who both defended the legitimacy of the Spanish Conquest as the secular expression of a "universalist" evangelizing mission, and the status of indigenous peoples as the bearers of limited rights, under what was still an essentially theological construct of international law. Vitoria reflects the intertwined Spanish and "colonial origins" of international law, which have also been highlighted by the Permanent People's Tribunal in a special session commemorating 500 years of indigenous resistance in 1991.[22]

The debates regarding the theological, ethical, and ultimately juridical implications of the Spanish Conquest also included a much more critical "counter-discourse" from within developed by Bartolomé de Las Casas and his disciples.[23] Las Casas served as the first Bishop of Chiapas from 1542–1544, when he was driven out of the diocese by angry Spanish landowners who rejected his insistence on peaceful means of evangelization; the capital of the Highlands region of Chiapas (Los Altos), was later renamed San Cristóbal de Las Casas in his honor. According to Dussel, Las Casas expressed the "most radical critique possible" of the injustices of the Spanish Conquest within the framework of the epoch's hegemonic discourse.[24] This was a critique which was deeply critical of the "myth" of modernity according to Dussel, but which Quijano and Mignolo might still situate within the epistemological cages of coloniality and Eurocentrism, analogous to the contemporary limitations in their view, on a global scale, of Marxism, Western post-Modernism and post-structuralism. Others such as León Portilla and Friede emphasize the extent to which Las Casas' critique evolved in an increasingly radical direction, was based on indigenous sources and translated aspects of indigenous knowledge, and included the defense of an early conceptualization of indigenous rights built upon the recognition of what we understand now to be rights of self-determination, autonomy, resistance, and rebellion, within an intercultural framework.[25]

Las Casas has been highlighted by Dussel (within the framework of his overall reconstruction of philosophical, ethical, and political theory from a global perspective centered around the concept of liberation and grounded in Latin America) and by Gustavo Gutiérrez, as the founder of a counter-hegemonic tradition within the church deeply engaged with the defense of the rights of indigenous peoples and African slaves and with ultimately anti-colonial, anti-imperialist, and anti-capitalist implications, which helped lay the basis for the emergence of the theology of liberation, but also according to Dussel for the philosophy, ethics, and politics of liberation.[26]

Las Casas continues to be a key point of reference and inspiration for many in Latin America who are deeply engaged in the kinds of liberation struggles and related reflections highlighted here; this includes a human rights center (the "Frayba") in Mexico named in his honor, founded in 1989 by Bishop Samuel Ruiz of Chiapas (who served in this position from 1960 to 2000), and an influential research center in Peru, also named for him, founded by Gustavo Gutiérrez. The Frayba, founded in San Cristóbal by Bishop Ruiz, was modeled on similar examples in El Salvador, Guatemala, and Chile where human rights centers were created under the auspices of bishops who did not necessarily consider themselves to be adherents or proponents of liberation theology as such, but understood their role to necessarily include the defense of human rights against repressive regimes and an alignment of the church with the most powerless sectors.

There is no necessary correlation here with a counter-hegemonic approach to law itself, or to human rights, but in the case of Monseñor Romero of El Salvador, who was quite conservative in traditional theological terms, all of this was in fact premised on a radical critique of law, in a manner to some extent reminiscent of Las Casas. Romero's point of departure was that "the law is like a serpent: it only bites those who are barefoot."[27] Bishop Ruiz took a similar approach to the founding of the Frayba, which continues today to emphasize the idea that the defense of human rights provides a basis for the critique of law itself, as it defends Zapatista political prisoners, EZLN base communities from incursions by government-backed, US-funded paramilitary forces, and pursues the cause of Las Abejas of Acteal through the labyrinths of the Inter-American System, but simultaneously before the Permanent People's Tribunal.

Bishop Ruiz played a key role in bringing liberation theology to Chiapas and rooting it deeply in its indigenous peoples, in the form of "indigenous theology," in a manner similar to Bishop Leonidas Proaño roughly during the same period in Ecuador. It is difficult to imagine the emergence of either the EZLN in Chiapas or the CONAIE in Ecuador in the absence of such efforts, in a manner equivalent to the complex, often conflictive but deeply intertwined relationship between liberation theology in Nicaragua or El Salvador and the FSLN and FMLN, or the legacies of Fathers Camilo Torres and Manuel Pérez and the ELN in Colombia (and for that matter of the Berrigans in the United States), and their equivalents elsewhere (including Bishop Fernando Lugo's election as president of Paraguay between 2008 and 2012). There are a series of complex convergences at play here that reflect an intertwined landscape of actors, hopes, and options.

Key contemporary Latin American thinkers such as Hinkelammert and Dussel (2013, in his *Ethics of Liberation*, as well as in the extensive histories of the Catholic Church and of the activism of its bishops in defense of indigenous rights, which he began to document in the 1960s and coordinated during the 1970s) have highlighted such continuities, including their affinities with Ernst Bloch's *Principle of Hope*, which Dussel has further elaborated in terms of his *Principle of Liberation*.[28]

An important guiding thread in the rich, evolving history of processes of resistance and rebellion in Latin America and in their theoretical elaborations since Las Casas, which continues to be reflected throughout the region today, is a complex convergence between church-based and secular discourses and praxis of liberation and human rights, with recurrent, utopian and millenarian dimensions. Such convergences are especially notable in contemporary contexts such as the defense of the rights of indigenous peoples in both Mexico and Colombia, and of the rights of migrants in transit (Mexico, where many of its own migrants and those with origins in other countries such as Guatemala and Honduras are of indigenous origin) and of persons who have been forcibly displaced (Colombia, where communities and regions where the population of African descent and of indigenous peoples are concentrated have been especially impacted by forced displacement).

Examples of this complex history which is still largely unwritten and cannot be adequately summarized here, include the rebellions of Tupac Amaru, Tupac Katari, and the Comuneros of Nueva Granada in the Andean region, and the Haitian Revolution, as key precursors to the Latin

American independence struggles of the nineteenth century, all the way up to more recent cases such as Mexico's Zapatistas (and related experiences in the Mexican context), and other indigenous movements (Ecuador, Bolivia, Colombia, Chile, Peru, Guatemala, among others) and movements of people of African descent, the landless, and unemployed (Colombia, Brazil, Argentina).

My approach here further assumes that contemporary human rights norms are the historical product of the struggles of social movements and their impact on evolving patterns of reflection, discourse, and policy. This includes the legacies and contributions of movements of the poor and excluded throughout history, against feudalism, colonialism, imperialism, slavery, racism and national oppression, the exploitation of workers, and the domination of women, for as Upendra Baxi has argued, from the perspective of those whose suffering has been consigned to "rightlessness," "the art of memory links responsibility and justice."[29] The largely unwritten history of the "making" of international human rights and international law is the history of the ebbs and flows in a non-linear trajectory as to the extent of recognition of the rights of those most exploited, oppressed, marginalized, and excluded in each historical period.[30] Such an approach also involves a distinct rupture with epistemological assumptions of a positivist, functionalist, and determinist character that are still prevalent in many circles. It also includes an insistence upon a critical understanding of legal definitions of rights in any specific historical period as minimums, not maximums ("floors and not "ceilings"), and thus as points of departure, not destinations in themselves.

All of this includes a recognition of how initially hesitant advances at one moment can be completed at a much higher level of complexity later, as the result of the pressure of vigorous social movements. A key example is the adoption of the Declaration of the Rights of Man and Citizen in 1789 in the context of the early stages of the French Revolution, which despite its classical liberal rhetoric of "liberty, equality, and fraternity," denied all three of these dimensions of human freedom to millions of African slaves within the French colonial empire, to women, and to males who were not property owners. The Declaration's failure to address the issue of slavery was not remedied until the rebellion of slaves in Haiti led by Toussaint Louverture in 1791 compelled the French National Assembly to finally abolish it in 1794 and despite such initial advances in France and then in the United Kingdom (and only much later in the United States and Brazil) the first enforceable international convention against slavery and the slave trade was not adopted until 1926.[31] Similarly the Nazi genocide was completely "legal" during the period it was carried out, and the first international convention against genocide was not adopted until 1948.

Haiti meanwhile was punished for its temerity in being the first state in the world to abolish slavery through the imposition of an indemnification clause in its ultimate recognition by France.[32] The United States eventually took on France's role as neocolonial enforcer.[33] Haiti continues to be marginalized today by the democratic currents flowing through most of its Latin American neighbors, and by their abandonment of solidarity amid its continuing occupation by US, UN, and OAS "peace-keeping" forces whose supposed defense of human rights produces persistent and recurrent violations. These include a cholera plague that killed and sickened thousands which was unleashed by UN troops, and which has led to a January 2015 US federal court ruling barring UN liability on the basis of immunity.[34] Haiti continues to symbolize the emptiness at the heart of the hegemonic versions of international human rights norms which emerged during the period of the transatlantic revolutions of the late eighteenth and early nineteenth centuries and their persistent limits and contradictions today.[35]

CHALLENGES TO HEGEMONIC PARADIGMS OF HUMAN RIGHTS

Latin American social movements along the lines described above have contributed to rethinking and reshaping key aspects of hegemonic paradigms of human rights characterized by largely unexamined assumptions as to the supposedly uniquely Western and specifically European character and origins of contemporary human rights and international law within the framework of the Enlightenment and modernity, liberalism, and neo-liberalism. Hegemonic approaches tend to privilege configurations of rights associated with interests related to liberty and property within a market framework, rather than to those of an economic, social, or cultural character, associated with imperatives of dignity and equality. In practice this has often meant the reduction of "liberty" to the defense of individual property rights, the dispossession of collective forms of property over land and natural resources, and the deprivation of legal recognition of such interests, and thus of their legitimacy, in the name of "progress," "modernization," "development," and so on.

The region's counter-hegemonic social movements have also vigorously questioned and sought to undermine the primacy given in this context to Westphalian nation-states as the most privileged subjects of rights and as "rights-givers" (as attributes of membership through citizenship in configurations of state power which trickle down from above), to structures of representative rather than participatory democracy, and to individual (rather than collective or group) rights of a civil or political character. These efforts have included ongoing activism and advocacy as to such issues at the grassroots through direct organizing and the construction of alternative spaces of power at the regional and local level through processes of autonomy, and also in many instances as influential voices to varying degrees "inside" or at the gate of state structures of power and influence, and their equivalents in transnational spaces such as the UN and the OAS.

Common threads throughout all of these cases, despite some of the achievements highlighted above, include the emergence of a form of "neo-developmentalism" or "neo-extractivism" which constitutes the Latin American version of the processes of "accumulation by dispossession" (via mega-projects, mining, and overall environmental devastation, forced migration and displacement, etc.) which David Harvey has described as the essence of contemporary forms of capitalist neoliberal globalization.[36]

My approach here converges with that of Zibechi, who has argued that despite the emergence of examples such as those cited above, the center of gravity as to the potential for fundamental transformations in Latin America remains with its most radical grassroots popular movements, and particularly with those most independent from state power and electoral machinations, and most committed to building alternatives to the state, from below and from spaces "outside" of its structures.[37]

"PARADIGM WARS" IN LATIN AMERICA

The intensification of such struggles throughout the region reflects what Jerry Mander and Victoria Tauli-Corpuz have described as a framework of "paradigm wars" regarding the meaning and impact of Western notions of "development."[38] These arise within the crucible of intensifying conflicts between indigenous people's movements and processes of neoliberal capitalist globalization.

According to Zibechi the interests of these underlying forces have driven a reconfiguration of regional hegemonies in a new political project which combines a fundamental accommodation to the demands of transnational capital and its local allies in a "post-neoliberal" mode; Dávalos, an Ecuadorian scholar who is very critical from the left as to the limits of the Correa régime of "citizen's revolution" in that country (as Zibechi is of its equivalent in Uruguay), has described such governments as examples of the emergence of a new "disciplinary" form of mass democracy in the region.[39] Key characteristics of this model include: relatively "progressive" social policies within a statist framework legitimized by revolutionary discourses, and focused on a critical stance toward US domination in the region and on alliance-building within a "South-South" framework in terms of foreign policy, and internally an emphasis on the reduction of poverty and inequality.

In all of these cases the strongest responses in resistance to processes of dispossession of resources and territories come from movements of indigenous peoples and people of African descent, other marginalized sectors (for example the urban poor and employed and youth), and environmentalists. Many of these sectors unite around the defense of the principles and rhetoric of the new constitutions of "refounded" states such as Ecuador and Bolivia which have redefined these polities as "plurinational" and "pluricultural," arguing that the Correa and Morales regimes are violating to varying degrees the precepts of the states which they helped create (like the African National Congress in South Africa or the sectors of the opposition that have come to occupy positions of power in Egypt, Tunisia, or Libya but have failed to act consistently with their origins or originally stated intentions).[40]

These same frameworks of "decolonized" constitutional law have redefined the traditional conceptual boundaries of international human rights principles to include the recognition of nature or "Mother Earth" as a subject of rights, as reflected in the indigenous cultures of the Andean regions of Latin America common to countries such as Ecuador, Bolivia, Peru, and Colombia through their shared roots in the Inca civilization, and its conception of "*Pacha Mama*" (Mother Earth in Quechua) and of a "good life" understood in terms of "*Sumak Kawsay*" or "*Suma Qamaña*" (as the concept is articulated respectively in the indigenous languages of the Quechua and Aymara peoples), this in turn is what is referred to as the basis for a "post-capitalist" paradigm framed in terms of the "common good of humanity" by Houtart.[41] These approaches go much further in the direction of the counter-hegemonic frameworks of human rights necessary to address issues of global systemic injustice reflected in persistent poverty and inequality, "from below," throughout the region, regardless of the ideological label attached to or embraced by the specific government at issue.

CURRENT LANDSCAPES OF LIBERATION IN LATIN AMERICA: THE LATIN AMERICAN SPRING, ORIGINS AND LIMITS

The current landscape of struggles for liberation in Latin America includes cases such as Venezuela, Ecuador, and Bolivia where social movements rooted in the poorest and most excluded sectors have both laid the foundation for state-centered processes of social transformation- as part of what Dussel has described as the "Latin American spring," prefiguring that which has swept the Arab world- and continue to shape and challenge their configurations and depth.[42] As a result Latin America is the single region in the world which has until recently been freest of US domination (a dramatic historical shift away from its longstanding status as "back yard"), and which as a result has been most successful in resisting the continued imposition of neoliberal hegemony, and in generating alternative models of plurinational, pluricultural, and participatory governance ("twenty-first century socialism," with all of its complexities and contradictions, plus decidedly more mixed cases such as Cuba and Nicaragua).

These experiences, beginning with the Zapatista rebellion in January 1994, have helped inspire equivalent expressions of resistance elsewhere ranging from the global justice (Seattle, Genoa, World Social Forum) and antiwar movements between 1999 and 2003, and the immigrant rights movement in the United States which mobilized millions in over a hundred cities between March and September 2006, to the *indignado/as* of Athens and Madrid, Occupy Wall Street, and so on, and the Arab Spring since 2010.

Key examples such as Venezuela, Ecuador, and Bolivia (to varying degrees, plus Colombia in a very different context which has included limited political advances, including the current peace process, but more wide-ranging innovations in terms of the human rights content of constitutional law) have included the "refoundation" of existing states, and the "decolonization" of their conceptual frameworks of constitutional law and as to legal pluralism.[43] The specific contours of this regional trend vary greatly in each case, and the extent to which this overall trend has actually contributed to the region's liberation from US domination and that of its domestic allies in each country is highly contested.[44] The electoral advances cited above, which are emphasized by Dussel in his conceptualization of a Latin American Spring, have at minimum opened spaces and opportunities for formal political, constitutional and legal ruptures with the "internal colonialism," "coloniality" or racist neocolonialism characteristic of Latin American states post-independence.[45]

A central tension which cuts across such examples is the contested relationship between social movements of the poor "from below," based in the most marginalized sectors of these societies, which are often focused on local and regional projects of resistance and autonomy, and processes of social transformation which seek to prevent, reduce, and/or eliminate poverty, which tend to be centered around the control and exercise of state power "from above," at the national level, and on concerted action among states in regional contexts such as Latin America, Africa, and the Arab world and on a global scale. An additional crosscutting tension is that between the marked tendency of state-centered processes to seek accommodation, to varying degrees, with the demands of global capitalist hegemony (e.g., through the application of neoliberal policies), and the anti-systemic character of movements from below which resist such tendencies more directly.

Given this approach, it is important to differentiate between two kinds of cases in this context: (1) those where state-centered processes of transformation have greatest weight and have ambivalent relationships to the social movements which made such state-led efforts possible (or where such movements played such a role initially but have faded in strength) (Venezuela, Brazil, Argentina, Uruguay, Nicaragua, El Salvador, South Africa); and (2) those where the center of gravity continues to lie in grassroots movements of the poor and the most excluded sectors (Ecuador and Bolivia), characterized by increasing tensions between these and the state-led processes which depend upon them in order to remain in power. This in turn provides us the basis for assessing which cases make the greatest contributions to the most fundamental kinds of changes, including those most capable of challenging regional and global capitalist systemic imperatives.

IMPACT OF CONSTITUTIONAL AND LEGAL TRANSFORMATIONS

Significant components of the international and regional human rights agendas associated with counter-hegemonic visions have been enacted into law and state policy in many key states in Latin America to varying degrees at least in formalistic terms, with many inconsistencies and gaps as to actual implementation throughout the last twenty years. Much of this has been accomplished at least in part through processes of legal and constitutional transformation in the context of "transitions to democracy" (often including Truth Commissions and/or trials of key human rights violators, to varying degrees) in the aftermath of US-backed authoritarian regimes.[46] These processes have also highlighted the direct incorporation ("constitutionalization") of international human rights standards into constitutional texts on a scale unprecedented elsewhere in the world, and made it possible to enforce these standards in domestic courts and where necessary through recourse to the Inter-American Human Rights Court of the OAS (which by contrast is of course not recognized as binding either by the United States or Canada), and in some cases have succeeded in translating such achievements into broader instruments of international law or policy in key normative spaces with significant potential impact beyond their country of origin. A key example is how Mexico's Zapatista rebellion in 1994 became the decisive spark not only for unprecedented efforts (only partially successful) to reform Mexico's own constitution, federal and state laws and overall state policy to finally recognize the cultural and linguistic dimensions of the existence and rights of the country's indigenous peoples, but also ultimately for the adoption of the UN's Declaration on the Rights of Indigenous Peoples by the General Assembly in September 2007, and for the intensification of an equivalent process within the OAS.

The critical, highly contradictory factor in this context was how the Zapatista uprising itself and its implications served to "name" and "shame" the Mexican state into becoming the leading rhetorical champion of the Declaration within the UN. Most of the heavy lifting in this complex process was ironically undertaken by leading Zapatista advisers from Mexico and indigenous advocates from elsewhere in Latin America.

Here as with the Mexican state's similar rhetorical championing in the UN of the rights of migrants, and of its version of market-friendly environmentalism as host of COP 16 in December 2010, there is a vast, uncharted gulf between its supposedly respectable standing as to such issues in the "international community" and its actual policies and practices on a daily basis with respect to its own people (which include the systematic violation of the rights of indigenous peoples and migrants, both Mexican and in transit through the country's territory from Central America and elsewhere, as especially notable patterns).

Despite such dialectical complexities, it is nonetheless crucial to recognize that the advances in UN recognition of indigenous rights symbolized by the adoption of the 2007 Declaration would not have been achieved without the impetus and leadership provided by the Zapatista rebellion and its effects. This case exemplifies the direct impact a counter-hegemonic movement can have "against the grain," from the "outside," and "from below" as to hegemonic structures and processes from above and the transformation of their normative content. Given the highly contested character of issues regarding indigenous and minority rights to self-determination and autonomy in the contemporary international arena, my argument here is that the Zapatista rebellion's contribution to reshaping the terrain as to such issues is equivalent to that of the Haitian Revolution and its impact leading to the abolition of slavery in Paris in 1794: slavery in effect had to be swept away "from below" before it could be "officially" abolished, in response, thereafter.

The Ecuadorian and Bolivian constitutions contributed to the emergence of counter-hegemonic paradigms of human rights and constitutional law by redefining and restructuring their states as "plurinational" and "pluricultural" and by directly incorporating international human rights standards into the constitutional text. But they also went further by recognizing the rights and legal standing of *Pacha Mama* (Mother Earth, according to the Andean indigenous cosmologies associated with Inca civilization and its environs, from Argentina to Colombia, and encompassing much of the Amazon Basin), and of the ethical system which mandates its protection (*Sumak Kawsay* or *Suma Qamaña*, the Andean indigenous paradigm of cosmic harmony and well-being, underpinning the possibility of a "decent life"). These measures in turn have led the Bolivian state to take a leading role in challenging hegemonic approaches to issues of climate change in the context of the UN summits held in Copenhagen in 2009 and Cancun in 2010, by convening an alternative Global People's Summit on Climate Change and the Rights of Mother Earth in Cochabamba in April 2010 and promoting the adoption of a resolution by the UN Human Rights Council and the General Assembly recognizing the "rights of Mother Earth" (the Earth itself as a planetary organism which is a bearer of rights) as an alternative paradigm and landscape within which issues of climate change, global warming, sustainable development, and environmentalism must be situated.

All of this is significantly more complex and contradictory in actual practice both in Ecuador and Bolivia (although in both contexts, notwithstanding increasing divisions within the ruling sectors, Presidents Rafael Correa and Evo Morales have both been re-elected to second terms). In Ecuador, the initial alliance between the CONAIE (Coordinadora de Nacionalidades Indígenas del Ecuador) and Correa, the key force behind indigenous and popular uprisings in 2000 and 2005 which eventually made it possible for him to emerge as a candidate of a united center-left front of opposition forces, broke down during the Constituent Assembly process which drafted the new constitution, and has sharpened during the last two years because of increasingly polarized differences over environmentalism and development policy (particularly as to oil extraction policy and mega-developments). In Bolivia, serious divisions within the ruling circle and between competing sectors of popular movements aligned for or against Morales have also intensified recently.

PERVASIVE STATE VIOLENCE AND PARAMILITARISM IN MEXICO

The Mexican state meanwhile is characterized by the continuing militarization of Chiapas (site of the 1994 Zapatista rebellion) and every other region in the country characterized by indigenous and popular unrest, and the unleashing of a US-backed counter-insurgency process, which has included reliance upon paramilitary forces responsible for massacres such as that of Acteal. Acteal was in turn reminiscent of, and reproduced, key symbolic, ideological and material elements of similar instances of state savagery in Guatemala and Peru, which have reappeared again in Mexico in a series of recent state crimes.

The massacre of seventy-two migrants in transit from Honduras, El Salvador, Guatemala, Ecuador, and Brazil in August 2010 in the municipality of San Fernando in the northern border state of Tamaulipas, which has been characterized in the context of the Mexican process of the Permanent People's Tribunal as the first massacre of its kind "with continental dimensions," plus the further discovery in April 2011 of mass graves with 196 remains, also primarily of migrants (Mexican and others), has completed the circle of inter-relationships between such tendencies and modalities of state terror, now reinforced in the context of the so-called "drug war."[47] The still unsolved mass disappearance of the forty-three students of the Ayotzinapa rural teacher's college in Guerrero in September 2014, primarily from the state's poorest indigenous communities, further underlines these tendencies.[48]

It was only relatively speaking a small step from Acteal to Mexico's current free fall, as exemplified in the Ayotzinapa case, into the latest example of generalized state terror (or "Colombianization") in the region (in the name of the "war against drugs") with the encouragement of persistent mechanisms of US domination such as the Security and Prosperity Accord of North America (the national security complement to NAFTA), the Mérida Initiative (Mexico's version of Plan Colombia, explicitly modeled after its predecessor), and Mexico's leading role with its Central American neighbors to the south in the Meso-American Project (formerly Plan Puebla Panamá), as Laura Carlsen has carefully documented.[49]

All of this has produced over 160,000 dead and 26,000 disappeared, mostly civilians, between 2007 and 2015 (more than for example Iraq, Afghanistan, or Syria during much of the same period).[50] Much of this violence has specifically included the criminalization of indigenous and other protest movements, including a series of targeted killings between 2009 and 2012 of activists involved in resistance movements to mega-development projects (mostly mining or hydroelectric, which together involve over 50 percent of the country's territory, mostly franchised to foreign investors) or in the defense of forests and environmental rights in regions such as Chiapas, Guerrero, Michoacán, Oaxaca, Chihuahua, Jalisco, and Colima, among others. These patterns have persisted and intensified since then amid the return to power in December 2012 of Mexico's former ruling party (the PRI, or Institutional Revolutionary Party), under Enrique Peña Nieto.

Alternative visions and projects of "human rights from below" grounded in the sectors most affected by the ravages of hegemonic policies and practices are more critical than ever under such circumstances. Our role as scholars and advocates based at least in part in both the Global North and the Global South must be to learn from, reflect upon, and accompany the construction of such processes.

NOTES

1. See Camilo Pérez-Bustillo, "Human Rights from Below," *CROP Newsletter*, May (2008), www.crop.org/viewfile.aspx?id=158. Also see Enrique Dussel, *Twenty Theses on Politics* (Durham: Duke University Press, 2008); Boaventura de Sousa Santos, *El caleidoscopio de las justicias en Colombia* (2 vols.) (Bogotá: Colciencias/Instituto Colombiano de Antropologia e Historia/Universidad de Coimbra-CEC/Universidad de los Andes/Universidad Nacional de Colombia/Siglo del Hombre Editores, 2004); Upendra Baxi, (2002) online compilation of his writings between 1960 and 2008: upendrabaxi.in/; and Richard Falk, *Human Rights Horizons: the Pursuit of Justice in a Globalizing World* (New York: Routledge, 2000).

2. See Balakrishnan Rajagopal, *International Law from Below* (New York: Cambridge University Press, 2003); Boaventura de Sousa Santos and César Rodriguez, *Law and Globalization from Below* (New York: Cambridge University Press, 2005); Michael Hardt and Antonio Negri, *Commonwealth* (Cambridge: Harvard University Press, 2009); Felix Patzi Paco, *Sistema Comunal: Una propuesta alternativa para salir de la colonialidad y del liberalismo* (La Paz: Centro de Estudios Alternativos, 2004); Walter Mignolo, "Delink-

ing, Decoloniality and Dewesternization" (2012) (Interview, Part II), online at: criticallegalthinking.com/2012/05/02/delinking-decoloniality-dewesternization-interview-with-walter-mignolo-part-ii/; and Raul Zibechi, *Territories in Resistance: A Cartography of Latin American Social Movements* (Oakland: AK Press, 2012); writings online at: www.surysur.net/autor/raul-zibechi/.

3. See Juan González, *Harvest of Empire: A History of Latinos in America* (New York: Penguin, 2011).

4. See Camilo Pérez-Bustillo, "Human Rights from Below," *CROP Newsletter*, May (2008), www.crop.org/viewfile.aspx?id=158.

5. See Leanne Weber and Sharon Pickering, *Globalization and Borders: Death at the Global Frontier* (New York: Palgrave MacMillan, 2011).

6. Forty-five dead, thirty-six of them women and children, all forcibly displaced indigenous persons with origins in several neighboring Tzotzil Mayan communities that have been among those most affected by state-promoted counter-insurgency and paramilitarism, which have constituted the Mexican government's principal response to the Zapatista rebellion, resulting in over 20,000 people internally displaced persons in Chiapas since 1994 (according to what are widely considered to be vastly under-estimated government figures); see: www.nytimes.com/2007/12/23/world/americas/23acteal.html?pagewanted=all&_r=0and regarding US complicity and knowledge as to the Mexican Army's US-funded collaboration with paramilitary groups in the Tzotzil Highlands ("Los Altos") and beyond, see: www.gwu.edu/~nsarchiv/NSAEBB/NSAEBB283/. All of this has led to a case brought against former Mexican President Ernesto Zedillo (1994–2000), currently head of Yale University's Center for the Study of Globalization and a high-paid consultant to the UN and member of boards or advisory groups to major transnational corporations such as Citibank, Alcoa, Procter and Gamble, Rolls-Royce, and British Petroleum, for his responsibility related to "crimes against humanity" associated with the massacre and the broader counter-insurgency campaign which it exemplified, see: www.nytimes.com/2012/09/09/world/americas/us-moves-to-grant-former-mexican-president-immunity-in-suit.html the Obama administration granted immunity to Zedillo regarding this case, at the request of the Mexican government, but this was challenged (and ultimately upheld) in courts in both the US and Mexico.

7. See dorsetchiapassolidarity.wordpress.com/2016/04/16/launch-of-national-campaign-in-defense-of-mother-earth-and-territory/.

8. See Walter Mignolo, "Geopolitics of sensing and knowing: on (de) coloniality, border thinking and epistemic disobedience, Postcolonial Studies," vol. 14 no. 3 (2011): 273–285.

9. See Enrique Dussel, *Ethics of Liberation in the Age of Globalization and Exclusion* (Durham: Duke University Press, 2013).

10. See Enrique Dussel, "Transmodernity and Interculturality: An Interpretation from the Perspective of Philosophy of Liberation," *Transmodernity* (2012): 28–59.

11. See Amarta Sen, *Development as Freedom* (New York: Anchor, 1999); Amarta Sen, *The Idea of Justice* (Cambridge: Harvard University Press, 2009); John Rawls, *Theory of Justice* (Cambridge: Harvard University Press, 1971); John Rawls, *The Law of Peoples* (Cambridge: Harvard University Press, 1999); Thomas Pogge, *Poverty and Human Rights: Cosmopolitan Responsibilities and Reforms* (London: Polity Press, 2002); Jeffery Sachs, *The End of Poverty: Economic Possibilities for Our Time* (New York: Penguin Press, 2005); Martha Nussbaum, *Frontiers of Justice: Disability, Nationality, Species Membership* (Cambridge: Harvard University Press, 2006); and Joseph Stiglitz, *The Price of Inequality* (New York: W. W Norton, 2012).

12. See Boaventura de Sousa Santos, *Sociología Jurídica Crítica* (Barcelona: Trotta, 2009).

13. See Upendra Baxi, (2002) online compilation of his writings between 1960 and 2008: upendrabaxi.in/.

14. See William Van Genugten, "The Use of Human Rights Instruments in the Struggle Against (Extreme) Poverty," Ch. 7 in Kjonstad, A. and Veit Wilson, J. H.,

Law, Power, and Poverty (1997) online at: poseidon01.ssrn.com/delivery.php?ID= 3181150651151181130010780790090180870170690640450690660750881180690730040221 2112501802210303010405612000102211509108900911205507302608500909400603102510 6118104070058087029004001071008016001115011087086095106071123069008104108116 115030019110031095&EXT=pdf.

15. See: saramago.blogspot.com/2005/02/utopa-y-esperanza-dos-palabras-que-no. html.

16. See saramago.blogspot.com/2005/02/utopa-y-esperanza-dos-palabras-que-no. html.

17. See Ernst Bloch *The Principle of Hope (3 vols.)* (Cambridge: MIT Press, 1995) and Enrique Dussel, *Ethics of Liberation in the Age of Globalization and Exclusion* (Durham: Duke University Press, 2013).

18. See Immanuel Wallerstein, *Utopistics: or, Historical choices of the 21st century* (New York: The New Press, 1998).

19. See Franz Hinkelammert, *La maldición que pesa sobre la ley: Las raíces del pensamiento crítico en Pablo de Tarso* (San José, Costa Rica: Editorial Arlekín, 2010).

20. See Gustavo Gutiérrez, *Las Casas: In Search of the Poor of Jesus Christ* (Maryknoll: Orbis Books, 1993).

21. See Jonathan Israel, *Democratic Enlightenment: Philosophy, Revolution, and Human Rights* (New York: Oxford University Press, 2013).

22. See Antony Anghie, "Francisco de Vitoria and the Colonial Origins of International Law" in *Social Legal Studies* 5:321(1996), on line at: teachers.colonelby.com/ krichardson/Grade%2012/Carleton%20-%20Int%20Law%20Course/Week%202/ ColonialOriginsIntLaw.pdf.

23. See Enrique Dussel *1492– El encubrimiento del otro* (Buenos Aires: CLACSO, 1992), online at: biblioteca.clacso.edu.ar/clacso/otros/20111218114130/1942.pdf.

24. See Enrique Dussel, *1492–El encubrimiento del otro*; and Franz Hinkelammert, *La maldición que pesa sobre la ley: Las raíces del pensamiento crítico en Pablo de Tarso* (San José, Costa Rica: Editorial Arlekín, 2010).

25. See Miguel Leon Portilla, *Visión de los vencidos* (México: Siglo XXI, 1959) and Juan Friede, *Bartolomé de Las Casas- Precursor del anticolonialismo: Su luch y su derrota* (México: Siglo XXI, 1974).

26. See Gustavo Gutiérrez, *Las Casas: In Search of the Poor of Jesus Christ* (Maryknoll: Orbis Books, 1993).

27. See Hans Offerdal, "Pope Paul VI's Plea for an Authentic International Social Justice," *Journal of the Institute of Justice and International Studies,* no.5, (2005): 55–73.

28. See Hinkelammert *La maldición que pesa sobre la ley: Las raíces del pensamiento crítico en Pablo de Tarso* (San José, Costa Rica: Editorial Arlekín, 2010); Enrique Dussel *Ethics of Liberation;* and Martinez Andrade and Jose Manuel Meneses, (eds.) *Esperanza y utopia: Ernst Bloch desde América Latina* (México: Ediciones de Medio Día, 2012).

29. See Upendra Baxi, (2002) online compilation of his writings between 1960 and 2008: upendrabaxi.in/.

30. See Edward Thompson, *The Making of the English Working Class* (New York: Vintage, 1963) and Upendra Baxi (2002) online compilation of his writings between 1960 and 2008: upendrabaxi.in/.

31. See C. L. R James, *Black Jacobins* (New York: Vintage, 1963) and Robin Blackburn, *The Making of New World Slavery: From the Baroque to the Modern* (New York: Verso, 2010).

32. www.margueritelaurent.com/pressclips/vertierre_08.html#vertieres.

33. ccrjustice.org/why-us-owes-haiti-billions-briefest-history-bill-quigley.

34. www.reuters.com/article/2015/01/10/us-un-haiti-lawsuit-idUSKBN0KJ0PX20150110.

35. See Robin Blackburn, *The Making of New World Slavery: From the Baroque to the Modern* (New York: Verso, 2010).

36. See Raul Zibechi, *Territories in Resistance: A Cartography of Latin American Social Movements* (Oakland: AK Press, 2012); writings online at: www.surysur.net/autor/raul-

zibechi/; and David Harvey, "The New Imperialism—Accumulation by Dispossession" in Socialist Register (2004), online at: socialistregister.com/index.php/srv/article/view/5811/2707#.V1MqryPhCCQ.

37. See Raul Zibechi, *Territories in Resistance: A Cartography of Latin American Social Movements* (Oakland: AK Press, 2012).

38. See Jerry Mander and Victoria Tauli-Corpuz, *Paradigm Wars: Indigenous Peoples' Resistance to Globalization* (San Francisco: Sierra Club Books, 2006).

39. See Pablo Dávalos, "La crisis del posneoliberalismo en Ecuador," (2011) online at: www.nacionmulticultural.unam.mx/portal/cultura_politica/pablo_davalos_201102 10.html. Also see Emir Sader, *Refundar el estado- Posneoliberalismo en América Latina* (Buenos Aires: CLACSO, 2008), online at: bibliotecavirtual.clacso.org.ar/ar/libros/coedicion/sader/sader.pdf and Raul Zibechi, *Territories in Resistance: A Cartography of Latin American Social Movements* (Oakland: AK Press, 2012).

40. See Boaventura de Sousa Santos, *Sociología Jurídica Crítica* (Barcelona: Trotta, 2009).

41. See François Houtart, "El concepto de Sumak Kawsay (Buen Vivir) y su correspondencia con el bien común de la humanidad" en *Ecuador Debate* no. 84 (2011): 57–76, online at: repositorio.flacsoandes.edu.ec/bitstream/10469/3523/1/RFLACSO-ED84-04-Houtart.pdf.

42. See Enrique Dussel, *Twenty Theses on Politics* (Durham: Duke University Press, 2008).

43. See Boaventura de Sousa Santos, *Epistemologies of the South: Justice Against Epistemicide* (Paradigm Publishers, 2014); Alejandro Medici "Teoría constitucional y giro decolonial: Narrativas y simbolismos de las constituciones- reflexiones a partir de la experiencia de Bolivia y Ecuador" (2009), online at: www.ceapedi.com.ar/otroslogos/revistas/0001/medici.pdf; Raul Prada, *Epistemología, pluralismo, y descolonización* (2012) online at: www.rebelion.org/docs/167277.pdf and Catherine Walsh, *Interculturalidad crítica y (de)colonialidad- Ensayos desde Abya Yala* (Quito: Abya-Yala, 2013).

44. See Barrett, Chávez, and Rodríguez Garavito, *The New Latin American Left: Utopia Reborn* (Amsterdam: Pluto Press, 2008) and Bruno Baronnet, Mora Bayo and Richar Stahler-Sholk (eds.) *Luchas "muy otras": Zapatismo y autonomía en las comunidades indígenas de Chiapas* (México: UAM/CIESAS/UNACH, 2011).

45. See Pablo González-Casanova, "Colonialismo interno: una redefinición" (2006) online at: bibliotecavirtual.clacso.org.ar/ar/libros/campus/marxis/P4C2Casanova.pdf; Edgardo Lander, *La colonialidad del saber: eurocentrismo y ciencias sociales- Perspectivas latinoamericanas* (Buenos Aires: CLACSO, 2006), online at: bibliotecavirtual.clacso.org.ar/clacso/sur-sur/20100708034410/lander.pdf; and Anibal Quijano, *Colonialidad del poder, eurocentrismo, y América Latina* (2000), marxismocritico.files.wordpress.com/2012/07/1161337413-anibal-quijano.pdf.

46. See Susan Eckstein and Timothy Wickham-Crowley (eds.), *Struggles for Social Rights in Latin America* (New York: Routledge, 2002).

47. See "Massacre in Tamaulipas" www.nytimes.com/2010/08/30/opinion/30mon3.html?_r=0, www.nytimes.com/2011/04/27/world/americas/27briefs-bodies.html?_r=0.

48. www.nytimes.com/2016/04/25/world/americas/inquiry-challenges-mexicos-account-of-how-43-students-vanished.html.

49. nacla.org/news/armoring-nafta-battleground-mexico%E2%80%99s-future, www.cipamericas.org/archives/3202.

50. www.ohchr.org/en/NewsEvents/Pages/DisplayNews.aspx?NewsID=16578&LangID=E.

BIBLIOGRAPHY

Anghie, Antony. "Francisco de Vitoria and the Colonial Origins of International Law." *Social Legal Studies* 5 (1996): 321. Online at: teachers.colonelby.com/krichardson/

Grade%2012/Carleton%20-%20Int%20Law%20Course/Week%202/
ColonialOriginsIntLaw.pdf.

Barrett, Patrick, Daniel Chávez, and Cesar Rodriguez Garavito. *The New Latin American Left: Utopia Reborn.* Amsterdam: Pluto Press, 2008.

Baronnet, Bruno, Mora Bayo, and Richard Stahler-Sholk. (eds.) *Luchas "muy otras": Zapatismo y autonomía en las comunidades indígenas de Chiapas.* México: UAM/CIE-SAS/UNACH, 2011.

Baxi, Upendra. Online compilation of his writings between 1960 and 2008: upendrabaxi.in/.

Benjamin, Walter. *Conceptos de filosofía de la historia.* Buenos Aires: Terramar Ediciones, 2007.

Blackburn, Robin. *The Making of New World Slavery: From the Baroque to the Modern.* New York: Verso, 2010.

Bloch, Ernst. *The Principle of Hope (3 vols.).* Cambridge: MIT Press, 1995.

Carlsen, Laura. "A Primer on Plan Mexico." May 5, 2008. Online at: www.cipamericas. org/archives/1474/.

Committee on Economic Social and Cultural Rights (CESCR-UN), Poverty and the International Covenant on ESC Rights. Online at: www2.ohchr.org/english/bodies/ cescr/docs/statements/E.C.12.2001.10Poverty-2001.pdf.

Dávalos, Pablo. "La crisis del posneoliberalismo en Ecuador." Online at: www. nacionmulticultural.unam.mx/portal/cultura_politica/pablo_davalos_20110210. html.

Dussel, Enrique. (1992, 1994) *1492–El encubrimiento del otro.* Buenos Aires: CLACSO. Online at: biblioteca.clacso.edu.ar/clacso/otros/20111218114130/1942.pdf.

———. "Beyond Eurocentrism: The World-System and the Limits of Modernity." In Fredric Jameson and Masao Miyoshi (eds.) *The Cultures of Globalization.* Durham: Duke University Press, 1998.

———. *Twenty Theses on Politics* (Durham: Duke University Press, 2008.

———. "Transmodernity and Interculturality: An Interpretation from the Perspective of Philosophy of Liberation." *Transmodernity* (2012): 28–59.

———. *Ethics of Liberation in the Age of Globalization and Exclusion.* Durham: Duke University Press, 2013.

Eckstein, Susan, and Timothy Wickham-Crowley. (eds.) *Struggles for Social Rights in Latin America.* New York: Routledge, 2002.

Falk, Richard. *Human Rights Horizons: the Pursuit of Justice in a Globalizing World.* New York: Routledge, 2000.

Friede, Juan. *Bartolomé de Las Casas- Precursor del anticolonialismo: Su luch y su derrota.* México: Siglo XXI, 1974.

González, Juan. *Harvest of Empire: A History of Latinos in America.* New York: Penguin Books, 2011.

González-Casanova, Pablo. "Colonialismo interno: una redefinición," (2006). Online at: bibliotecavirtual.clacso.org.ar/ar/libros/campus/marxis/P4C2Casanova.pdf.

Gutiérrez, Gustavo. *Las Casas: In Search of the Poor of Jesus Christ.* Maryknoll: Orbis Books, 1993.

———. *A Theology of Liberation. History, Politics and Salvation.* Maryknoll: Orbis, 1973.

Hardt, Michael, and Antonio Negri. *Commonwealth.* Cambridge: Harvard University Press, 2009.

Harvey, David. "The New Imperialism- Accumulation by Dispossession." In *Socialist Register,* (2004). Online at: socialistregister.com/index.php/srv/article/view/5811/ 2707#.V1MqryPhCCQ.

Hinkelammert, Franz. *El mapa del emperador.* Costa Rica: Instituto de Estudios Teológicos, 1996.

———. *La maldición que pesa sobre la ley: Las raíces del pensamiento crítico en Pablo de Tarso.* San José, Costa Rica: Editorial Arlekín, 2010.

Houtart, François. "El concepto de Sumak Kawsay (Buen Vivir) y su correspondencia con el bien común de la humanidad." En *Ecuador Debate,* no. 84 (2011): 57–76.

Online at: repositorio.flacsoandes.edu.ec/bitstream/10469/3523/1/RFLACSO-ED84-04-Houtart.pdf.

Internal Displacement Monitoring Centre (IDMC) Annual Report (2015). Online at: www.internal-displacement.org/assets/library/Media/201505-Global-Overview-2015/20150506-global-overview-2015-en.pdf.

Israel, Jonathan. *Democratic Enlightenment: Philosophy, Revolution, and Human Rights.* New York: Oxford University Press, 2013.

James, C. L. R. *Black Jacobins.* New York: Vintage, 1963.

Lander, Edgardo. *La colonialidad del saber: eurocentrismo y ciencias sociales- Perspectivas latinoamericanas.* Buenos Aires: CLACSO, 2000. Online at: bibliotecavirtual.clacso.org.ar/clacso/sur-sur/20100708034410/lander.pdf.

León Portilla, Miguel. *Visión de los vencidos.* México: Siglo XXI, 1959.

Mander, Jerry, and Victoria Tauli-Corpuz. *Paradigm Wars: Indigenous Peoples 'Resistance to Globalization.* San Francisco: Sierra Club Books, 2006.

Martinez-Andrade, Luis, and Jose Manuel Meneses. (eds.) *Esperanza y utopia: Ernst Bloch desde América Latina.* México: Ediciones de Medio Día, 2012.

Medici, Alejandro. "Teoría constitucional y giro decolonial: Narrativas y simbolismos de las constituciones- reflexiones a partir de la experiencia de Bolivia y Ecuador."(2009). Online at: www.ceapedi.com.ar/otroslogos/revistas/0001/medici.pdf.

Mignolo, Walter. "The Zapatistas's Theoretical Revolution: Its Historical, Ethical, and Political Consequences." In Review (Fernand Braudel Center) 25 no. 3, *Utopian Thinking* (2002): 245–275. Online at: www.jstor.org/stable/40241550?seq=1#page_scan_tab_contents.

———. "Globalizacion, doble traduccion y interculturalidad." Edited by Edmundo Mercado y Alvaro Canon, *Revista Educativa Cultural Saint Andrew's.* Special Issue on Colonialidad del Saber y Educación, 1 no. 2 (2006): 52–61, Colegio Saint Andrew's, La Paz, Bolivia.

———. "Who Speaks for the "Human" in Human Rights?" Edited by Anna Forcinito, Raul Marrero-Fonte and Kelly McDonough, *Hispanic Issues* on Line. Special Issue: Human Rights in Latin America and Iberian Cultures, 5 no. 1 (2009): 7–25.

———. "Geopolitics of sensing and knowing: on (de) coloniality, border thinking and epistemic disobedience, Postcolonial Studies." 14 no. 3 (2011): 273–285.

———. "Delinking, Decoloniality and Dewesternization." (Interview, Part II), (2012). Online at: criticallegalthinking.com/2012/05/02/delinking-decoloniality-dewesternization-interview-with-walter-mignolo-part-ii/.

Nussbaum, Martha. *Frontiers of Justice: Disability, Nationality, Species Membership.* Cambridge: Harvard University Press, 2006.

Offerdal, Hans. "Pope Paul VI's Plea for an Authentic International Social Justice." *Journal of the Institute of Justice and International Studies,* no.5 (2005): 55–73.

Patzi Paco, Felix. *Sistema Comunal: Una propuesta alternativa para salir de la colonialidad y del liberalism.* La Paz: Centro de Estudios Alternativos, 2004.

Pérez-Bustillo, Camilo. "Human Rights from Below." CROP Newsletter, May (2008). Online at: www.crop.org/viewfile.aspx?id=158.

———. "Ningún ser humano es ilegal." In *Balance de los Derechos Humanos en el Sexenio de Fox.* Mexico City: UACM/PRD, 2007.

Pogge, Thomas. "Poverty is a Massive Crime Against Humanity." (2013). Online at: www.dw.com/en/poverty-is-a-massive-crime-against-humanity/a-16936635.

———. "Q and ASAP- After the MDGs- Thomas Pogge Sees Some Promise, Many Potential Pitfalls in First Official Recommendations for Millennium Development Goals Replacement Effort." (Interview by Amy Gordon), (2013). Online at: academicsstand.org/2013/06/q-asap-after-the-mdgs-thomas-pogge-sees-some-promise-many-potential-pitfalls-in-first-official-recommendations-for-millennium-development-goals-replacement-effort/.

———. "Comment: Are We Violating the Human Rights of the World's Poor?" *Yale Human Rights & Development L. J.* 14 no. 2 (2011): 14–33. Online at: www.law.yale.edu/documents/pdf/LawJournals/1._Pogge.pdf.

———. (ed.) *Freedom from Poverty as a Human Right: Who Owes What to the Very Poor?* Oxford: Oxford University Press/UNESCO, 2007.

———. *Poverty and Human Rights: Cosmopolitan Responsibilities and Reforms.* London: Polity Press, 2002.

Pogge, Thomas, and Christian Barry. (eds.) *Global Institutions and Responsibilities: Achieving Global Justice.* London: Wiley-Blackwell, 2006.

Prada, Raul. *Epistemología, pluralismo, y descolonización.* (2012). Online at. www. rebelion.org/docs/167277.pdf.

Quijano, Anibal. *Colonialidad del poder, eurocentrismo, y América Latina.* (2000). Online at: marxismocritico.files.wordpress.com/2012/07/1161337413-anibal-quijano.pdf.

Rajagopal, Balakrishna. *International Law from Below.* Cambridge: Cambridge University Press, 2003.

Rawls, John. *A Theory of Justice.* Cambridge: Harvard University Press, 1971.

———. *The Law of Peoples.* Cambridge: Harvard University Press, 1999.

Sachs, Jeffery. *The End of Poverty: Economic Possibilities for Our Time.* New York: Penguin Press, 2005.

Sader, Emir. *Refundar el estado- Posneoliberalismo en América Latina.* Buenos Aires: CLACSO, 2008. Online at: bibliotecavirtual.clacso.org.ar/ar/libros/coedicion/sader/sader.pdf.

Sen, Amarta. *Development as Freedom.* New York: Anchor, 1999.

———. *The Idea of Justice.* Cambridge: Harvard University Press, 2009.

Sousa Santos, Boventura. *El caleidoscopio de las justicias en Colombia* (2 vols.). Bogotá: Colciencias/Instituto Colombiano de Antropologia e Historia/Universidad de Coimbra-CEC/Universidad de los Andes/Universidad Nacional de Colombia/Siglo del Hombre Editores, 2004.

———. *Sociología Jurídica Crítica.* Barcelona: Trotta, 2009.

———. *Another Knowledge is Possible: Beyond Northern Epistemologies.* London: Verso, 2008.

———. *Epistemologies of the South: Justice Against Epistemicide.* Boulder: Paradigm Publishers, 2014.

Sousa Santos, Boaventura, and Cesar Rodriguez. *Law and Globalization from Below.* Cambridge: Cambridge University Press, 2005.

Stiglitz, Joseph. *The Price of Inequality.* New York: W. W Norton, 2012.

Thompson, Edward. *The Making of the English Working Class.* New York: Vintage, 1963.

Van Genugten, William. "The Use of Human Rights Instruments in the Struggle Against (Extreme) Poverty." In Kjonstad, A. and Veit Wilson, J. H., *Law, Power, and Poverty* (1997). Online at: poseidon01.ssrn.com/delivery.php?ID=318115065115 118113001078079009018087017069064045069066075088118069073004022121125018022103030104056120001022115091089009112055073026085009094006031025106118104070058087029004001071008016001115011087086095106071123069008104108116115030019110031095&EXT=pdf.

Wallerstein, Immanuel. *Utopistics: or, Historical choices of the 21st century.* New York: The New Press, 1998.

Walsh, Catherine. *Interculturalidad crítica y (de)colonialidad- Ensayos desde Abya Yala* Quito: Abya-Yala, 2013.

Weber, Leanne, and Sharon Pickering. *Globalization and Borders: Death at the Global Frontier.* New York: Palgrave MacMillan, 2011.

Zibechi, Raul. *Territories in Resistance: A Cartography of Latin American Social Movements.* Oakland: AK Press, 2012. Online at: www.surysur.net/autor/raul-zibechi/.

———. *Descolonizar el pensamiento critico y las rebeldías: autonomías y emncipaciones en la era del progresismo.* México: Bajo Tierra Ediciones/JRA, 2016.

Part IV

The Arizona Ban and
Forty-Three Disappeared Students

ELEVEN

Racial Interpellation, Civic Education, and Anti-Latina/o Racism

Andrea J. Pitts

The analysis in this essay focuses on a case of anti-Latina/o racism in the US Southwest, namely, a series of legislative documents that led to the banning of Mexican American Studies (MAS) in Tucson, Arizona. I aim to show that even in fact-stating cases of third-personal address, an implicit "you" or "you all" is invoked by the speaker and that such hails bear normative weight. I conclude by pointing to responses to the banning of MAS in Tucson to demonstrate a multiplicity of forms of uptake resulting from the cases of third-personal address that I discuss.

To elaborate the role of what I describe as *racial interpellation,* I discuss three interrelated sets of norms that surface throughout the legal documents that supported the banning of MAS in the district. The three normative trends are nativism, individualism, and, what Leo Chavez calls the "Latino-threat narrative." Each set of norms, I argue, bear implicit second-personal vocatives that support anti- Latina/o racism. In what follows, I first outline some of the historical background of the banning of MAS in Tucson. In the second section, I clarify my account of anti-Latina/o racism. Then, I turn to specific language within the Arizona legislation involved in the ban to specify indirect second-personal hails that surface via each set of norms—that is, nativism, individualism, and via the "Latino-threat narrative." The penultimate section analyses the relationship between multicultural liberalism and the banning of MAS in Tucson. The final section offers some responses from groups that have been resisting the ban, and I conclude by addressing their invocations toward non-individualist forms of collective pedagogy and action.

Banning Mexican American Studies in the Tucson Unified School District

On May 11, 2010, Governor of Arizona Jan Brewer approved House Bill 2281. HB 2281 contains the following mandates: a school district or charter school in this state shall not include in its program of instruction any courses or classes that include any of the following:

1. promote the overthrow of the US government.
2. promote resentment toward a race or class of people.
3. are designed primarily for pupils of a particular ethnic group.
4. advocate ethnic solidarity instead of the treatment of pupils as individuals.

In December of 2010, then superintendent, Tom Horne, filed a motion to find the Tucson Unified School District's (TUSD) Mexican American Studies program to be in violation of the Arizona statute that came out of HB 2281, A.R.S. 15–112. In June of 2011, the newly elected superintendent of schools, John Huppenthal, issued another finding, stating again that TUSD was in violation of the new state statute. In December of that year, an Arizona judge agreed that the TUSD was indeed violating the mandates of A.R.S 15–112. The concerns expressed by Horne and Huppenthal were that the Mexican American Studies program in the district, also known as "La Raza Studies," was teaching "a kind of ethnic chauvinism that the citizens of Tucson should no longer tolerate."[1] Underlying Horne and Huppenthal's claims was the view that "people are individuals, not exemplars of racial groups."[2] In a statement written by Horne, he states: "What is important about people is what they know, what they can do, their ability to appreciate beauty, their character, and not what race into which they were born [sic]."[3] One of the primary textbooks for the Mexican American Studies program was Paulo Freire's *Pedagogy of the Oppressed*, a classic text in the discipline of critical pedagogy, which discusses how to reformulate educational models by starting from the lived realities of those who face oppression. Horne writes regarding this text·

> Most of [the parents and grandparents of students in the Mexican American studies program] came to this country legally, because this is the land of opportunity. They trust the public school with their children. Those students should be taught that this is the land of opportunity, and that if they work hard they can achieve their goals. They should not be taught that they are oppressed.[4]

Moreover, referring to books that discuss the Chicano rights movement and the movement's conception of *Aztlán* as a homeland for Mexicans in the US southwest whose land was stolen by the United States in 1848, Horne writes that such books that outline the importance of resignifying this geographic region for Mexican Americans should not be paid for by American taxpayers. The reason for this is that these books promote the overthrow the US government and create racial resentment among students. Following the court ruling, many books were banned from the district's curricula, including Gloria Anzaldúa's *Borderlands/La frontera*. Such books were removed from classrooms and prohibited from being studied in the district's schools. In addition, any school found not to comply with the new state statute would risk losing state financial support which would result in the loss of millions of dollars. Interestingly, Horne and Huppenthal's complaints only targeted Mexican American Studies in the school district, and did not affect other curricula that included course material on African American, Asian American, and European history. Since the ruling in 2011, supporters of MAS have attempted to revive parts of the program, but Huppenthal remains skeptical of the program's ability to comply with the mandates of A.R.S. 15–112.

At the heart of this controversy is a question regarding what counts as a proper public educational curriculum for US citizens. Huppenthal and Horne claim that teaching students to endorse forms of ethnic and racial solidarity and the continued promotion of programs that examine historical analyses of oppression in the United States are obstacles to the betterment of US political goals. The targeting of Mexican American Studies in particular, in Arizona, is important. That is, much of Horne and Huppenthal's worries about Mexican American Studies in the TUSD often refer to the contemporary immigration debates within the US Southwest. At one point in Horne's findings, he states that books taught in the MAS program are "gloating over the difficulty we are having in controlling the border," suggesting that the MAS program wrongly teaches students to feel discontent with the current immigration policies of the United States.[5] Huppenthal and Horne seem to agree that other programs that teach about histories of violence or other forms of systemic marginalization and disenfranchisement of US minorities (e.g., African American or Asian American studies) were not found to be in violation of the mandates of A.R.S. 15–112. The last major ruling on the banning of MAS occurred in March of 2013. There, a US district court judge ruled that the appeals filed by teachers and administrators of the program did not sufficiently "meet the threshold needed to establish a constitutional violation."[6] In this document, a federal judge ruled in favor of the constitutionality of the wording and mandates of A.R. S. 15–112. Thus, current litigation has been denied for proponents of MAS in the district.

ANTI-LATINA/O RACISM AND STRUCTURAL WHITE SUPREMACY

Given this contextual framing of the example, I will add here a brief note about the conception of anti-Latina/o racism that I use throughout this essay. It is important to note that while African American, Native American, and Asian American Studies programs were not targeted in the debate, the displacement of Mexican-American Studies points to what Andrea Smith considers one of the "pillars of white supremacy." Smith argues that making sense of the power relations that different groups of people of color experience under white supremacy (e.g., Native peoples, Latinas/os, Arab and Muslim Americans, Asian Americans, African Americans, etc.) requires that we interpret the notion of white supremacy as operating via three distinct but related logics.[7] These three logics or "pillars" are slavery/capitalism, genocide/colonialism, and Orientalism/war.[8] The first pillar is the commodification of people of color, and in particular the commodification of Black peoples through the brutality of the Middle Passage, the violence and exploitation of African and African-descended peoples in slave economies in the Americas and the Caribbean, the regulation and control of Black Americans via Jim Crow laws, and the perpetual criminalization of Black Americans within the current era of mass incarceration. The second pillar, Smith argues, operates via the elimination of indigenous peoples, either through violence or through assimilation. In particular, Smith underscores the "present-absence" of Native peoples in the United States and the "temporal paradox" wherein "living Indians [are] induced to 'play dead,' as it were, in order to perform a narrative of manifest destiny in which their role, ultimately, was to disappear."[9] The third pillar of white supremacy, "Orientalism," drawing here from the work of Edward Said, names specific peoples or nations as "inferior and as posing a constant threat to well-being of empire."[10] Orientalism, in turn, provides global justifications for military violence. Smith cites here the US "War on Terror," which justifies harassment and violence against Arab and Muslim Americans, and which justifies military aggression against predominantly Muslim and Arab nations. The logics of these three pillars of white supremacy serve to reinforce one another and often effectively separate communities of color that may be distinctly affected by one or another specific form of racial oppression. She argues that resistance to only one logic of white supremacy makes that form of resistance complicit with the structural domination of other groups affected by the remaining logics of white supremacy.

By referring to structural facets of white supremacy, I am claiming that racism is not an individualistic set of biases or beliefs about people of differing racial groups. This latter claim is taken usually to mean that racism is the result of individual prejudices and discrimination. Against this view I claim that what makes white supremacy *structural* in nature are the material differences among racial groups in terms of rewards and harms sanctioned via institutional social practices. Or put another way, following Eduardo Bonilla-Silva, we can consider the development of racialized social systems that afford material benefits to whites as a social group against a background of racial hierarchy as the *structural* characteristic of white supremacy.[11]

Thus, anti-Latina/o racism functions under multiple logics of white supremacy, and as Smith states, "these logics may affect peoples differently depending on whether they are black, Indigenous, Mestizo, etc."[12] The targeting of MAS in Tucson, while it unjustly targets Mexican Americans and, by extension, other Latinas/os more broadly, it bolsters white supremacy via the perpetuation of the logic of Orientalism or, what I will refer to more broadly as *nativism*—a racialized conception of a group as foreign and inherently inferior due to characteristics of that group. Moreover, the language of individualism endorsed throughout A.R.S. 15–112 also undergirds Smith's second pillar of white supremacy. Namely, inclusion or assimilation within a specific form of American individualism serves as a way to erase or diminish the importance of non-Anglo-American cultural, ethnic, and racial identities.

NATIVISM AND RACIAL INTERPELLATION

To clarify what I mean by nativism, consider the examples of anti-Latina/o racism that Alcoff points to in her piece, "Comparative Race, Comparative Racisms." Alcoff states that often forms of anti-Latina/o racism surface via claims regarding the foreignness of Latinas/os and the refusal of Latinas/os to assimilate to "American culture." Alcoff cites the work of political theorist Samuel Huntington as an illustration of this form of discrimination. Huntington states, for instance, that "There is no *Americano* dream. There is only the American dream created by the Anglo-Protestant society. Mexican Americans will share in that dream and in that society only if they dream in English."[13] This form of racial discrimination targets Latinas/os as foreign and as unable to endorse and uphold the democratic values of the state.[14] The targeting of the MAS program stemmed from this particular logic of white supremacy—or what Alcoff calls an "axis of racism"—that places the cultural practices and norms of non-Anglo-American groups as unworthy of social inclusion and political representation.[15] As I'll argue in a moment, some normative hails socially locate Mexican American peoples and cultures as potential threats to the order of the nation. To clarify this point, we can trace a form of racialized nativism that functions within the legal documents presented against the Mexican American Studies Program in Tucson. This analysis is then the first context in which we can see how racial norms function via indirect second-personal interpellations.

Before turning to those texts, we can briefly revisit some views on the pragmatic functions of speech acts to specify some potential normative dimensions of the language I will analyze in the documents that led to the banning of MAS. First, recall that at the end of J. L. Austin's essay titled, "Performative Utterances," Austin returns his readers to the distinction between performative utterances (of the kind that he has been discussing through the essay) and declarative statements. Austin states that in many cases of illocutionary speech acts such as "I warn you to . . . ," "I advise you to . . . " proper assessment of the normative dimensions of such utterances requires an assessment of the justification of the warning in question or the soundness of the advice given.[16] At first blush, such speech acts appear distinct in kind from other forms of speech, and, perhaps, most clearly as distinct from declarative utterances regarding statements of fact. However, he follows this claim with a query regarding the nature of declarative statements. He writes:

> But actually—though it would take too long to go on about this—the more you think about truth and falsity the more you find that very few statements that we ever utter are just true or just false. Usually there is the question are they fair or are they not fair, are they adequate or not adequate, are they exaggerated or not exaggerates? . . . 'True' and 'false' are just general labels for a whole dimension of different appraisals which have something or other to do with the relation between what we say and the facts. If, then, we loosen up our ideas of truth and falsity we shall see that statements, when assessed in relation to the facts, are not so very different after all from pieces of advice, warnings, verdicts, and so on.[17]

In this sense, Austin seems to suggest that all third-person statements can bear second-person claims and function in a normative valence. Thus, even seemingly agent-neutral utterances are hails to an audience. However, such hails, when spoken in the third-person, pragmatically erase the normative locatedness of the speaker. Accordingly, many third-person utterances do successfully do this and those that do create norms.

Through this lens, I propose that third-person addresses within the context of the banning of MAS in Tucson include second-person addresses to differing racial groups. Consider, for example, the impact of the statement within the Arizona statute A.R.S. 15–112 that prohibits district schools from offering courses that "Advocate ethnic solidarity instead of the treatment of pupils as individuals." Such a statement contains indirect vocative addresses, although such a statement might appear on its surface to avoid implicating specific racial or ethnic groups and to be broadly applied to all ethnic groups. For instance, one indirect second-person hail may be "those of you who think that racial and ethnic identity matter for success in the nation are mistaken," or "in order to be considered an American citizen you ought not consider yourself a member of a racial or ethnic groups." In these cases, conceptions of individualism and nativism are placed outside the context of ethnicity, culture, and race. Rather than connecting these views to dominant Anglo-Protestant norms and values, the statement in A.R.S. 15–112 attempts to place individualism outside of any cultural or historical context.

To better situate nativism in Tucson, however, we can look more closely at the history of ethnic studies in the state. In "The Nativistic Legacy of the Americanization Era in the Education of Mexican Immigrant Students," René Galindo writes that although Mexicans helped establish private and public schools in the mid-nineteenth century, by the end of the century, "schools were firmly in the hands of Anglo administrators and school boards."[18] He cites that, following the 1870s, nearly sixty years passed before a Mexican administrator served on the district's school board. Also during that period, he argues, Mexicans were targeted by Americanization policies and many were forced to repatriate. For example, during the years of 1929 and 1937 approximately 458,000 people of Mexican-origin, both immigrant and native-born to the United States, were either deported or repatriated to Mexico.[19]

Within Tucson schools, Americanization policies were strictly enforced. In 1919, English-only instruction became required by law in the state of Arizona and Tucson developed the 1C Program, which segregated schools by English-speaking ability and required mandatory immersion programs for Spanish-speaking students. Many students who went through the 1C Program reported feeling threatened and reported being abused by instructors[20] Many cases of abuse were enacted as forms of punishment for speaking Spanish in the classroom. Eventually, the 1C program was replaced by the state's first bilingual educational program in 1969.[21]

Regarding racial interpellation more broadly, during this period many Spanish-speaking Americans were normatively hailed to conform to Anglo-American cultural values and ways of life, including English-only norms of linguistic communication. Consider, for example, Gloria Anzaldúa's discussion of the Americanization program that she endured during her primary education in southern Texas. She describes her teacher stating: "If you want to be American, speak 'American.' If you don't like it, go back to Mexico where you belong."[22] Anzaldúa describes being hit on the knuckles with a ruler for pronouncing her own name in a Tejano dialect of Spanish. In these cases, there are direct second-person hails made to students in schools. The claim appears to be that national identity or inclusion as a potential contributor to the nation requires stripping oneself of cultural or linguistic relations to Mexican cultures and histories.

In Arizona, in response to these forms of discrimination, as Gómez and Gabaldón argue, the Tucson Unified School District was also a major center for political resistance to racism and for civil rights activity since the 1960s. For example, following a desegregation lawsuit in 1979, it was the first district in the state to create a Black Studies Department. Also several lawsuits spanning over the late 1970s to the 1990s secured tax revenue to renovate and restructure schools that primarily served Mexican American and Native American students.[23] One significant development that points toward the current debate over ethnic studies in the TUSD was that, while a Native American Studies Department was created in response to the Native American Languages Act of 1990, no call had been made for a Mexican American Studies program in the district at that time. Despite both the severe treatment that both groups suffered through the Americanization programs that affected the district, and despite the prominence of Mexican Americans within the school district (Mexican Americans comprised the majority of students in the district), there was no specific program that would address the needs of this portion of the student body that comprised the TUSD. While the 1990 federal mandate legally codified the claim that "It is the policy of the United States to preserve, protect, and promote the rights and freedom of Native Americans to use, practice, and develop Native American languages," no such federal mandate was ever enacted for the Spanish language of inhabitants of the US Southwest.[24] Such policies might have led to implicit hails to Latinas/os in the state such as "your language and culture are not worth preserving in schools," or "the histories of abuse against Native Americans outweigh the abuses that Mexicans and other Latin Americans have suffered at the hands of the US government." Moreover, as Gómez and Gabaldón state, "Mexican American students did not have a department that could provide the kind of vital support (parental involvement, dropout prevention, college preparation, and so on) that the other minority groups enjoyed."[25] This was especially important because drop-out rates among students enrolled in the 1C program had never moved below 60 percent over its forty-seven years in operation and because drop-out rates remained high after the district's development of the Bilingual Education Department in 1969.

Stemming from growing dissatisfaction with the treatment of Mexican American students in the district, over the years 1997 and 1998 a series of audits were conducted by three distinct subcommittees that would address the status of the Bilingual Education Department. These concerns were raised by faculty members who called for the district to act in the interest of Mexican American and other Latina/o students. Finally, in 1999, upon the request of the subcommittees involved, the district established its first Hispanic Studies Department, which included a project for a new curriculum that would address K-12 education in the district.[26] Following this decision, a Pan-Asian Studies Department was also created that would serve Asian and Pacific Islander students in the district. Finally in 2002, the Hispanic Studies Department developed the Mexican American Studies program to serve in Tucson schools throughout the district.

Gómez and Gabaldón also state that these structural developments incited a backlash against minority programs in the district. A public debate emerged as to whether programs designed to aid minority students should be eligible to receive increased state funding. One of the previous court decisions that allowed for the governing school board to increase desegregation funding had, in effect, served to shift a great deal of taxpayer money toward minority students.[27] The increase from $2 million in 1980 to $63 million in 2008 caused controversy at the state level due to conservative legislators' disapproval of spending state funds on minority students, which included potentially offering funds to students who were undocumented. In this backlash, for example, Gómez and Gabaldón cite several initiatives that targeted the bilingual education programs in the state, including the "English for the Children" initiative in 1998 which proposed Arizona Proposition 203 that would serve to replace many bilingual education programs with English immersion programs. Proposition 203 restricted the use of bilingual programs to very limited circumstances and created waivers that would grant students entry into its programs. The document states:

> [English is] the leading world language for science, technology, and international business, thereby being the language of economic opportunity. . . . Immigrant parents are eager to have their children acquire a good knowledge of English, thereby allowing them to fully participate in the American Dream of economic and social advancement.[28]

While the proposition was voted in by 63 percent of the constituents of the state, the document assumes that knowledge of English will be a strong enabling capacity for success in the United States. However, what the policy does not offer is an analysis of other structural barriers to social mobility, such as forms of racial discrimination in terms of access to employment, education, and housing for Latinas/os.

Following this legislative trend, Tom Horne, in his campaign running for superintendent of schools attacked his opponent, Jaime Molera, because of Molera's policies concerning the waivers that granted students access to the bilingual education programs. In his years as superintendent, Horne also explicitly targeted Mexican American students in the TUSD. As Gómez and Gabaldón write, "His office called for investigations to determine whether Mexican students were illegally attending public schools in US border towns; criticized schools for sponsoring Spanish spelling bees; proposed to set cutoff scores on the state's high school graduation test so that 10 percent of high school seniors would be denied graduation; revised the English proficiency test so that English learners could be pushed into regular classes even when they were not proficient in reading or writing; threatened to dismiss teachers who spoke with an accent; and lowered the amount of preparation teachers were required to have when serving English learners."[29] Such actions create second-person hails that suggest, for example, that "those of you with accents are deserving of unequal treatment" or "you, Spanish-speaking persons, ought not support and promote excellency in Spanish via spelling bees or similar programs/events." These hails normatively place English as a more valuable language than other languages. By discouraging the use of Spanish among school children in the district, these efforts suggest that this language cannot offer something valuable to its speakers. Furthermore, this disparagement of the language coincides with claims regarding "authentic" forms of American identity, which, as I discuss in the next section, requires a form of liberal individualism.

INDIVIDUALISM AND RACISM WITHOUT RACISTS

In 2006, just after his re-election, Horne crafted "An Open Letter to the Citizens of Tucson," a document that sparked the debate about the role of Mexican American Studies in the district and called to terminate the program. Horne and others involved in this backlash were taking a stand against funding for programs that supported the use of the Spanish language in schools. The indirect interpellative claims here appear to suggest that educational instruction in Spanish, and any encouragement of cultural norms, practices, and values of non-Anglo-American groups constituted potentially harmful practices. Such beliefs seem to stem from the form of nativism that I describe above, and are intimately related to a specific conception of individualism. Moreover, as I argue below, the racial interpellative content of Horne's position mirrors that of some contemporary multicultural liberal views.

First, turning to the language of Horne's early documents about MAS in the district, we can see traces of the Americanization rhetoric of the early twentieth century. Woodrow Wilson, in a speech in 1915 to recently naturalized citizens of the United States, expressed suspicion over the loyalties of citizens who maintain group-based ethnic identities in the United States. Wilson states:

> You cannot dedicate yourself to America unless you become in every respect and with every purpose of your will thorough Americans. You cannot become thorough Americans if you think of yourselves in groups. *America does not consist of groups.* A man who thinks of himself as belonging to a particular national group in America has not yet become an American, and the man who goes among you to trade upon your nationality is no worthy son to live under the Stars and Stripes.[30]

From this excerpt, we can see that Wilson is invoking a sense of US American identity that divorces itself from specific non-Anglo American cultural identities, which would presumably include rejecting non-white and non-Anglo-American ethnic and racial identities. This language positively hails non-Anglo-Americans to adopt an individualistic conception of identity, an identity that feels no social or political ties to groups or interests outside of those of mainstream Anglo-American people. Also individualism in this sense is assumed to be a universal good, which precludes other forms of political and social identification.

In Horne's letter to citizens of Tucson, the author offers several statements regarding US national identities that are very similar to those of Woodrow Wilson from 1915. For example, in an introductory section titled "Philosophy," Horne writes:

> I believe people are individuals, not exemplars of racial groups. What is important about people is what they know, what they can do, their ability to appreciate beauty, their character, and not what race into which they are born. They are entitled to be treated that way. It is fundamentally wrong to divide students up according to their racial group, and teach them separately.[31]

Both Wilson's address to recently naturalized citizens of the US of 1915 and Horne's "Philosophy" express a claim that focuses heavily on US identity being constituted via a commitment to a strict form of individualism.

Regarding this racialized individualism, Bonilla-Silva argues that since the 1950s, racism has shifted in several significant ways, one of which includes an invocation of liberal and individualist ideologies that treat notions such as "equality, fairness, reward by merit, and freedom" in an "abstract and decontextualized manner."[32] Bonilla-Silva argues that this new form of liberal individualism, in his words, "is a formidable rhetorical mine that allows Whites extreme argumentative flexibility on racial and racially perceived matters and enables them to raise liberal arguments to support and/or pursue illiberal ends."[33] Following this claim, we can excavate the "rhetorical mine" of the banning of MAS in Tucson to unearth second-person vocatives that create racial norms. The rhetoric of individualism found in the legal documents of the banning of MAS in Tucson denies forms of dependency and shared vulnerability among non-white citizens. While white citizens are treated as a vulnerable group—that is, teaching about the political relationship between Mexico and the United States promotes resentment against white persons—other racial groups are denied any form of vulnerability. Thus, here, as in various other discourses, norms of whiteness becomes invisible and universally applicable within the district's curriculum. The school district members do not call for an audit to analyze the content of the core state curriculum for its racial content, nor is there any discussion of ethnic solidarity among white students or faculty in the district.

In this latter vein, another potentially implied second-person hail of the A.R.S. 15–112 legislation is "you, white persons, have no ethnicity, nor any race that bears relevance in this matter." However, as Nakayama and Peñaloza ask rhetorically, "If whiteness is everything and nothing, if whiteness as a racial category does not exist except in conflict with others, how can we understand racial politics in a social structure that centers whites, yet has no center?"[34] The claim here is that judging from the history of the Americanization programs in Arizona and the lack of public funding for schools that primarily serve minority students that existed prior to the 1970s, the district claims that whiteness played no role in the historical disenfranchisement of Latina/o students. To claim as much would be to "promote resentment" toward white persons as a racial group. The second-person implication here appears to be "you, white readers, bear no responsibility for addresses the disenfranchisement of Latinas/os in the state of Arizona." Whiteness, when implicitly engaged via second-person racial norms, functions as a kind of anonymity and this kind of racial normativity supports the epistemic ignorance and insensitivity of whiteness. However, this analysis of second-personhood seeks to mark the ways in which mutual dependency functions as a precondition for ethical engagement. The anonymity of whiteness depends upon the perpetual marking and denigration of other racial groups.

Consider also that Horne's claim that "people are individuals, not members of racial groups" is a claim about the social ontology of persons. In particular, in his appeal to "the citizens of Tucson" he opens the document by stating that "The citizens of Tucson, of all mainstream political ideologies, would call for the elimination of the Tucson Unified School District's ethnic studies program if they knew what was happening there."[35] Thus, he assumes a third-person position to defend the proposal that he will offer in the document, stating that "The purpose of this letter is to bring these facts out into the open."[36] Horne assumes in this letter an agent-neutral stance on the claims he's making regarding the social ontology of persons. By appealing to "the citizens of Tucson," he assumes that if the "facts" of the program are made clear to his audience, they too would feel the call for the termination of the program.

Here, at one level, we see an appeal to a presumably anonymous body of potential readers who will understand and interpret his claims in a manner that would be in agreement with the prescriptive claims that he offers (i.e., the call for the termination of the program, the claims regarding ethnic solidarity, etc.). The following claims that Horne makes regarding the status of social groups and individuals thus is meant as a preface for the more direct criticism that he will make of the program. His statement about "what is important about people" is asserted in the declarative voice as well, proposing that his claim again is addressed to the anonymous Tucson citizen, and calls for her/his/their agreement. The final statement of the paragraph, "It is fundamentally wrong to divide students according to their racial group, and teach them separately," makes a similar rhetorical move.

Notice, however, within this kind of assertoric speech, Horne implicitly excludes specific readers from his pronouncement. Namely, while some moderate readers may not initially disagree with the "what is important about people" statement, he suggests through this utterance that racial group membership plays no role in determining features of one's identity such as their aesthetic views, the perception and legibility of their character, their credibility as knowers, or their relative ability to act within a given social space. This form of individualism proposed by Horne indirectly suggests that citizens of Tucson *ought not* believe that such features of one's identities are affected by race and processes of racialization. Thus, he assumes that the general readers of his document must also be persons who shares his conception of individualism.

In a next paragraph of the document, Horne writes that "the evidence is overwhelming that ethnic studies in the Tucson Unified School District teaches a kind of destructive ethnic chauvinism that the citizens of Tucson should no longer tolerate."[37] The "evidence" that Horne then proceeds to cite includes a criticism of the name used for the program ("La Raza Studies"), the textbooks that the program uses, and some of the material used in activities associated with the program. Interestingly, while Horne does make several prescriptive claims regarding the content of the curriculum in the program (e.g., "ethnic chauvinism should not be tolerated," and "students should not be taught that they are oppressed"), he does not explicitly provide an interpretation of the "evidence" that he proposes. The primary rhetorical move is to assume that his readers will use the same "background [individualist] philosophy" to interpret his claim that ethnic group identification is harmful to students.

Here again Bonilla-Silva's work is relevant. As he states, the language of individualism becomes a tool through which terms like "equality" and "fairness" can be abstractly wielded by interlocutors in a way that rejects material inequalities and patterns of discrimination. Consider the low graduation rates that Gómez and Gabaldón cite in their analysis of the history of the 1C program in the Tucson school district. Horne's rhetorical move is to locate claims about individualism as "background" information to support his position about the interests of students in the Tucson school district. However, if one were to cite the empirical research on educational metrics for success for students in the district, there would be more (third-person articulated) evidence to endorse a normative position that would *support* funding for MAS. For example, a 2012 report conducted by researchers in education studies at the University of Arizona analyzed graduation rates and statewide assessment test results from 2008–2011 to determine the impact of MAS in Tucson on student achievement. The report concluded that "there is a consistent, significant, positive relationship between MAS participation and student academic performance.[38]

Like most empirical research, this study offers a series of third-person statements regarding the impact of MAS in Tucson. However, an important difference here is that social scientists, like those who conducted the 2012 study, usually must make their methodologies explicit and hence available for public scrutiny. Regarding scientific knowledge more broadly, Helen Longino describes "objectivity" in scientific practice as the inclusion of intersubjective criticism and "the degree to which both its procedures and its results are responsive to the kinds of criticisms described."[39] She continues, that scientific methods must be considered social processes and that "objectivity" in science depends on factors such as the existence of shared avenues for criticism, shared standards of practice, the responsibility to respond to criticism, and a fair distribution of epistemic authority among the participants in the practice (Ibid.). In this sense, while empirical research shares a third-person grammatical structure with the forms of background knowledge that Horne invokes, the practices that the researchers of University of Arizona engage in and those of Horne differ to a large degree. Namely, Horne's background claims are not offered explicitly for public scrutiny, nor does he attempt to distribute epistemic authority to those who are critics of his version of individualism.

MULTICULTURAL POLITICS AND
INDIVIDUALISM IN THE BANNING OF MAS

Also along these lines, a claim found in A.R.S. 15–112 is that public schools should not "advocate ethnic solidarity." This statement makes the broader claim that identification with one's ethnic group is antithetical to the goals of public education in the nation, perhaps something like "your non-Anglo cultural identity is an obstacle to the meeting the demands of US citizenship." Along these lines, Horne writes in his "Open Letter to the Citizens of Tucson":

> On the TUSD website, it says the basic text for this program is "the pedagogy of oppression." Most of these students' parents and grandparents came to this country, legally, because this is the land of opportunity. They trust the public schools with their children. Those students should be taught that this is the land of opportunity, and that if they work hard they can achieve their goals. They should not be taught that they are oppressed.[40]

Referring to Freire's *Pedagogy of the Oppressed,* Horne makes an implicit claim here regarding the families of Tucson students, and a claim that is not uncommon to liberal discourses of multiculturalism in terms of their second-personal normative content. Namely, the implication is that there is a strict division among Latinas/os within the US Southwest with respect to migration status and Latinas/os ought to be understood in this manner.

To elaborate the relationship between Horne and some versions of contemporary liberal political theory, let us briefly consider here a version of liberal multiculturalism that defends a distinction between native-born and nonnative born Latinas/os in the United States. The view I will analyze is that of Will Kymlicka's, an important figure in contemporary liberal multiculturalism. What is similar between Horne's views about migration status and Kymlicka's is that both normatively endorse the claim that there should be stark distinctions among Latina/o groups in the United States with respect to their relationship to the state. Namely, while their positions differ in many respects and appear to be unlikely bedfellows, both Horne and Kymlicka claim that Mexican Americans who voluntarily come to the country should be expected to adopt the dominant language and culture of that country.

To clarify Kymlicka's position, we can briefly discuss his stance on voluntary Latina/o migrants. In 1995, Kymlicka's book *Multicultural Citizenship: A Liberal Theory of Minority Rights* made a huge impact on contemporary Western liberalism. Its central focus was a set of thorny issues involving special state accommodations for cultural minority groups within the nation-state.[41] He argues that post WWII, many Western nation-states adopted the model of universal human rights, which held that rights should be "assigned to individuals regardless of group membership."[42] This meant that, despite some accommodations made through affirmative action and reparations (which are still largely contested within liberal theory), there cannot be group-specific rights to accommodate cultural or religious differences. Cultural and religious practices are considered part of private life on this view, and thus cannot be endorsed by the state without violating the cultural and religious neutrality of the state.

Yet, as Kymlicka and others have pointed out, a doctrine of universal human rights is "simply unable to resolve some of the most important and controversial questions relating to cultural minorities: which languages should be recognized in the parliaments, bureaucracies, and courts? Should each ethnic minority or national group have publicly funded education in its mother tongue? Should internal boundaries . . . be drawn so that cultural minorities form a majority within a local region? Should governmental powers be devolved from the central level to more local regional levels controlled by particular minorities . . . .should the traditional homelands of indigenous peoples be reserved for their benefit and so protected from encroachment by settlers and resource developers? What are the responsibilities of minorities to integrate . . . " and so on.[43] To address these issues, Kymlicka developed a theoretical apparatus for liberal theorists that he proposed would resolve some of these difficult issues. The proposal would retain a central role for individual autonomy, which he proposed as a core commitment of liberalism.

Kymlicka's version of liberal multiculturalism, then, relies heavily on a distinction between different minority groups within the state, a distinction that corresponds to the distinction that Horne draws in the documents he proposes that called for the termination of the Mexican American Studies Program in Tucson. Kymlicka's distinction is between what he calls *national minorities* and a separate form of cultural minority group that he calls *polyethnic groups*. National minorities are those groups that seek rights to self-government alongside majority cultures. Polyethnic groups, Kymlicka claims, often attempt to become integrated into majority cultures, but also attempt to transform the institutions of the majority culture to better accommodate their own relevant cultural differences. Unlike polyethnic groups, Kymlicka argues, national minorities were involuntarily incorporated into new political jurisdictions, and such groups thereby hold special rights to self-government. Polyethnic groups, he claims, are comprised of immigrant groups that voluntarily migrated into a new national setting. The voluntariness of the patterns of migration, Kymlicka argues, denies self-governing rights to polyethnic groups. However, given the involuntary, and hence, unjust nature of the existence of national minorities, such groups should be granted special rights to self-government within the state. Examples of national minorities, Kymlicka states, are aboriginal groups and the Québécois of Canada, as well as Puerto Ricans and Native Americans in the United States. Kymlicka also considers some Mexican Americans relevant members of national minorities.

The qualification, for Kymlicka, of being considered a national minority is tied to the notion of voluntariness. Whether or not an individual chose to enter into a new national context should thereby dictate the amount of special accommodations that that individual should expect to find within the state. In addition, Kymlicka does defend rights for polyethnic groups to practice their cultural customs in private life, but sees "their distinctiveness [as] manifested primarily in their family lives and in voluntary associations, and is not inconsistent with their institutional integration."[44] Such a distinction—between national minorities and polyethnic groups—remains even within his later work, including his 2007 book *Multicultural Odysseys*, wherein the author distinguishes between "'old minorities, who were settled on their territory prior to it becoming part of a larger independent country, and 'new' minorities, who were admitted to a country as immigrants after it achieved legal independence."[45]

The important point with respect to Mexican Americans for Kymlicka's and Horne's view is that he draws a distinction between "the descendants of Mexicans (Chicanos) living in the south-west when the United States annexed Texas, New Mexico, and California after the Mexican War of 1846–48" and other "Spanish speaking-immigrants recently arrived from Latin America . . . who come to the United States with the intention to stay and become citizens."[46] With respect to normative interpellation, this distinction proposes that subgroups of Latinas/os ought to view themselves as distinct in relation to the state depending on their familial and historical lineages. For example, Mexican Americans who descended from persons who migrated after the 1840s should understand themselves as unable to request accommodation rights from the state, including linguistic rights. One potential hail from this claim could be "you, Mexican Americans, ought to make different claims on the state depending on the manner in which your families came under the juris-diction of the US government." However, as Juliet Hooker has pointed out about such a distinction,

> In the case of Mexican Americans, [according to Kymlicka] it would seem that some Chicanos, those whose ancestors historically resided in the Southwest, might be entitled to greater terms of accommodation of their original culture, whereas more recent, voluntary immigrants would more properly be considered an ethnic group entitled to certain polyethnic rights but not full accommodation. Setting aside the ques-tion of whether the two groups could even be easily distinguished, such an outcome, however unlikely in practice, would clearly lead to significant problems with regard to solidarity. The issue is not simply whether Latinos should be thought of as a single group or as multiple groups and of what kind but, rather, how to conceive of Latino identity itself.[47]

As Hooker notes, for identity and solidarity purposes, there is usually no distinction made among many Mexican Americans between the volun-tariness and involuntariness of those who lived in the United States prior to the annexation of the territory of the now US Southwest and those who migrated afterward. The implication of this critique of Kymlicka's dis-tinction is that the special accommodations that should be granted to national minorities according to Kymlicka's version of multicultural lib-eralism cannot address the rights-based claims developed by Chicanos as a cultural minority in the United States. This is so because the political demands of the Chicano rights movement, for example, were not pref-aced on a view about the native status of Mexicans in the United States prior to the Gladsden Purchase or the Treaty of Guadalupe. Rather, many of the demands came from the systemic disenfranchisement of and dis-crimination against Mexican Americans in the United States, with their demands ranging from claims to national sovereignty, immigration re-form, housing and property rights, to fighting for labor rights for farm-workers and for domestic workers.

Another line of criticism against the distinction between voluntary and involuntary migrants is, as Jorge Gracia points out, that "it is disin-genuous to claim that immigrants subject to political persecution immi-grate voluntarily . . . even those who come to the United States because of economic exigency, one could argue, do not have a choice: starving is not a realistic option."[48] Gracia claims here that the distinction that Horne and Kymlicka propose, which, too, bears roots in a form of nativism (albeit at a more sophisticated level in the work of Kymlicka), ignores important facets of agency that question the relative "voluntariness" of decisions to migrate. We can consider here the ways in which an individ-ual's practical agency is interdependent with others. Both Horne and Kymlicka's claims regarding the norms that should be taken up by voluntary immigrants deny this mutual dependency and instead treat practical agency as something that is divorced from historical, social, and political constraint.

Importantly, Hooker's and Gracia's criticisms makes reference to how Latinas/os understand themselves, and not how Kymlicka's theory proposes that they ought to define themselves. That is, they attempt to create agential discursive space for persons who are potentially affected by policy decisions regarding English-only educational curricula or decreases in state funds for Latina/o students. Both authors propose that the ability to make claims on the state should depend on how one is concretely located within a broad range of normative positions with respect to the history of that state and its treatment of racial and ethnic minorities. Neither Kymlicka nor Horne's respective positions rely on such a non-ideal account of agency. Namely, the conception of choice and voluntariness that functions within each of their respective accounts appears to foreclose the kinds of mutually dependent forms of agency that I defend in this project. The protection of individual rights, on their views, appears to be enough for fair treatment in the United States. Moreover, in both cases, the decision to immigrate to another country is viewed as an autonomous decision, one for which the agent decides independently and is thus willing to take on the full responsibility of her/his/their actions. Both Kymlicka and Horne's model of agency and migration presume a model of independent moral deliberation and one that is stripped of context, which prevents the agent from sharing responsibility with other agents.[49]

In addition to this commonality among Horne and Kymlicka's position, the role that histories of violence and conquest play within their models of civic education is significant. In a recent discussion regarding the question of whether to include polyethnic groups (i.e., "new" immigrant minorities) under the umbrella of national minorities and granting them the same forms of accommodation rights, Kymlicka states: "the logic of liberal multiculturalism does attach importance to facts of history and territory. Across Western democracies, the policies adopted for 'old' homeland minorities across the West differ from those adopted for 'new' immigrant minorities."[50] Thus, we can see from Kymlicka's recent account that history does play an important role in the granting of accommodation rights to cultural minorities.

Unfortunately, for our purposes here, his emphasis on history is attached to territory rights, which does not yet address the question of Mexican Americans in Arizona who do not distinguish between those individuals and families inhabiting US Southwestern territories prior to the annexation of land to the United States and those arriving afterward. As such, whether or not the Tucson Unified School District ought to take on a special obligation to recognize the cultural and historical influences of Mexican Americans in Arizona—as it does for Native Americans—remains unresolved under such a liberal framework. As a state-supported institutional practice, whether MAS should be permitted is a matter of *precisely how* the state should recognize its relationship with Mexico and Mexican-descended peoples within the nation-state. If treated as a voluntary immigrant group—which is how Horne discusses the matter—that is, the parents and grandparents of students in the Mexican American Studies program coming to the United States legally and seeking a "land of opportunity"—the state need not protect certain forms of historical framing. This bears implicit claims such as "it is your responsibility to learn English if you migrated here legally" and the claim that "you, Latinas/os, will be afforded equal opportunity to succeed if you simply identify as individuals and assimilate to Anglo-American cultural norms and values." The conception of voluntariness that both Horne and Kymlicka propose thereby erases the histories of violence and continued forms of economic exploitation that exist between the United States and Mexico. Moreover, the denial of accommodation rights for Mexican Americans, including language rights, effectively attempts to separate people of color in the US Southwest by recognizing the harms committed against Native Americans, for example, but denying and suppressing the harms committed against Mexican Americans. As I point out above via Smith's work, this divisive tactic effectively supports structural white supremacy.

THE LATINO THREAT AND RESPONSES TO THE BANNING OF MAS

Following this form of individualism in Horne's account, returning to the language of A.R.S.15–112, it is clear that Horne's statement that "people are individuals, not exemplars of racial groups" endorses an assimilationist model of identity for Mexican Americans. Horne's later statement: "What is important about people is what they know, what they can do, their ability to appreciate beauty, their character, and not what race into which they were born," proposes that none of these factors—that is, knowledge, ability, taste, and character—are relevantly assessed in terms of group membership within an historically marginalized group. Unlike African Americans and Native Americans, on Horne's view, Mexican Americans have no reason *not* to believe "that this is the land of opportunity, and that if they work hard they can achieve their goals."[51] Although the histories of disenfranchisement and marginalization outlined through the Mexican American Studies program provide a counterhistory to this narrative, Horne treats such narratives as divisive and leading to forms of resentment and anti-white sentiment among students within the TUSD.

Also, the link that Horne draws between the banning of MAS and the recent immigration debates is telling. Primarily, because the focus on immigration presupposes, as does Kymlicka's distinction between polyethnic groups and national minorities, that ethnic solidarity among US

Chicanos is considered destabilizing to the nation because cultural and political representation for Mexican Americans does not currently exist within the state of Arizona (this is what Kymlicka refers to as the threat of an "ethnic revival" in *Multicultural Citizenship*). Kymlicka's blindspot as well as Horne's is that a stark division between immigrant and native-born citizen within many politically mobilized Latina/o communities does not exist, as we can see, for example, in the 1960s with the Chicano Rights Movement.

Along these lines, Leo Chavez has recently argued that expressed fears of the "reconquest" of the US Southwest have lingered throughout the last two centuries, and much anti-Latina/o racism (which includes Mexican American, Central American, and South American ethnic groups) can be attributed to this fear of destabilizing the cultural and political climate of the United States.[52] In Horne's 2010 document titled "Finding by the State Superintendent of Public Instruction of Violation by Tucson Unified School District Pursuant to [Arizona Revised Statute] 15–112 (B)," Horne cites the new Arizona statute that prohibits "courses or classes that . . . 1) Promote the overthrow of the United States Government. 2) Promote resentment toward a race or class of people."[53] Horne's concerns coincide with what Chavez calls the "Latino Threat Narrative." This narrative, Chavez argues, is a series of interwoven themes within US political discourses regarding immigration and national security that construct Latinas/os as criminals, sexually licentious and reproductively irresponsible, recalcitrant to integration within US mainstream culture, and potentially dangerous to national security. As early as the 1920s, undocumented Mexican immigrants were viewed as criminals; however, by the 1970s, this view shifted to include the idea that Mexican immigrants were *invading* the United States.[54] Chavez cites major US national magazines that featured headlines depicting the "out of control behavior" of Mexican immigrants, including pieces from the *US News and World Report, Atlantic Monthly,* as well as *Time Magazine.* Emerging out of this trope was the idea that Mexican Americans were planning a *Recon quista* [reconquest] of the US Southwest. By the 1980s, the theme of reconquest became widespread, with headlines worrying over a "Disappearing Border" and that "Los Angeles is being invaded."[55] Likening this narrative to the Gramscian notion of "common sense"—that is, "the largely unconscious and uncritical way of perceiving the world that is widespread within any given historical epoch—Chavez argues that the Latino Threat Narrative overshadows and homogenizes the lived experiences of Latinas/os in the United States.

Horne's statements regarding the educational material that encourages students to "overthrow the United States government" thus fits within the Latino Threat Narrative. This narrative assumes a third-person, agent-neutral stance that implicitly creates racial norms for Latinas/os in the state. Namely, when heard by Latinas/os, it may target them as potential threats to the stability of the nation, casting them as criminals or enemies of the state. Such implicit hails could be something like "citizens of the United States, you should be concerned about Latinas/os in the United States" or as in the letter to Sheriff Joe Arpaio that I cite at the beginning of this project states, "you, Latinas/os, pose a threat to the well-being of the nation." Much of the recent forms of criminalization of immigrants in Arizona, via SB1070 for example, append criminal charges to violations of civil immigration law. That is, migrants in Arizona who are stopped by local police and who are not carrying alien registration documents can be given a misdemeanor charge and fines up to $1,000 and/or be imprisoned for up to six months. Criticisms of such forms of criminalization are that policies that allow local police officers to question and detain persons who they suspect of being undocumented will encourage racial profiling in the state. Thus, specific sets of racial norms are supported that also encourage law enforcement officers to view persons who appear to be Latina/o as unlawful. This potential hail, "You, officer, should carry out the duties of your job by suspecting persons who appear to be of Mexican and Central American descent to be unlawfully present in the state," thereby creates a normative directive whereby racial discrimination becomes legally sanctioned.

Turning to other second-person implications of Horne's writings, we can also see the impact of Horne's statement on the constitution of specific forms of ethnocentric racial normativity. In the "Testimony by Witnesses" section of Horne's document, he cites an anonymous teacher:

> Impressionable youth in TUSD have literally been reprogrammed to believe that there is a concerted effort on the part of a white power structure to suppress them and relegate them to a second-class existence. This fomented resentment further encourages them to express their dissatisfaction through the iconoclastic behavior we see—the contempt for all authority outside of their ethnic community and their total lack of identification with a political heritage of this country.[56]

Part of what this quotation demonstrates is a third-personal claim about the status of "a political heritage" in the United States that excludes the historical, cultural, and social impact of Latina/os and Chicanas/os. In addition, it renders ethnic solidarity among Latinas/os and Chicanas/os as merely a vehicle of contempt and hate-mongering. However, we can also find indirect forms of second-person vocatives within these declarative utterances. It suggests to students in the TUSD that they themselves are subject to "reprogramming" by the educational curricula of the district, which overshadows any non-public educational means by which students acquire knowledge of the political and social contexts around them. Furthermore, it denies any agency to their decisions and their parents and guardians to choose to participate in the MAS program. Finally, it indirectly tells students of the TUSD that they currently do not bear "a second-class existence," and, rather, it suggests to them that they are already treated with equal recognition and respect within the "political heritage" of the country. This last indirect vocative, perhaps something like, "You, Latina/o and Chicana/o students of the TUSD, are not subject to racism, racial oppression, political disenfranchisement, and marginalization," functions both third-personally and second-personally. It both makes a claim about the racial politics of the United States, as well as addresses students indirectly through the interpellative call that they should not view the racial climate of the United States as one that bears any traces of racism, racial oppression, political disenfranchisement, or marginalization for Latinas/os and Chicanas/os.

Furthermore, this statement bears racial norms for white citizens of the district as well. The implicit first-person plural of the letter, that is, "we, teachers of the district who oppose the program," appears to suggest that the political heritage of the country is not associated with cultural or ethnic group-based distinctions. It thereby diminishes the responsibility of white citizens in the district to be responsible knowers of histories of discrimination against Mexican Americans in the nation. This kind of ignorance and insensitivity to the experiences of people of color stems from the belief that formal equality can provide equal opportunities within the nation. As I state above via Bonilla-Silva's writings, the presumption that moral agents all come from the same social, cultural, and historical backgrounds effectively creates a misleading conception of moral deliberation, and such a view supports structural white supremacy.

In this vein, consider briefly Horne's statements about the parents of Tucson students. He assumes that the parents and guardians of Tucson students will not want to encourage their children to learn about the histories of oppression that affect Mexican Americans in the country. Although Horne relies on this claim to defend his position about the content of MAS, he does not include any testimonial evidence from parents or guardians of students in the program. While Horne's documents contain many direct quotations from teachers, students, and school administrators, they do not cite parents or guardians to support his claim that such speakers would endorse his claims.

Importantly, responses to the banning of MAS such as that of SaveEthnicStudies.org suggest that there is a plurality of forms of uptake regarding the significance of the MAS program. Along these lines, consider the "No history is illegal!" campaign organized by the Network of Teacher Activists. This group of educators responded via a slogan that affirms a third-person declarative. Interestingly, the campaign effectively responded to the implicit hails of the racial speech of Horne et al. While the ban never claimed directly that any specific form of *history* would be considered illegal, resistance to the ban mobilized around that indirect claim. Namely, they asserted that A.R.S. 15–112 made the teaching of Mexico-US political relations and teaching the history of the Chicano rights movement illegal in the state. The campaign organized public teach-ins and shared curricula in an effort to help distribute information in support of the program in Tucson. The campaign's website also focused heavily on testimonial evidence from educators from diverse geopolitical contexts who expressed their support of MAS programs. This method of resistance thereby endorsed a form of pluralism with respect to civic education, and rejected the implicit individualism and erasure of non-Anglo ethnic identities that surfaced through the normative content of the ban.

Other resistance groups also formed following the ban, including, for example, the Arizona Ethnic Studies Network, and MAS received letters and forms of support from such organizations as the Modern Language Association, the Asian/Pacific American Librarians Association, the Black Caucus of the American Library Association, and the National Council of Teachers of English. These diverse forms of uptake thereby indicate that there are a variety of "you"s that are invoked through this ban. Consider another slogan from "No history is illegal!," the phrase "A campaign to save our stories." This phrase utilizes a first-person plural position to defend a variety of marginalized perspectives. Citing Martin Luther King, Jr., the campaign's website also uses King's statement, "Injustice anywhere is a threat to justice everywhere." Thus, the campaign rallies around a shared commitment to including various forms of cultural and historical curricula in public schools. Finally, they conclude "What is happening in Arizona is not only a threat to Mexican American Studies, it is a threat to our right to teach the experiences of all people of color, LGBT people, poor and working people, the undocumented, people with disabilities, and all those who are least powerful in this country."[57] Thus, directly, the campaign states that it is committed to a pluralistic conception of civic education and the importance of differing perspectives and voices within public discourses in the United States.

NOTES

1. Tom Horne, "An Open Letter to the Citizens of Tucson," State of Arizona Department of Education. June 11, (2007): 1. Accessed June 6, 2016. nau.edu/uploadedFiles/Academic/CAL/Philosophy/Forms/An%20Open%20Letter%20to%20 Citizens%20of%20Tucson.pdf

2. Tom Horne, "An Open Letter to the Citizens of Tucson," State of Arizona Department of Education. June 11, (2007): 1. Accessed June 6, 2016. nau.edu/uploadedFiles/Academic/CAL/Philosophy/Forms/An%20Open%20Letter%20to%20 Citizens%20of%20Tucson.pdf.

3. Tom Horne, "An Open Letter to the Citizens of Tucson," State of Arizona Department of Education. June 11, (2007): 1. Accessed June 6, 2016. nau.edu/uploadedFiles/Academic/CAL/Philosophy/Forms/An%20Open%20Letter%20to%20 Citizens%20of%20Tucson.pdf.

4. Tom Horne, "An Open Letter to the Citizens of Tucson," State of Arizona Department of Education. June 11, (2007): 2. Accessed June 6, 2016. nau.edu/

uploadedFiles/Academic/CAL/Philosophy/Forms/An%20Open%20Letter%20to%20
Citizens%20of%20Tucson.pdf.
　　5. Tom Horne, "An Open Letter to the Citizens of Tucson," State of Arizona Department of Education. June 11, (2007): 3. Accessed June 6, 2016. nau.edu/
uploadedFiles/Academic/CAL/Philosophy/Forms/An%20Open%20Letter%20to%20
Citizens%20of%20Tucson.pdf.
　　6. Acosta, et al. v. Huppenthal, et al. (2013): 1.
　　7. Andrea Smith, "Heteropatriarchy and the Three Pillars of White Supremacy," in
The Color of Violence: The INCITE! Anthology (Cambridge: South End Press, 2006).
　　8. Andrea Smith, "Heteropatriarchy and the Three Pillars of White Supremacy," in
The Color of Violence: The INCITE! Anthology, edited by INCITE! Women of Color
Against Violence. (Cambridge: South End Press, 2006), 67–69.
　　9. Andrea Smith, "Heteropatriarchy and the Three Pillars of White Supremacy," in
The Color of Violence: The INCITE! Anthology, edited by INCITE! Women of Color
Against Violence. (Cambridge: South End Press, 2006), 68.
　　10. Andrea Smith, "Heteropatriarchy and the Three Pillars of White Supremacy," in
The Color of Violence: The INCITE! Anthology, edited by INCITE! Women of Color
Against Violence. (Cambridge: South End Press, 2006), 67–69.
　　11. Eduardo Bonilla-Silva, *White Supremacy and Racism in the Post-Civil Rights Era*
(Boulder: Lynne Rienner Publishers, 2001), 44.
　　12. Andrea Smith, "Indigeneity, Settler Colonialism, White Supremacy," *Global Dialogue* 12 no. 2 (2010): 3.
　　13. Samuel Huntington, "The Hispanic Challenge," *Foreign Policy* 14 no. 12 (2004):
30–45.
　　14. Linda Alcoff "Comparative Race, Comparative Racism," in *Race or Ethnicity?:
On Black and Latino Identity* (Ithaca: Cornell University Press, 2007), 176.
　　15. Linda Alcoff "Comparative Race, Comparative Racism," in *Race or Ethnicity?:
On Black and Latino Identity* (Ithaca: Cornell University Press, 2007).
　　16. John Austin, *Philosophical Papers* (New York: Oxford University Press, 1979), 250.
　　17. John Austin, *Philosophical Papers* (New York: Oxford University Press, 1979),
250–251.
　　18. René Galindo "The Nativistic Legacy of the Americanization Era in the Education of Mexican Immigrant Students," *Educational Studies* 47, no. 4 (2011): 333. 323–346.
　　19. René Galindo "The Nativistic Legacy of the Americanization Era in the Education of Mexican Immigrant Students," *Educational Studies* 47, no. 4 (2011): 323–346.
　　20. René Galindo "The Nativistic Legacy of the Americanization Era in the Education of Mexican Immigrant Students," *Educational Studies* 47, no. 4 (2011): 339.
　　21. Conrado Gómez and Saldavor Gabaldón, "A Legacy of Memory: The Debate
over Ethnic Studies in Arizona Public Schools," *Aztlán: A Journal of Chicano Studies* 38,
no. 2 (2013): 166.
　　22. Gloria Anzaldúa *Borderlands/La frontera: The New Mestiza* (San Francisco: Aunt
Lute Books, 1999), 75.
　　23. Gloria Anzaldúa *Borderlands/La frontera: The New Mestiza* (San Francisco: Aunt
Lute Books, 1999), 144–167.
　　24. Public Law, "Native American Languages Act," October 30 (1990): 4.
　　25. Conrado Gómez, Conrado and Saldavor Gabaldón, "A Legacy of Memory: The
Debate over Ethnic Studies in Arizona Public Schools" *Aztlán: A Journal of Chicano
Studies* 38, no. 2(2013):168.
　　26. Conrado Gómez, Conrado and Saldavor Gabaldón, "A Legacy of Memory: The
Debate over Ethnic Studies in Arizona Public Schools" *Aztlán: A Journal of Chicano
Studies* 38, no. 2 (2013): 166.
　　27. Conrado Gómez, Conrado and Saldavor Gabaldón, "A Legacy of Memory: The
Debate over Ethnic Studies in Arizona Public Schools" *Aztlán: A Journal of Chicano
Studies* 38, no. 2 (2013): 169.
　　28. Arizona Proposition 203, "English Language Education for Children in Public
Schools," (2000).

29. Conrado Gómez, Conrado and Saldavor Gabaldón, "A Legacy of Memory: The Debate over Ethnic Studies in Arizona Public Schools" *Aztlán: A Journal of Chicano Studies* 38, no. 2 (2013): 170.

30. Emphasis added. Woodrow Wilson, "Address to Naturalized Citizens at Convention Hall," Philadelphia, May 10, 1915" *The American Presidency Project*. Accessed June 6, 2016. www.presidency.ucsb.edu/ws/?pid=65388.

31. Tom Horne, "An Open Letter to the Citizens of Tucson," State of Arizona Department of Education. June 11, (2007): 1. Accessed June 6, 2016. nau.edu/uploadedFiles/Academic/CAL/Philosophy/Forms/An%20Open%20Letter%20to%20Citizens%20of%20Tucson.pdf.

32. Eduardo Bonilla-Silva, "'This Is a White Country': The Racial Ideology of the Western Nations of the World-System." Sociological Inquiry 70, no. 2 (2000): 189.

33. Eduardo Bonilla-Silva, "'This Is a White Country': The Racial Ideology of the Western Nations of the World-System." Sociological Inquiry 70, no. 2 (2000): 190.

34. Nakayama, Thomas and Lisa Peñaloza. "Madonna T/races: Music Videos through the Prism of Color," in *The Madonna Connection: Representational Politics, Subcultural Identities and Cultural Theory* (Boulder: Westview Press, 1993), 54.

35. Tom Horne, "An Open Letter to the Citizens of Tucson," State of Arizona Department of Education. June 11, (2007): 1. Accessed June 6, 2016. nau.edu/uploadedFiles/Academic/CAL/Philosophy/Forms/An%20Open%20Letter%20to%20Citizens%20of%20Tucson.pdf.

36. Tom Horne, "An Open Letter to the Citizens of Tucson," State of Arizona Department of Education. June 11, (2007): 1. Accessed June 6, 2016. nau.edu/uploadedFiles/Academic/CAL/Philosophy/Forms/An%20Open%20Letter%20to%20Citizens%20of%20Tucson.pdf.

37. Tom Horne, "An Open Letter to the Citizens of Tucson," State of Arizona Department of Education. June 11, (2007): 2. Accessed June 6, 2016. nau.edu/uploadedFiles/Academic/CAL/Philosophy/Forms/An%20Open%20Letter%20to%20Citizens%20of%20Tucson.pdf.

38. Nolan Cabrera, Jeffrey Milem and Ronald Marx, "An Empirical Analysis of the Effects of Mexican American Studies Participation on Student Achievement within Tucson Unified School District," *University of Arizona College of Education*, June 20, (2012): 7. Accessed June 6, 2016. www.coe.arizona.edu/sites/default/files/MAS_report_2012_0.pdf.

39. Helen Longino, *Science as Social Knowledge: Values and Objectivity in Scientific Inquiry* (Princeton: Princeton University Press, 1990), 76.

40. Tom Horne, "An Open Letter to the Citizens of Tucson," State of Arizona Department of Education. June 11, (2007): 2. Accessed June 6, 2016. nau.edu/uploadedFiles/Academic/CAL/Philosophy/Forms/An%20Open%20Letter%20to%20Citizens%20of%20Tucson.pdf.

41. Importantly, Kymlicka does not discuss racial minorities such as African Americans, a point which is worthy of its own criticism, but for which I do not have the space here.

42. Will Kymlicka, *Multicultural Citizenship* (New York: Oxford University Press, 1995), 6.

43. Will Kymlicka, *Multicultural Citizenship* (New York: Oxford University Press, 1995), 4–5.

44. Will Kymlicka, *Multicultural Citizenship* (New York: Oxford University Press, 1995), 14.

45. Will Kymlicka, *Multicultural Odysseys: Navigating the New International Politics of Diversity* (New York: Oxford University Press, 2007), 77.

46. Will Kymlicka, *Multicultural Citizenship* (New York: Oxford University Press, 1995), 16.

47. Juliet Hooker, *Race and the Politics of Solidarity* (New York: Oxford University Press, 2009), 79.

48. Jorge Gracia, *Latinos in America: Philosophy and Social Identity* (Malden: Wiley-Blackwell, 2008), 114.
49. Such other relevant agents and factors might include employers, families, friends, state representatives, educational resources, threats of violence, dire poverty, and so on.
50. Will Kymlicka, *Multicultural Odysseys: Navigating the New International Politics of Diversity* (New York: Oxford University Press, 2007), 226.
51. Tom Horne, "An Open Letter to the Citizens of Tucson," State of Arizona Department of Education. June 11, (2007): 2. Accessed June 6, 2016. nau.edu/uploadedFiles/Academic/CAL/Philosophy/Forms/An%20Open%20Letter%20to%20Citizens%20of%20Tucson.pdf.
52. Leo Chavez, *The Latino Threat: Constructing Immigrants, Citizens, and the Nation* (Stanford: Stanford University Press, 2013).
53. Tom Horne, "An Open Letter to the Citizens of Tucson," State of Arizona Department of Education. June 11, (2007): 2. Accessed June 6, 2016. nau.edu/uploadedFiles/Academic/CAL/Philosophy/Forms/An%20Open%20Letter%20to%20Citizens%20of%20Tucson.pdf.
54. Leo Chavez, *The Latino Threat: Constructing Immigrants, Citizens, and the Nation* (Stanford: Stanford University Press, 2013), 26.
55. Leo Chavez, *The Latino Threat: Constructing Immigrants, Citizens, and the Nation* (Stanford: Stanford University Press, 2013), 29–30.
56. Tom Horne, "An Open Letter to the Citizens of Tucson," State of Arizona Department of Education. June 11, (2007): 5. Accessed June 6, 2016. nau.edu/uploadedFiles/Academic/CAL/Philosophy/Forms/An%20Open%20Letter%20to%20Citizens%20of%20Tucson.pdf.
57. Network of Teacher Activist Groups, "No History Is Illegal," Network of Teacher Activist Groups. Accessed October 2, 2014. www.teacheractivistgroups.org/tucson/.

BIBLIOGRAPHY

Acosta, V. Huppenthal, et al. 2013. See United States District Court District of Arizona Memorandum Order online at: www.azag.gov/sites/default/files/Acosta%20Dkt%20227.pdf.
Alcoff, Linda Martín. "Comparative Race, Comparative Racism." In *Race or Ethnicity?: On Black and Latino Identity*. Edited by Jorge J.E. Gracia. Ithaca: Cornell University Press, 2007.
Anzaldúa, Gloria. *Borderlands/La frontera: The New Mestiza*. San Francisco: Aunt Lute Books, 1999.
Arizona Proposition 203. "English Language Education for Children in Public Schools." 2000.
Austin, J. L. *Philosophical Papers*. Oxford University Press, 1979.
Bonilla-Silva, Eduardo. "'This Is a White Country': The Racial Ideology of the Western Nations of the World-System." Sociological Inquiry 70, no. 2 (2000): 188–214.
———. "White Supremacy and Racism in the Post-Civil Rights Era. Boulder: Lynne Rienner Publishers, 2001.
Cabrera, Nolan L., Jeffrey F. Milem, and Ronald W. Marx. "An Empirical Analysis of the Effects of Mexican American Studies Participation on Student Achievement within Tucson Unified School District. University of Arizona College of Education, June 20, 2012. Accessed June 6, 2016. www.coe.arizona.edu/sites/default/files/MAS_report_2012_0.pdf.
Chavez, Leo. *The Latino Threat: Constructing Immigrants, Citizens, and the Nation*. Stanford: Stanford University Press, 2013.
Galindo, René. "The Nativistic Legacy of the Americanization Era in the Education of Mexican Immigrant Students." *Educational Studies* 47, no. 4 (2011): 323–346.

Gómez, Conrado L., and Saldavor A. Gabaldón. "A Legacy of Memory: The Debate over Ethnic Studies in Arizona Public Schools." *Aztlán: A Journal of Chicano Studies* 38, no. 2 (2013): 163–74.

Gracia, Jorge J. E. *Latinos in America: Philosophy and Social Identity*. Malden: Wiley-Blackwell, 2008.

Hooker, Juliet. *Race and the Politics of Solidarity*. New York: Oxford University Press, 2009.

Horne, Tom. "An Open Letter to the Citizens of Tucson." State of Arizona Department of Education. June 11, 2007. Accessed June 6, 2016. nau.edu/uploadedFiles/Academic/CAL/Philosophy/Forms/An%20Open%20Letter%20to%20Citizens%20of%20Tucson.pdf

———. "Finding by the State Superintendent of Public Instruction of Violation by Tucson Unified School District Pursuant to Arizona Revised Statute 15–112 (B)." TUSD Ethnic Studies Findings. December 30, 2010. Accessed June 6, 2016. www.azag.gov/sites/default/files/sites/all/docs/TUSD_Ethnic_Studies_Findings.pdf

Huntington, Samuel P. "The Hispanic Challenge." *Foreign Policy* 1412 (2004): 30–45.

Kymlicka, Will. *Multicultural Citizenship*. New York: Oxford University Press, 1995.

———. *Multicultural Odysseys: Navigating the New International Politics of Diversity*. New York: Oxford University Press, 2007.

Nakayama, Thomas, and Lisa Peñaloza. "Madonna T/races: Music Videos through the Prism of Color." In *The Madonna Connection: Representational Politics, Subcultural Identities and Cultural Theory*. Edited by Cathy Schwichtenberg: 39–55. Boulder: Westview Press, 1993.

Network of Teacher Activist Groups. No History Is Illegal. Network of Teacher Activist Groups. Accessed October 2, 2014. www.teacheractivistgroups.org/tucson/.

Public Law 101–477. "Native American Languages Act." October 30, 1990.

Smith, Andrea. "Heteropatriarchy and the Three Pillars of White Supremacy." In *The Color of Violence: The INCITE! Anthology*. Edited by INCITE! Women of Color Against Violence. Cambridge: South End Press, 2006.

———. "Indigeneity, Settler Colonialism, White Supremacy." *Global Dialogue* 12(2): 2010.

Wilson, Woodrow. "Address to Naturalized Citizens at Convention Hall, Philadelphia, May 10, 1915" The American Presidency Project. Accessed June 6, 2016. www.presidency.ucsb.edu/ws/?pid=65388.

TWELVE

Ayotzinapa

An Attack Against Latin American Philosophy

Amy Reed-Sandoval

In the midst of the extensive news coverage of the Ayotzinapa tragedy there has been at least some reference to the political activism of the forty-three disappeared students of the Raúl Isidro Burgos *escuela normal*, or normal school. A normal school, in Mexico, is one in which young adults study to become accredited K-12 public school teachers in Mexico. Normal schools are not, strictly speaking, universities, but they are popular spaces of university-level learning. Many people outside of Mexico, including within the United States, who have followed this story are aware that prior to being disappeared, the forty-three students were *en route* to a protest that irritated some important figures in the Mexican government. Less well-known, however, are the philosophical dimensions of this and other political activities the forty-three *normalistas* (or normal school students), and of how these philosophical dimensions are connected to a broader philosophical history and ideology of Mexican normal schools. In this chapter I aim to explore these issues in order to argue that the Aytozinapa tragedy is, and has been, an attack against normal school philosophizing and Latin American philosophy itself.[1]

I should clarify from the outset that in arguing that the Ayotzinapa tragedy is, and has been, an attack against Latin American philosophy, I absolutely do not wish to diminish what are clearly some of the cruelest and most horrible aspects of this tragedy. Ayotzinapa has been, most importantly and saliently, a tremendous and disgusting violation of human rights. This raises the question: what can be gained from understanding the Ayotzinapa tragedy in the manner I am proposing? If we already understand the tragedy in terms of murders, kidnappings, and other physically violent acts, and also as a violation of the freedom of expression of the forty-three disappeared students, why bother to think of Ayotzinapa as an attack against Latin American philosophy?

The first reason for which I consider this exploration to be important—a reason that I shall soon "unpack" in greater detail—is that it can help honor with greater detail and understanding the intellectual contributions of these forty-three students. I believe that sometimes, when society celebrates "activists" (as it often ought to) it ignores and simplifies their philosophical contributions. Activists, as many are aware, often get represented in the mass media like mere "parts of a machine," and not as philosophically complex and interesting actors.[2] Therefore, in exploring the Ayotzinapa tragedy as an attack against Latin American philosophy, I want to articulate conceptual resources for humanizing and thus respecting the normal school victims themselves. The second reason for which I consider this exploration worthwhile is that Latin American philosophy continues to be a marginalized philosophical subfield (including in the context of some universities in Latin America). Thus, if my argument is successful, we should consider the Ayotzinapa tragedy to be a threat to an already-marginalized philosophical tradition—a tradition that, apart from being intrinsically philosophically valuable, also serves as a vehicle for activism and social change.

My argument is organized as follows. I begin by defining, at least in broad strokes, what I mean by Latin American philosophy. I then move on to explore the philosophical history of Mexican *escuelas normales*. My goal is to argue that Mexican normal schools have historically been, and continue to be, "philosophical spaces" in which Latin American philosophy has flourished. Then, I argue, partly by way of an "expressivist argument," that Ayotzinapa was and continues to be an attack against Latin American philosophy. Not only were forty-three young philosophers violently disappeared through Ayotzinapa, the tragedy also sends a message that marginalized Others engaged in Latin American philosophical methodology are vulnerable. And finally, I discuss why I believe it is useful to think about Ayotzinapa (at least in part) as I am advocating.

Prior to beginning, allow me to make a few notes about some terminology I shall employ. First, I shall use the term "normal schools" and "*escuelas normales*" interchangeably (as they mean the same thing, though one term is in English and the other is in Spanish). Second, I will also use the terms "normal school students" and "normalistas" interchangeably for the same reasons. Finally, when I use the term "Ayotzinapa," I am referring not to the town of Ayotzinapa, but to the infamous tragedy itself. In this sense, I am tracking current, popular usage of the term in contemporary political discourse.

DEFINING LATIN AMERICAN PHILOSOPHY

Let me begin by turning my attention to an important question to which I will definitely not be able to respond satisfactorily: namely, "what is Latin American philosophy?" In fact, this metaphilosophical question has been a very important part of Latin American philosophy itself.[3] Although a number of different answers to this question have been provided, I shall focus here on just two different possible definitions of this broad area of thought.

First, we might define Latin American philosophy as any philosophical work to have been produced within the geographical space that is Latin America. This definition is, in many respects, inclusive and intuitive. However, it also raises questions and is vulnerable to objections. For instance, can a philosophical work "count" as "Latin American philosophy" if it is produced outside of Latin America? It would be bizarre to claim that the work of, say, a Peruvian philosopher ceases to "count" as Latin American philosophy should the philosopher choose to spend a few years writing and publishing philosophy in the United States or France. On the other hand, one might wonder whether philosophical works produced within the geographical spaces that is Latin America that do explicitly engage philosophical works produced by Latin Americans and Latina/os should "count" as Latin American philosophy. My intention is certainly not to resolve this complicated debate; rather, it is merely to signal that this definition of Latin American philosophy— though inclusive and intuitive in many respects— is nevertheless vulnerable to objections and criticisms.

A second possible conception of Latin American philosophy suggests that it involves philosophical engagement with a somewhat precise philosophical tradition. According to this understanding, Latin American philosophy is noteworthy, in part, for its philosophical concern for questions of Latin American identity, and also for its emphasis on engaging the perspectives of marginalized "Others." Of course, the philosophy, pedagogy, and theology of liberation have played an important role in the development of this tradition.[4] This conception seems to improve upon the first in that it is not limited to work produced in the geographical space of Latin America, and in that it requires some form of engagement with the philosophical works of Latin American and Latina/o philosophers.

However, this definition also raises questions. For example, is it really fair *not* to "count" as Latin American philosophy those philosophical works that are, in fact, produced by Latin Americans and Latina/os but that do not engage with works produced by other Latin Americans and Latina/os? Shouldn't philosophers located in Latin America "just philosophize" about life's most important questions without having to adhere explicitly to the philosophical precedent of an established canonical figure?[5] With these thoughts in mind, one might argue that this second conception of Latin American philosophy is also problematically exclusionary in nature.

In fact, I am not going to select a particular definition of Latin American philosophy; it is beyond the burden of this chapter to engage the robust literature on this matter, and as we have seen, even two particularly straightforward and intuitive conceptions feature both merits and disadvantages. I am going to argue, however, that the Ayotzinapa tragedy has been, and continues to be, an attack against Latin American philosophy under both conceptions of such philosophy that I identified. Ayotzinapa, I shall argue, represents an attack against philosophical work that has been produced within the geographical space that is Latin America (conception one), and also against a "philosophical tradition" that is concerned with Latin American identity, and with engagement with the philosophical perspectives of marginalized "others" (conception two). With this in mind, I shall now argue that Mexican *escuelas normales* are, in fact, philosophical spaces where Latin American philosophy has flourished.

A PHILOSOPHICAL HISTORY OF MEXICAN *ESCUELAS NORMALES*

Let us review what we already know about the most notorious tragedy to have occurred involving normal school students in Mexico: on September 26, 2014, in Iguala, Guerrero, forty-three students of the Raúl Isidro Burgos normal school in Ayotzinapa were disappeared. The students of this *escuela normal* have been linked in the mass media to militant Marxist activity—particularly, but not exclusively, in the form of protests. We also know that on the day of the forced disappearances, the students were at a political protest in Iguala. That same day, a conference had been organized by the Igualan mayor's wife, who had her own political ambitions. Stated very broadly, the *estudiantes normalistas* were protesting against discriminatory practices on the part of the Mexican government.

Those unfamiliar with Mexican *escuelas normales* might regard this as an exceptional and horrific case of a random group of student activists being targeted for their militant activity. It is important to note, however, that the majority of normal schools in Mexico have a reputation for progressive political activism that often opposes actions on the part of the Mexican government. Students who attend *escuelas normales* tend to be working class, and in the south of Mexico (where the state of Guerrero is located), many normal school students are indigenous and/or Afro-Mexican. While these facts are common knowledge in Mexico, there has not yet been an extended analysis of Mexican normal schools as philosophical spaces. However, a short historical overview of the *escuelas normales* of Mexico will demonstrate that this is precisely what they are.

First, note that the history—philosophical and otherwise—of these schools begins in 1921, the year that the Mexican Revolution officially ended. At that time, various *escuelas normales* were founded, in part, by the famous Mexican philosopher José Vasconcelos.[6] They were constructed primarily in poor and rural areas of Mexico. Vasconcelos and other founders of the *escuelas normales* saw in these schools an opportunity to generate community leaders all over Mexico. Vasconcelos also conceived of these schools as a means for solidifying the *Raza Cósmica*, or cosmic race, in Mexico.[7] As many are aware, Vasconcelos believed that Mexican racial identity can be described in terms of a cosmic race or a "fifth race," that is, in essence, a "blend" of the different races of the world. In his controversial work, Vasconcelos regarded this as a positive aspect of Mexican racial identity—in part because he believed that the conscientious development of the Raza Cósmica would eventually serve to counteract Anglo-American political and philosophical hegemony.

Vasconcelos' book *La Raza Cósmica* is, of course, an extremely prominent philosophical text in the Latin American philosophical tradition. However, the important connection between this book and the early founding of Mexican normal schools is somewhat less well-known. I have drawn out this connection in order to note that Mexican *escuelas normales* were connected to Latin American philosophy from the moment of their very founding.

There are additional ways in which Vasconcelos and philosophical ideas shaped *escuelas normales*. In fact, he influenced greatly the very pedagogical orientation of these schools. Vasconcelos argued that aesthetics and artistic creation should figure prominently in normal school education, and he therefore took steps to incorporate his "aesthetic monism" into the day-to-day practices of normal school teachers' pedagogy.[8] According to Vasconcelos' aesthetic monism (in broad strokes, as helpfully articulated by Eric Chávez) "without emotions . . . abstract reality as it is presented by science and logic can never be comprehended and unified solely by the human intellect."[9] Instead, Vasconcelos argued, "human intellect, human emotions, and all human senses have to work together in order for humans to achieve a true knowledge of reality."[10] Importantly, Vasconcelos believed that the cosmic race—or, as he sometimes called it, the Mexican race—possesses an intimate connection to the sorts of aesthetic experiences that underlie and unify all human knowledge. We can see then, that the philosophy of Vasconcelos, in terms of his theory of the cosmic race, and his theory of aesthetic monism, have played a fundamental role in the founding and vision of Mexican *escuelas normales*.

As many are aware, Vasconcelos' Raza Cósmica project is controversial for a variety of reasons. For instance, Vasconcelos ignored (intentionally or unintentionally) important distinctions between ethnoracial groups in Mexico. The harms that have occurred against many indigenous and Afro-Latino groups in Latin America as the result of an uncritical and politically prominent "mestizo consciousness" in Latin America have been widely noted in the social sciences. However, the philosophical milieu of Mexican normal schools is not limited a politics and ideology of *mestizaje*. In fact, Mexican normal schools have also been spaces in which indigenous philosophies of what is now Mexico have been discussed, articulated, and developed.

For example, as explored in detail by Oaxacan anthropologist Alejandra Aquino Moreschi, toward the end of the 1970s Mexico experienced what has been called an "indigenous emergence." Moreschi explains that "there appeared in Mexico the first Mexican state-independent, identity-based indigenous social movements and organizations. The surge of these first self-defined "Indian" or "indigenous" social movements in Mexico [in this decade] marked the inauguration of what some experts and Mexican indigenous rights activists have called the "indigenous awakening" or the "indigenous emergence," or the "Indian return" or the "fourth wave of indigenous mobilizations." [11]

This so-called "indigenous emergence," as it were, was very prominent in Oaxaca (particularly in the Sierra Juárez). And, importantly, this movement was itself very philosophical.

Some of the most important conceptual work of the "indigenous emergence" was the development of the political concept of Oaxacan autonomy—a political autonomy inspired and informed by traditional Oaxacan indigenous (and particularly Zapotec) concepts like an interpretation of *usos y costumbres*, *guelagetza*, *tequio*, and *cooperación*. As explained by a prominent Oaxacan indigenous activist of the "indigenous emergence," "in time we understood that autonomy was not merely a political instrument, but also a life project, a way of being . . . a form of constructing a new pact between the state of Mexico and indigenous communities—one that would guarantee to us direct access to our collective and individual rights." [12]

So, what does this clearly philosophical "indigenous emergence" that transpired in Oaxaca the 1970s and 1980s have to do with Mexican normal schools? It is important to note, as does Aquino Moreschi, that Mexican normal schools were spaces in which indigenous Oaxacans from many parts of Oaxaca came together to articulate a unique pan-Oaxacan political philosophy—a Oaxacan conception of political autonomy—based upon traditional Oaxacan philosophical notions. For many rural Oaxacans, attending a normal school in Oaxaca City was one of the only affordable options for post-high school study. Upon arriving at a popular *escuela normal* in Oaxaca's capital city, indigenous Oaxacans from across the state of Oaxaca entered into dialogue about the ways in which Oaxacan indigenous ideas could be translated into a political philosophy of indigenous survivance in Mexico. Oaxacan normal schools rapidly became spaces of philosophical output and protest.

Thus far, we have seen that there are three senses in which Mexican *escuelas normales* have constituted philosophical spaces. First, they were founded in 1921 by Mexican philosopher José Vasconcelos as part of his efforts to promote the development of a Raza Cósmica that would eventually counteract Anglo-American hegemony. In addition, the pedagogical orientation of the first *escuelas normales* was strongly influenced by Vasconcelos' aesthetic monism. Third, we saw that in the context of Oaxaca's "indigenous emergence" of the 1970s and 1980s, the *escuelas normales* were also spaces in which Oaxacan indigenous philosophies were called upon to generate a political philosophy of indigenous survivance.

Moving on, we should also note, as has been observed in the limited *philosophical* attention that the mass media in Mexico, the United States, and elsewhere has paid to the Ayotzinapa tragedy, that Mexican normal schools have, indeed, been influenced significantly by Marxist philosophy. In particular, *escuelas normales* have been and continue to be spaces where the works of important figures of the established Latin American Marxist tradition are studied. Students in the *escuelas normales*—including students in the Ayotzinapa normal school in question—read figures such as José Carlos Mariátegui, Emilio Frugoni, and Adolfo Sánchez Vázquez, and then put this theory into practice through political activism in a true spirit of philosophical praxis.[13] And, finally, it is important for us to reflect upon the fact that *escuelas normales*—understood, now, as places where philosophy is read and articulated and developed and put into practice—are spaces in which marginalized "Others" participate in significant, creative philosophical exchanges. As mentioned previously, many students of Mexican *escuelas normales* are working class and of indigenous and/or Afro-Mexican descent. Thus, Mexican *escuelas normales*, in offering such a philosophical space to marginalized "Others," accord with Latin American liberation theology, pedagogy, and philosophy.

For all of these reasons, I submit that Mexican normal schools are, and historically have been, philosophical spaces. That is, they are spaces in which philosophy is read, debated, articulated, developed, exchanged, questioned, understood, written down, presented, and put into practice for liberatory purposes. With this in mind, I turn to the following question are they also spaces in which Latin American philosophy flourishes? Yes, indeed they are, on both of the conceptions of Latin American philosophy identified at the outset.

First of all, Mexican *escuelas normales* are spaces in which philosophy is produced within the geographical boundaries of Latin America. And second, Mexican *escuelas normales* are spaces in which young philosophers engage with canonical and otherwise important works (expressed in written and verbal form) of the Latin American philosophical tradition—including those of José Vasconcelos, Mariátegui, and Sánchez Vázquez, and also prominent elements of Oaxacan indigenous (particularly Zapotec) traditions.

The forty-three disappeared students of the Raúl Isidro Burgos normal school in Ayotzinapa, as well as the other students who continue to study in that school, participated in this normal school tradition of engaging, producing, learning about, and putting into practice Latin American philosophies. On the day of their disappearance, they were attempting to participate in precisely the sort of philosophical praxis that tends to be identified as characteristic of this philosophical tradition. Is it correct to assume, then, that Ayotzinapa was, among other things, and attack against Latin American philosophy itself? In the next section I argue that it is.

AYTOZINAPA AS AN ATTACK
AGAINST LATIN AMERICAN PHILOSOPHY

How might we understand Aytozinapa as an attack against Latin American philosophy? To address this question we must first consider what it means to "attack" a philosophical tradition. In the context of Anglo-American analytic philosophy, the usage of war metaphors is common when describing acts of critical engagement of others' philosophical works. One frequently hears statements such as "I *attacked* your second premise," or "her argument was *defeated*," or "his entire project was *destroyed*." Allow me to clarify that when I say that Ayotzinapa can be understood, at least in part, as an attack against Latin American philosophy, I am not employing the term "attack" in this particular sense.

Rather, I mean to say that a philosophical tradition may be "attacked" when it is publicly undermined: either explicitly, deliberately and/or physically, or less explicitly, as a result of widespread disrespect toward and disregard of it. For example, indigenous knowledge systems were very explicitly and violently attacked in the early colonial period. Today, when violent, forced religious and philosophical conversations of indigenous peoples are not so common, indigenous knowledge continues to be "attacked" through widespread disrespect and disregard.

Ayotzinapa, I argue, was and continues to be an attack against Latin American philosophy in both of these senses. On the one hand, the students of Ayotzinapa, as Latin American philosophers (broadly understood) were physically attacked while engaging in the sort of philosophical praxis that is characteristic of the Latin American philosophical tradition. Thus, Ayotzinapa was *literally* a violent attack against Latin American philosophers, and *literally* an act of physical suppression of Latin American philosophical praxis in action.

On the other hand, however, Ayotzinapa also represents an attack against Latin American philosophy in the second, somewhat subtler way—in that it also constitutes disrespect and disregard (albeit less explicit) toward this philosophical tradition. Note that it is not clear, and it is in fact unlikely, that those who are responsible for the disappearances of the forty-three students were necessarily *thinking about* Latin American philosophy when they committed the atrocities in question. Furthermore, no one ever made an explicit statement about Latin American philosophy over the course of the development of the tragedy. In addition, I am also not suggesting that the forty-three disappeared students necessarily felt a personal sense of identification with the Latin American philosophical tradition *as such* (though I acknowledge that this is certainly a possibility). And yet, I submit that the Ayotzinapa tragedy nevertheless makes a statement about Latin American philosophy in the absence of any specific references toward Latin American philosophy.

Here, I am thinking in terms of an "expressivist" argument of the sort that is often made in the contexts of medical ethics and, in particular, disability studies.[14] In employing an "expressivist argument" I am maintaining that a certain social practice, occurrence, or event can have a damaging effect on a social group, even in the participants in the practice or occurrence or event were not intending, or even considering, the damaging effect in question. A prominent example of an expressivist argument is that which is made by some disability rights activists to the effect that when pre-natal testing is performed to determine if one's future baby will be born with a disability—with the understanding that one's embryo or fetus will be aborted if it is determined that the future baby will have a disability—this sends the message that the life of a person with a disability is not worth living. According to this version of the expressivist argument, this holds even if the people who get pre-natal testing did not intend this particular message.

Another illustration of the expressivist argument that sometimes gets employed is that of a person who hangs up a flag bearing a swastika merely because she likes the design. Let us imagine a person who, for whatever reason, is completely unaware of the cruelty and the history of hatred, racism, and murder that the swastika represents. According to the expressivist argument, when this person hangs a swastika flag outside of her home she is still sending out a message of hatred, racism, and cruelty even if she did not intend that message.

With this general sketch of the expressivist argument in mind, let us return to the Ayotzinapa tragedy. I have acknowledged that the primary participants in the tragedy, so to speak (that is, both the victims and the aggressors), may not have been thinking about Latin American philosophy before and during the violent tragedy in question. Furthermore, and as such, those at fault for the disappearances may not have intended to send out a message about Latin American philosophy as such through their reprehensible actions. And as I mentioned previously, Latin American philosophy as such has not, thus far, been connected explicitly to the Ayotzinapa tragedy itself. It may seem, then, that even though the Ayotzinapa tragedy was a violent attack against Latin American philosophical actors (and thus an attack against Latin American philosophy in the first sense), it is not an attack against Latin American philosophy in the second sense of constituting widespread disrespect and disregard toward this philosophical tradition.

However, this argument works only if we fail to recognize that Mexican normal schools are, in fact, philosophical spaces in which Latin American philosophy has historically flourished, and in which it continues to be produced. But we have seen that these *escuelas normales* are, indeed, spaces of Latin American philosophy in at least two senses. Not only are they spaces of higher learning in the geographical space that is Latin America, they are also spaces in which young philosophers do work that engages and responds to works and ideas that are situated in the recognized Latin American "philosophical tradition." Even though many citizens of Mexico may not be familiar with the specific philosophical history of *escuelas normales* (i.e., their connection with the work of Vasconcelos, etc.), these schools are widely regarded as spaces in which politically progressive philosophies and strategies of praxis are both articulated and put into praxis. On these grounds, I submit that the Ayotzinapa tragedy—the forced disappearance of forty-three normal students—expressed an attack against Latin American philosophy independently of the beliefs of any of the "actors" in question.

Ayotzinapa was and is an attack against Latin American philosophy, first of all, because forty-three Latin American philosophers were disappeared and thus silenced over the course of this tragedy. However, Ayotzinapa did far more than violently silence the forty-three students in question. The violence also threatens Mexican philosophers in highly marginalized positions who dare to do philosophy in accordance with Latin American philosophical ideas and methodologies, which are largely praxis-oriented, frequently Marxist, and developed from the perspective of marginalized Others in Latin America who confront local political corruption and Anglo-American/Western hegemony in the realms of philosophy, history, and politics. So it does not matter that the "primary actors" in the tragedy may not have actively thinking about Latin American philosophy as such. Ayotzinapa was, and continues to be, an attack against this philosophy.

Prior to concluding this chapter, allow me to consider an objection. One might insist that the violence against the forty-three disappeared students was not an attack against Latin American philosophy, but rather, an attack against their bodily integrity and freedom of expression as expressed in a protest against prominent political figures in Guerrero. Furthermore, one might argue that even if the forty-three disappeared students were passionately committed to Latin American philosophy per se, it does not follow that this commitment was itself the subject of the attack.

In response, I wish to reiterate that I, of course, acknowledge that the Ayotzinapa tragedy was, first and foremost, physically violent and obscenely cruel independently of the issues I have tried to raise over the course of this chapter. However, I also want to make clear that the forty-three students in question were also attacked *as normalistas*—that is, as poor, indigenous, mestiza/o, and/or Afro-Mexican students in a southern Mexican normal school known for the aforementioned philosophical activities—*and that is part of what made them seem to be such easy targets of violence.*[15] Once we get clear on the philosophical history of Mexican *escuelas normales*, we can come to see the incredibly intimate connections between Latin American philosophy, as a politically and philosophically marginalized subfield, and the vulnerable social identities of normal school students not only in Ayotzinapa, but across Mexico (and particularly in states like Guerrero, Oaxaca, and Chiapas, which feature significant representation of indigenous peoples). I submit, then, that in addition to being a truly horrid violation of human rights, Ayotzinapa is also a dangerous attack against Latin American philosophy and those marginalized Others who dare to engage in it.

CONCLUSION

I have argued, in this chapter, the Mexican *escuelas normales* are philosophical spaces in which Latin American philosophy, in particular, has historically flourished. Founded, in part, by Mexican philosopher José Vasconcelos in order to promote his vision of a developed and politically solidified *Raza Cósmica*, these *escuelas normales* have also featured a pedagogical orientation that is strongly influenced by Vasconcelos' aesthetic monism. In addition, pan-Oaxacan indigenous philosophies, not to mention Latin American Marxist ideas, have been and continued to be developed and debated in *escuelas normales*. Finally, Mexican normal schools are spaces in which marginalized Others in Mexico philosophize and engage in the sort of philosophical praxis that is often regard as characteristic of the Latin American philosophical tradition. Furthermore, I have argued, by way of an expressivist argument that Ayotzinapa is an attack against Latin American philosophy. Not only did the Ayotzinapa tragedy entail the violent forced disappearance of the forty-three *normalistas* in question, it also sends a message that it is quite literally dangerous for marginalized Others to engage in Latin American philosophical scholarship and praxis.

To conclude this chapter, I want to respond very briefly to the question of how useful it is to think of Ayotzinapa along these lines given that we have already come to understand Ayotzinapa in terms of human rights violations and political oppression, broadly understood. First, as I stated at the beginning, I believe that understanding Ayotzinapa as an attack against Latin American philosophy enables us to humanize a bit more the forty-three students in question. Indeed, we can come to think about their actions and beliefs in more pluralistic and complex terms. While the *normalistas* have often been associated, in the mass media, with Marxist and subversive political activity, we need to understand that the philosophical output of *escuelas normales* (and individual *normalistas*) cannot be reduced to militant Marxism. From the early writings of Vasconcelos to pan-Oaxacan indigenous political philosophies, *escuelas normales* are ideologically complex spaces where students are exposed to a diversity of views and perspectives. We should understand the forty-three *normalistas* not simply as "militant Marxist activists," but as young philosophers engaged in complex philosophical praxis that cannot be reduced to the ideas of a particular thinker.

Second, I believe that in understanding Ayotzinapa as an attack against Latin American philosophy we can, in fact, expand the conversation about justice for Ayotzinapa. We have, thus far, been focused on incredibly important issues of locating the victims, holding the violent perpetrators accountable for the death and violence they caused, and engaging in productive dialogue with the parents of the disappeared. These are, of course, the most important concerns at hand. In addition to these concerns, however, I propose that we start to consider what precise philosophical ideas, and what particular values, have been undermined in this violent tragedy, so that we can come to understand the full reach of this violence in hopes of preventing it from occurring again. We should ask how, as a society, we can promote and protect the development of these ideas and ideals. And we should explore why philosophical acts on the part of marginalized Others are sometimes responded to so very violently.

I believe that as academics, in particular, we should approach the Ayotzinapa tragedy with the philosophical complexity it deserves—in part by entering into dialogue with the philosophical ideas that were studied, produced, and put into practice by the forty-three disappeared students of Ayotzinapa. The poet David Huerta wrote that "Quien esto lea debe saber también/Que a pesar de todo/Los muertos no se han ido/ Ni los han hecho desaparecer (Whoever reads this should also know/That despite everything/The dead have not gone/Nor were they made to disappear)."[16] In approaching the Ayotzinapa tragedy with additional philosophical complexity, in part by connecting Ayotzinapa to the philosophical spaces that are Mexican *escuelas normales*, we can continuously reassert through our work that the dead are not gone or truly "disappeared," and that the meaning of the work of forty-three students will not go unacknowledged.

NOTES

1. Previous versions of this essay were presented at the X Conferencia Latinoamericana de Crítica Jurídica entitled "Justicia para Ayotzinapa" in Ciudad Juárez, Mexico, and at American Philosophical Association Committee on Hispanics Panel entitled "43 Disappeared Students: Philosophical Perspectives on Ayotzinapa" at the 2016 Eastern Division meeting in Washington, DC. I am grateful to the attendees of both of these sessions for useful feedback and discussion.

2. For a very interesting discussion of the ethics and representation of activists in a Latin American context, see Luis Ruben Díaz Cepeda, "En defensa del otro: Reflexiones sobre la subjetividad ética-política de los activistas sociales desde la filosofía de Enrique Dussel" (Unpublished Dissertation).

3. For a particularly helpful overview of various metaphilosophical debates about the nature of Latin American philosophy, see Susana Nuccetilli (2003), "Latin American Philosophy: Metaphilosophical Foundations" in the *Stanford Encyclopedia of Philosophy*, accessible at plato.stanford.edu/entries/latin-american-metaphilosophy/.

4. For further discussion see Iván Márquez, ed., *Contemporary Latin American Social and Political Thought: An Anthology* (Lanham: Rowman and Littlefield Publishers, Inc., 2008).

5. For more on this point, see Carlos Pereda Falaiche, "Latin American Philosophy: Some Vices," in the *Journal of Speculative Philosophy* 20 no. 3 (2006): 192–203.

6. For further discussion see Javier Ocampo López, "José Vasconcelos y la Educación Mexicana," *Revista Historia de la Educación Latinoamericana* (2005): 137–157.

7. See José Vasconcelos, *The Cosmic Race/La Raza Cósmica* (Los Angeles: California State University, 1979).

8. See José Vasconcelos, *Filosofía Estética* (Mexico City: Trillas, 2009).

9. See Eric Chávez, "José Vasconcelos: Life, Education, and Aesthetics," accessible at www.academia.edu/8342254/Jose_Vasconcelos_Life_Education_and_Aesthetics.

10. See Eric Chávez, "José Vasconcelos: Life, Education, and Aesthetics," accessible at www.academia.edu/8342254/Jose_Vasconcelos_Life_Education_and_Aesthetics.

11. See Alejandra Aquino Moreschi, *De Las Luchas Indias al Sueño Americano: Experiencias Migratorias de Jóvenes Zapotecos y Tojolabales en Estados Unidos* (México, D.F.: Centro de Investigaciones y Estudios Superiores en Antropología Social, 2012). This and all subsequent English to Spanish translations are my own.

12. See Alejandra Aquino Moreschi, *De Las Luchas Indias al Sueño Americano: Experiencias Migratorias de Jóvenes Zapotecos y Tojolabales en Estados Unidos* (México, D.F.: Centro de Investigaciones y Estudios Superiores en Antropología Social, 2012), 51.

13. See Adolfo Sánchez Vázquez, *La Filosofía de la Praxis* (Mexico, D.F., Siglo XXI Editores Mexico, 2003).

14. See, for instance, Adrienne Asch, "Prenatal Diagnosis and Selective Abortion: A Challenge to Practice and Policy," *American Journal of Public Health* 89 no. 11 (1999): 1649–1658.

15. For additional analysis of the representational meaning of Ayotzinapa, I recommend to the reader the spring 2016 issue of *Cuadernos Fronterizos*, which features a special section devoted to Ayotzinapa. It is accessible at: www.uacj.mx/ICSA/CF/Documents/NumerosAnteriores/Cuadernos%20Fronterizos%2035.pdf.

16. See David Huerta, "Ayotzinapa," in *Aristegui Noticias*, accessible at: aristeguinoticias.com/0311/lomasdestacado/poema-de-david-huera-sobre-ayotzinapa-en-el-maco-de-oaxaca/.

BIBLIOGRAPHY

Asch, Adrienne. "Prenatal Diagnosis and Selective Abortion: A Challenge to Practice and Policy." *American Journal of Public Health* 89 no. 1 (1999): 1649–1658

Chávez, Eric. "José Vasconcelos: Life, Education, and Aesthetics." Unpublished manuscript. accessible at: www.academia.edu/8342254/Jose_Vasconcelos_Life_Education_and_Aesthetics.

Díaz Cepeda, Luis Ruben. "En defensa del otro: Reflexiones sobre la subjetividad ética-política de los activistas sociales desde la filosofía de Enrique Dussel" (Unpublished Dissertation).

Huerta, David. "Ayotzinapa." In *Aristegui Noticias,* accessible at: aristeguinoticias.com/0311/lomasdestacado/poema-de-david-huera-sobre-ayotzinapa-en-el-maco-de-oaxaca/.

Márquez, Iván. (ed.) *Contemporary Latin American Social and Political Thought: An Anthology.* Lanham: Rowman and Littlefield Publishers, Inc., 2008.

Moreschi, Alejandra Aquino. *De Las Luchas Indias al Sueño Americano: Experiencias Migratorias de Jóvenes Zapotecos y Tojolabales en Estados Unidos.* México, D.F.: Centro de Investigaciones y Estudios Superiores en Antropología Social, 2012.

Nuccetilli, Susana. "Latin American Philosophy: Metaphilosophical Foundations." In *Stanford Encyclopedia of Philosophy* (2003). Accessible at plato.stanford.edu/entries/latin-american-metaphilosophy/.

Ocampo López, Javier. "José Vasconcelos y la Educación Mexicana." In *Revista Historia de la Educación Latinoamericana,* (2005): 137–157.

Pereda Falaiche, Carlos. "Latin American Philosophy: Some Vices." In the *Journal of Speculative Philosophy* 20 no.3 (2006): 192–203.

Sánchez Vázquez, Adolfo. *La Filosofía de la Praxis.* Mexico, D.F.: Siglo XXI Editores Mexico, 2003.

Vasconcelos, José. *The Cosmic Race/La Raza Cósmica.* Translated by Didier T. Jaén. Los Angeles: California State University, Los Angeles, 1979.

Vasconcelos, José. *Filosofía Estética.* Mexico City: Trillas, 2009.

THIRTEEN

Addressing Ayotzinapa

*Using Dussel's Analectic Method for Establishing an
Ethical Framework for Complex Social Movements*

Luis Rubén Díaz Cepeda

On the night of September 26, 2014, three civilians and three student-teachers of the Raul Isidro Burgos Rural Teachers School were shot to death by members of the police force. In the same attack forty-three *normalistas*, student teachers, were kidnapped by these armed forces, and to this day they have not been found.[1] These events have outraged the national and international community. This indignation has been channeled into mass social mobilization that has possibly created the necessary material conditions for the transition to a truly democratic government in Mexico.

In order to achieve this change of regime, it is necessary to switch the balance of power. And, in the case of Mexico, given the complicity between political and economic elites, this can be attained only through contentious actions in the form of social movements that unite the victims of the system and people that stand in solidarity with them. Social movement theory—Tarrow[2] and Tilly,[3] for example—says that the larger membership a social movement has, the stronger the political power it holds. Achieving a large membership may require the building of coalitions. Mexico is no exception. The history of the last decade of social mobilization in Mexico shows that when social movements gain empathy for their causes, their membership grows, to the point where they become more complex social movements that involve several social organizations. However, history also shows the difficulties they face when agreeing on a common agenda and strategies.

With this problem in mind, I contend that in order for the Ayotzinapa social movement to avoid repeating the mistakes of previous social movements, they need a way to solve their internal differences. I argue in favor of the analectic method developed by Enrique Dussel as the best option for the Ayotzinapa social movement to reach the agreements that may bring about the necessary political force to effectively challenge the current Mexican state. My argument is that when members of a simple social organization operate with a parochial subjectivity, they are not open to the alterity of divergent social organizations. This closeness may prevent the organization of complex social movements. In order to prove my argument, first, I demonstrate the historical need of such a method. Second, I show why the Ayotzinapa social movement may also need it. Third, I present the analectic method. Finally, I analyze the benefits that it may bring to the Ayotzinapa social movement.

HISTORICAL BACKGROUND

The first step in developing my case in favor of the analectic method as the best tool to achieve a critical consensus is to demonstrate the need for such a mechanism. In order to do so, I will show the difficulties of transitioning from a simple social movement, which I define as a social movement where there is a singular unifying identity, to a complex social movement where there are several social organizations, each with its own identity attempting to unify efforts. I will present the last two major social movements in Mexico hoping that these case studies show that in some cases the social activists' parochial subjectivity has negatively affected the structure of a complex social movement. Hence, there exists the need for an agreement method that includes divergent positions.

The first case is the social mobilization against the war on drugs that former President Felipe Calderon started on December 11, 2006, with the creation of the "Michoacan Join Operation." This operation included constitutional reforms that permitted military personnel to police the streets.[4] This strategy created a surge in violence, where over 20,000 people disappeared and an estimated 120,000 people were killed. In response to this violence, a number of social organizations, each one with their own specific group identity, strongly opposed Calderon's strategy. All of these organizations agreed that the military strategy should end, yet they disagreed on how and when it should be terminated. I identify two main different positions: On one hand, since 2008, a radical movement located in Ciudad Juarez demanded an immediate end to the militarization and did not recognize the federal government as a counterpart in the dialogue, since they considered the government to be the cause of the surge in violence. On the other hand, starting in 2011, the Movement for Peace with Justice and Dignity (MPJD), led by the poet Javier Sicilia, demanded an end of violence through a dialogue with the federal government and the care of the victims. The different social organizations and concerned citizens gathered in Cd. Juarez on June 10, 2011, to discuss the *Pacto Nacional por la Paz con Justicia y Dignidad*, a pact that should have produced a common statement. It was signed and publicly announced on the night of June 10, only to be broken the next day in El Paso, Texas, as some of the organizations were not able to reach an agreement on the demands of the movement.

I argue that an agreement was not reached because it was unclear who was in control of the decision-making processes. One group believed that the people should make decisions directly by casting votes in an assembly. The other group believed that only a few select representatives should make decisions for the movement as a whole. Given their different political agendas and subjectivities, both social movements were unable to work together. Each organization continued to pursue their respective agendas and eventually lost political power as a complex social movement.[5]

The second case study I would like to present is #*Yo soy 132*. After years of resistance to President Calderon's strategy in combatting the drug war, social organizations and the Mexican people were exhausted. By 2012, the country itself seemed to have entered a dormant phase in which social movements failed to thrive. As the presidential elections neared, and with Enrique Peña Nieto as the central-right candidate representing the *Partido Revolucionario Institucional* (PRI), a sure victory seemed promising. However, opposition arose from an unexpected group, Iberoamerican University (Universidad Iberoamericana), a private Jesuit school. Iberoamericana students, supported by students of other private universities such as the Mexico Autonomous Technologic Institute (Instituto Tecnológico Autónomo de Mexico, ITAM) started the movement #*Yo Soy 132* in protest of EPN and to demand fair elections.[6] The # *Yo Soy 132* movement managed to awaken a new generation of students who no longer considered the Zapatista Army of National Liberation (EZLN) its main reference.[7] They utilized social networks as a tool to achieve political gains. # *Yo soy 132* garnered the support of Mexican civil society through social networks, and people flocked to support their platform. Additionally, what I call the *usual suspects*, long-time leftist social organizations, responded to their call. These organizations contributed their experience as well as their strategies and agendas. They proposed the movement go beyond the presidential election and strive for profound social and economic change. Even though this proposal was accepted, once again, they were not able to reconcile the visions of the different groups, and the movement essentially disappeared after Peña Nieto was elected president.[8]

With these two case studies I showed the difficulties of building a complex social movement. I also highlighted the challenges that emerge when different social organizations with different subjectivities attempt to work together. Hence the need for a method that would allow them to achieve a critical consensus. In the next section, I will critically evaluate the Ayotzinapa social movement in order to determine if it faces the same difficulties.

THE AYOTZINAPA SOCIAL MOVEMENT

With Peña Nieto's administration, the old PRI resumed power and continued its neoliberal economic agenda through the use of any necessary tactics, including physical repression against political opponents. The policy of repression became evident when members of the Normal Isidro Burgos Student Organization and other social organizations in solidarity with the students, denounced the attack on their classmates by policemen. I will not elaborate on the details of the attack and kidnapping of the students, as by now these details have been widely spread by media outlets. Rather, I want to focus on the social mobilization that demands finding the students alive and obtaining justice for the victims either killed or injured that night.

The strong social mobilization for Ayotzinapa can be explained by the sum of several factors: (1) The social organizations' discourse making the state responsible for the levels of violence had permeated to the general population,[9] (2) evidence that local government officers were involved in the *normalistas'* disappearance, (3) the slow response of the federal government to find them, and (4) the normal Raul Isidro Burgos' network of social organizations. For the purposes of this essay, let me focus on the latter factor.

In a country with over 10,000 missing people in the first two years of the EPN administration, the disappearance of forty-three students could have been easily overlooked. However, one factor that prevented this from happening was that Normal Isidro Burgos is part of the Front of Socialist Peasant Students of Mexico (*Federación de Estudiantes Campesinos de México*, FECSM), which in turn, is in contact with the State Coordinator of Education Workers of Guerrero (*Coordinadora Estatal de Trabajadores de la Educación de Guerrero*, CETEG), as well as many other leftist social organizations. Additionally, the Normal school has a history of social struggle, which has allowed them to gain experience on how to respond to an attack by the State. In the words of Cesar Enrique Pineda, a founding member of Youth in Alternative Resistance (*Jóvenes en Resistencia Alternativa*, JRA) "When I heard of the attack on the students, I knew that there would be a strong reaction . . . I knew that the network to which they belong would mobilize to pressure the federal government."[10]

During its first days, the Ayotzinapa movement had a local reach. It was not until the annual October 2 march in Mexico City in memory of the victims of the Tlatelolco massacre that it began to gain momentum and thereby reach a national audience. During this march, one could hear the participants chanting and demanding justice for those killed, as well as demanding that the forty-three missing students be returned alive. Then, a group of social activists, in conjunction with parents of missing *normalistas*, helped create a platform of solidarity with Ayotzinapa. This platform of solidarity called for the first global day of action, which culminated in organized social unrest. This first global day of action started an *in crescendo* period of protests, and reached its climax with the march on November 20, 2014. Since this march, massive mobilization has decreased, but has not come to an end.

In addition to massive public demonstrations, the Ayotzinapa social movement allowed for the development of two organizations that promote a new constituent assembly. These initiatives were not born with Ayotzinapa, but had been drafted for some time. However, the levels of social mobilization and mass discontent created by the Ayotzinapa social movement have created ideal conditions for the proposal of a new constituent that may be accepted by a majority of the population.

The first initiative is the Popular Citizen Constituent (*Constituyente Ciudadana Popular*, PCC). The PCC was convened by Raul Vera, the Bishop of the Diocese of Saltillo and a well-known promoter of human rights of migrants and victims of violence, as well as an advocate for many other causes. This initiative was the result of over two years of work with different social organizations and was officially launched in Mexico City on February 5, 2014. Its goal is to create a new social contract against the implementation of neoliberal policies made by the last federal administrations. Other important activists like Father Alejandro Solalinde, Javier Sicilia, Lydia Cacho, as well as social organizations such as the Mexican Electricians Union (SME) have joined this organization in solidarity.

The goal of the PCC is to found a new state and a new nation "starting from the creation of a new community-oriented subject that builds, from grassroots movements, a way of doing politics opposed to the surrender and destruction of the country that anti-national groups have made."[11] The process of building this new social pact begins with having a process of national organization, where social activists share the initiative with the population. Once the initiative has been adopted by the people, it will boost the movement to its specific goal: a new constitution before February 2017. To announce this new constitution, there will be a new Congress. The members of this new Congress will be elected from the people and not from the current political system. In the words of Father Alejandro Solalinde, "when the time comes, we will surround the Congress but not as a symbolic decision, no, no. Thousands of people come to tell you gentlemen [the current political class] that based on the article 39 of the

Constitution, we have elected a new Congress and you are out of work."[12]

On the other hand, there is the People's National Convention (*Convención Nacional Popular*, PNC). The PNC is primarily made up by local and state-level organizations that first collaborated with the *normalistas* and their parents. Some of these organizations such as Coordinara Estatal de Trabajadores de la Educación en Guerrero (State Coordination of Guerrero Education Workers, CETEG) are known for using highly disruptive tactics to push their demands. The PNC was officially convened by parents and Students Association Raul Isidro Burgos, in collaboration with the National Popular Assembly (ANP) the same day, February 5, 2015, that the PCC was announced. PNC has called civil society and social organizations together, especially the members of the National Indigenous Congress and la *otra campaña*, in order to create the PNC as a "coordination space that allows us to create a national benchmark, a political agenda and a plan for the short, medium and long term. This will allow the national movement to have a direction." Over 200 organizations responded to the call and met in Ayotzinapa on February 5 and 6, 2015, and signed the plan.

It is important to note that even though these two social movements have different origins and strategies, they agree that Mexico is being ruled by a criminal state. Through its neoliberal policies and association with organized crime, this criminal state has caused the killing and disappearance of hundreds of thousands of people and have caused a large segment of the population to live in poverty and unsustainable conditions. In consequence, the organizations claim that this regime must fall, and the people must return to rule. Commonly shared goals have inspired the movements to unite efforts, as denoted in the joint statement, "[we follow] parallel but not opposite directions. The objectives of each project lead to dialogue. In the next few days we will continue to strengthen the bridges of dialogue, communication, understanding and action to contribute to the liberation of this shameful and unjust neoliberal system."[13] Other organizations are also supporting their efforts. In a vast majority of states in Mexico there are small organizing committees that are creating the networks necessary to promote such ambitious goals. There is also the solidarity platform, which since the beginning of the Ayotzinapa social movement, has been fighting the narrative of the State in order to maintain the level of mobilization.

Despite their intentions of working together, their ideological differences may divide them. On one hand, PCC consists of organizations and individuals close to or belonging to Christianity and other faiths that promote non-violence. On the other hand, PNC, for the most part, is made up of Marxist organizations that because of their ideology, conceive of the world as a class struggle where the conquest of power may come through a direct and violent confrontation with the repressive

State. In order to maintain their alliance, these two groups must find a mechanism to mediate their divergent attitudes regarding violence and long-term political goals. This method should have an ethical basis that allows them to look past their ideological and strategic differences for the sake of building of a larger social movement. As previously mentioned, I argue that the appropriate procedure is the analectic method developed by Dussel. In the following paragraphs I will elaborate on this method.

LIBERATION ETHICS

Certainly there are several theories that explain the cycles of social protest. Within the Anglo- American sociology there is the resource mobilization theory, developed by Tilly,[14] and in political philosophy the works of Hardt and Negri[15] are essential. Closer to the geopolitical coordinates of Latin America, the works of Holloway[16] and Laclau are notable.[17] Such references are of great value, but I contend that they lack an overall vision, while the political philosophy of Enrique Dussel has a global vision, as it treats the material, formal, and feasibility aspects of political actions.

Because of the extent of the liberation political theory, I will not analyze it here in detail, but I will limit myself to the relevant part for this study: reaching a consensus in social movements. In *Twenty Theses on Politics*, Dussel[18] argues that the way to retain and exercise power (which always belongs to the people) is through the active and direct participation of the community that is alert to recover, through *hiperpotentias*, the power of the institutions when they become corrupt and oppressive. *Hiperpotentias* frequently take the form of social movements. Since social movements are essential actors in the endless process of liberation, it is vital that they have a process that allows them to reach agreements which allow them to fulfill the ethical duty to the other.

In *Ethics of Liberation in the Age of Globalization and Exclusion*, Dussel says that a critical consensus is achieved when "excluded victims having formed a community . . . participate symmetrically in agreements . . . based on rational argument."[19] I consider that achieving such consensus is easier within simple social movements, for they already have a common set of beliefs, which most of the time already include a conflict-solving process as casting votes, adopting the leader decision, and so on. In other words, the biggest challenge emerges when social organizations with disparate ideologies want to form complex social movements. This implies that a participant should be open to work with people outside of one's own ideological system. The analectic method provides this advantage.

ANALECTIC METHOD

Because of its complexity, the full development of the analectic method, also called ana-dialectic method, went through several stages. In Dussel's words, "all previous thinking [first edition of *Method for a Philosophy of Liberation*] was inscribed on the ontological totality, whereas now we could open ourselves to the meta-physical otherness."[20] In this work, I use the finished version that Dussel presents in the second edition of the same book, where he says that the analectic method is "inherently ethical [. . . because] the acceptance of the other as other means an ethical choice, a choice and a moral commitment: it is necessary to reject ourselves as a totality, to assert ourselves as finite, being atheist of foundation as identity."[21]

It is only after adopting the category of exteriority of the other in *Para una ética de la liberación l atinoamericana Vol. I*,[22] that Dussel fully developed the analectic method. The first two steps of the method are part of a closed dialectic. It is not until the third moment when it is possible to see the full development and power of the analectic method. The first movement occurs when the entities manifest themselves to the persons in their daily lives. These entities head, dialectically and ontologically, toward the fundament. In a few words, they make a movement from the ontical to the ontological. The second movement is when the entities are epistemically demonstrated as existential possibilities. Up to this point, being is fixed within identity, everything comes and goes back to the same. This limitation clearly sets the limits of the negative dialectic, where otherness is denied, as all entities are included in the totality of being.

In order to open being, Dussel subsumes the concept of exteriority, presented by Levinas in *Totalité et Infini*,[23] where the Lithuanian philosopher takes the opposite direction of Heidegger and wondered not for the ipseity of being, but for the diversity of beings. Levinas posts, then, the thesis of an irreducible otherness than cannot be contained by the categories of being. In the third step, by subsuming this category, Dussel opens the dialectic method through alterity. This openness is defined by him as the affirmation of the negated by the entire system. Dussel notes that from all the entities that are subject to the intentional consciousness of the subject, there is one that refuses to be absorbed into the totality of the subject's categorical horizon: the face of the other. The face of the other opens the fourth movement: the revelation of the exteriority. From the exteriority, the face of the other—the oppressed one—challenges the pretended ontological totality of the system and demands a new ethical relation. This new ethical relation is metaphysical as it goes beyond the limits of being. The critical position from the exteriority allows the fifth step, which is to modify the ontic possibilities so that the order is affected, in an ontological level, in the service of justice for the other qua other.

Allow me to elaborate on the analectic method. In a closed under-standing of the dialectic method, there is a negation of what is affirmed in the first place. It is from this negation that a new situation comes to be. This is a closed system where all the elements are already contained within the system. Think of the situation where the bourgeoisie starts a class struggle by creating an opposite class, the proletariat. An orthodox reading of Marx would say this class struggle will be solved by the prole-tariat, factory workers. It is easy to see that this perception comes from a belief system for a European-urban-post-industrial reality, where all its elements, the bourgeoisie, the proletariat, and the new situation, are al-ready contained in the system. On the contrary, in the analectic system, which is open to exteriority, there are elements that are against the bour-geoisie; not because of they were created by the bourgeoisie, but because even in their full novelty they are different and already opposed to it. When the system is open to other realities such as the Latin American one, other classes such as farmers and indigenous people reveal that the contradiction of capital goes beyond an urban reality. With their novelty, farmers and indigenous people bring new forms of resistance that are of use to a larger class struggle.

In a few words, a close reading of the dialectic method is overcome by adding a positive moment where the analectic method through external-ity introduces novelty or otherness to a system, thus allowing the voice of the other to be heard. Now, I will go back to my original line of argumen-tation and analyze how subjectivity and the analectic method can be combined in favor of social movements.

SUBJECTIVITY AND THE ANALECTIC METHOD

Obviously, a social movement is made up of people and every person has a subjectivity from which he/she interacts with the world. The concept of world in Dussel's philosophy is a little more elusive than it seems, so allow me to briefly explain. For Dussel, the world is "all the (real, poten-tial or imaginary) entities that are related to the actual person and not just of their own."[24] The world is opposed to the cosmos, which Dussel de-fines as "the totality of real things, known or unknown to the human being."[25] The world, then, is what is known to humankind, but obviously the categorical horizons (knowledge) of a person cannot include all knowledge of humankind. A person has to do only with certain parts of that knowledge, and therefore, it is possible to talk about the world in a primary sense. In this sense, Dussel defines world as "the daily horizon from which we live. The world of my home, my neighborhood, my coun-try, the working class."[26]

This immediate world begins to form from the moment a newborn, let's name her Violet, moves away from the proximity of the mother who nursed her and met her needs. When Violet grows and start to be independent of her mother, she is subject to an endless number of stimulus by the entities around her. As she grows these entities are explained to Violet, by her parents, brothers and sisters, friends, and so on. They explain to her the sense of things within the culture where Violet was born. A culture is thus a world where the daily life of each person develops. In that sense, one can speak of different worlds, for example, a Latin American world, a European world, and so on, where each of them is a totality that gives meaning to things within their own *logos*.

These daily horizons should not to be confused with the World, in the sense of all things known by humankind. In order to not to fall into this error, it is necessary to question reality itself, for persons living uncritically in their categorical horizon (world) may take it as if it were universal. Dussel claims that living in an acritical routine is like living "in an inadvertent prison. We look at the world from the bars of our cell and we believe they are the bars of the cell where the others are prisoners."[27] In other words, uncritical people inhabit their categorical horizon (world) and takes it as if it were universal. From this, it can be foreseen that when there is the need to reach an agreement, uncritical people will act according to the categories that are already given in their world and will not go beyond their categorical horizon, for they are incapable of substituting the victim.

When participants of a social movement have a parochial subjectivity they confuse their own world as the World and believe their knowledge to be the universal truth. They deny the other the right to have a voice with the excuse of having a greater and better knowledge of the World. Denying the other may then lead to the application of the same forms of exclusion that have already been rejected from the philosophy of liberation, as they could easily lead to a quick fetishization of the power of social movement. Also, by blindly following their belief system, uncritical social activists disregard the position of other activists. Clearly this attitude inhibits the dialogue among differing positions and prevents social activists from organizing a complex social movement.

This limitation of having a closed and intolerant subjectivity that is adverse to alterity shows the need of the analectic method, of the need to be open to the other, to the one beyond one's own world. Since to hear the voice of the other is to do justice, one must go beyond one's own conception of the categorical world in order to truly liberate the oppressed. A critical complex social movement, then, must be inclusive of the different organizations (worlds) involved in it. This requires a subject that approaches other social activists with the intention of reaching an understanding that allows for the formation of a critical consensus in favor of the victims, which in turn allows for the organization of larger, more powerful social movements.

AYOTZINAPA AND THE ANALECTIC METHOD

To this point in this paper I have proved that having parochial subjectivities prevents social activists from creating or sustaining complex social movements, and that the analectic method developed by Enrique Dussel gives uncritical social activists an ethical ground on which to overcome their limited perspectives. Based on this argument, I consider that this method would be suitable for the Ayotzinapa social movement, as it may help the organization avoid the mistakes of past social movements. I argue this to be true because in a close reading of the dialectic method, families and the social organizations that operate in solidarity with them, would work only to find the forty-three missing students alive and, more importantly, they will do so within their belief system, be it Marxist, Christian, Autonomist, Anarchist, and so forth.

On the contrary, if, how the dialectic method proposes, the system is broken by the exteriority of the face of the other, they will be able to negotiate their ideological differences and extend their solidarity not only to the forty-three missing students, but to the over one hundred thousand missing people in Mexico by creating and sustaining social movements as the ones they are already proposing. To achieve this, social activists must be a bit skeptical of their world-life or ideology so as to not totalize the other, and they must be open to irreducible otherness.

Before I finish and following the advice of this essay, having a certain level of skepticism of one's own ideas, I must point out possible limitations on this research. This work is based on the premise that the success of a complex social movement requires that different social organizations participating share if not visions, at least strategies and actions that allow them to reach the common goal. However, I see at least two reasons why this might not be the case: (1) Since different organizations have access to different resources through their respective strategies, it is possible that a variety of strategies may benefit the movement, and (2) the effort of keeping the different organizations together may be too high, and may end up distracting organizations of their efforts to archive their priority: to help the other. It is important to know that this is a discussion that is also taking place inside the movement and it will take time to be resolved assertively.

In conclusion, I say that to the extent that participants in social movements are able to assume the responsibility we have for the other, which is beyond one's categorical system, we will be able to build a long-winded movement with the capacity to challenge repressive states, as is the current Mexican state, that by attacking future teachers undermine the foundation of the social structure of the country.

NOTES

1. On January 27, 2015, Murillo Karam, then the attorney general claimed that the historic truth was that the *normalistas* have been killed and incinerated by member of *Guerreros Unidos*, a local drug cartel, in a trash dump in Cocula, Guerrero. This version was doubted by many social organizations and the parents of the missing students. On February 10, 2016, an Argentine Forensic Anthropology Team *(Equipo Argentino de Antropología Forense*, EAAF) concluded than according to their expertise, there is no evidence to prove that forty-three bodies were incinerated in the site where PGR claims.

2. See Sidney Tarrow, *Power in Movement. Social Movements and Contentious Politics* (New York: Cambridge University Press, 2011).

3. See Charles Tilly, *From Mobilization to Revolution* (New York: McGraw-Hill, 1978).

4. See Jorge Chabat, *La respuesta del gobierno de Calderón al desafío del narcotráfico: entre lo malo y lo peor* (México D.F: Centro de Investigación y Docencia Económicas (CIDE), División de Estudios Internacionales, 2010).

5. See Luis Díaz Cepeda, "Breve análisis de la relación Estado-movimientos sociales en contextos de violencia extrema: Ciudad Juaréz durante el periodo de militarización," in *De La Democracia Liberal a la Soberanía Popular. Vol. II Gobiernos Latinoamericanos: Los Desafíos del Estado, La Acummulacción y la Seguridad* (Buenos Aires, Argentina: Consejo Latinoamerican de Ciencias Sociales., 2015).

6. See Gloria Muñoz Ramírez, *# Yo Soy 132 voces del movimiento* (México, D.F.: Ediciones Bola de Cristal, 2011).

7. See Massimo Modonesi, "De la generación zapatista al # Yo Soy 132. Identidades y culturas políticas juveniles En México" in *Observatorio Social de América Latina* (Buenos Aires, Argentina: Consejo Latinoamericano de Ciencias Sociales., 2102), 119–142.

8. See Luis Díaz Cepeda, "#Yo Soy 132, a Networked Social Movement of Mexican Youth" in *Waves of Social Movement Mobilizations in the Twenty-First Century: Challenges to the Neo-Liberal World Order and Democracy* (Lanham: Lexington Books, 2015), 41–58.

9. See Kathleen Staudt and Zulma Mendez, *Courage, Resistance and Women in Ciudad Juárez: Challenges to Militarization in Ciudad Juárez* (Austin: The University of Texas Press, 2015).

10. (cuando me entere del ataque a los estudiantes, supe que se venía una fuerte reacción, . . . la red a la que ellos pertenecen, iba a presionar al gobierno federal). Enrique Cesar Pineda, Entrevista. Interview by Luis Rubén Díaz Cepeda, March 24, 2015.

11. (El nuevo sujeto comunitario que construya *desde las bases* una política contraria a la entrega y destrucción del país que los grupos antinacionales han realizado.) Patricia Gutiérrez-Otero, "Qué Es La Constituyente Popular," February 14, 2015, sec. *Cultura en México*. Accessed March 25, 2015. See online at: www.siempre.com.mx/2015/02/que-es-la-constituyente-ciudadana-popular/.

12. (cuando llegue el momento rodeamos los congresos pero no así como toma simbólica, no, no. Miles de personas señores, venimos a decirles [a la actual clase política] que ya hemos elegido un nuevo congreso en base al artículo 39 de la constitución y se acabó su chamba). Arturo Gallo Ramírez, "Obispo Raúl Vera propone creación de nueva Constitución." *Milenio. Jalisco*, enero 2015, sec. Región. www.milenio.com/region/Obispo-Raul-Vera-creacion-constitucion_0_448155374.html.

13. ([seguimos] caminos paralelos pero no opuestos. Los objetivos de cada proyecto nos llevan a dialogar. En los días subsiguientes seguiremos fortaleciendo los puentes de diálogo, comunicación, entendimiento y acción para contribuir a la liberación de este oprobioso e injusto sistema neoliberal). Convención Nacional Popular, and Constituyente Ciudadana Popular. "Declaración Conjunta Ayotzinapa y Constituyente Ciudadana-Popular," February 5, 2015. Accessed February 6, 2015. constituyenteciudadana.org/?p=305.

14. See Charles Tilly, *From Mobilization to Revolution* (New York: McGraw-Hill, 1978).
15. See Michael Hardt and Antonio Negri. *Multitude* (New York: The Penguin Press, 2004).
16. See John Holloway, "Cómo cambiar el mundo sin tomar el poder" (Buenos Aires: Herramienta, 2002).
17. See Ernesto Laclau, *La Razón Populista* (México: Fondo de Cultura Económica, 2005).
18. See Enrique Dussel, *20 Tesis de Política*. *20 Tesis de política* (México: Siglo XXI: Centro de Cooperación Regional para la Educación de Adultos en América Latina y el Caribe, 2006).
19. (habiendo constituido una comunidad las víctimas excluidas . . . participan simétricamente en los acuerdos de aquello que les afecta, sosteniendo además que dicho consenso crítico se fundamenta por argumentación racional y es motivado por co-solidaridad pulsional). Enrique Dussel, *Ética de La Liberación En La Edad de La Globalización Y de La Exclusión* 7th ed. (Madrid: Trota, 2011), 464.
20. ("todo el pensar anterior estaba inscrito en la totalidad ontológica, mientras que ahora podíamos abrirnos a la alteridad meta-física"). Enrique Dussel, *Método para una Filosofía de La Liberación*. *Superación analéctica de la dialéctica hegeliana*, (Salamanca: Ediciones Sigueme, 1974), 13.
21. (intrínsecamente ético [. . . pues] la aceptación del otro como otro significa ya una opción ética, una elección y un compromiso moral: es necesario negarse como totalidad, afirmarse como finito, ser ateo del fundamento como identidad). Enrique Dussel, *Método para una Filosofía de La Liberación*. *Superación analéctica de la dialéctica hegeliana*, 1974), 17.
22. See Enrique Dussel, *Para Una Ética de La Liberación Latinoamericana. Tomo I. Para una ética de la liberación latinoamericana. Tomo I* (México: Siglo veintiuno editores, 2014).
23. See Emmanuel Levinas, *Totalité et Infini* (Paris: Le livre de poche. Biblio essaís, 1987).
24. (la totalidad de los entes [reales, posibles o imaginarios] que son por relación a las persona y no solo reales, de suyo). Enrique Dussel, *Filosofía de la liberación* (México: Fondo de Cultura Económica, 2011), 54.
25. (la totalidad de las cosas reales, conocidas o no por el ser humano). Enrique Dussel, *Filosofía de la liberación* (México: Fondo de Cultura Económica, 2011), 54.
26. (el horizonte cotidiano desde el cual vivimos. El mundo de mi hogar, de mi barrio, de mi país, de la clase obrera). Enrique Dussel, *Filosofía de la liberación* (México: Fondo de Cultura Económica, 2011), 53.
27. (en una prisión inadvertida. Miramos al mundo como desde los barrotes de nuestra celda y creemos que son los barrotes de la celda donde esta encarcelados los otros). Enrique Dussel, *Filosofía de la liberación* (México: Fondo de Cultura Económica, 2011), 66.

BIBLIOGRAPHY

Chabat, Jorge. *La respuesta del gobierno de Calderón al desafío del narcotráfico: entre lo malo y lo peor*. México D.F: Centro de Investigación y Docencia Económicas (CIDE), División de Estudios Internacionales, 2010.
Convención Nacional Popular, and Constituyente Ciudadana Popular. "Declaración Conjunta Ayotzinapa y Constituyente Ciudadana-Popular," February 5, 2015. Accessed February 6, 2015. constituyenteciudadana.org/?p=305.
Díaz-Cepeda Luis Rubén. "Breve análisis de la relación Estado-movimientos sociales en contextos de violencia extrema: Ciudad Juaréz durante el periodo de militarización." In *De La Democracia Liberal a la Soveranía Popular. Vol. II Gobiernos Latinoamericanos: Los Desafíos del Estado, La Acummulacción y la Seguridad*, edited by

Francisco J. Cantamutto, Adrian Velázquez, and Agostina Costantino. Buenos Aires: Consejo Latinoamerican de Ciencias Sociales., 2015.

———. "#Yo Soy 132, a Networked Social Movement of Mexican Youth." In *Waves of Social Movement Mobilizations in the Twenty-First Century: Challenges to the Neo-Liberal World Order and Democracy*, edited by Nahide Konak and Rasim Özgür Dönmez, Lanham: Lexington Books, 2015, 41–58.

Dussel, Enrique. *20 Tesis de política*. México: Siglo XXI: Centro de Cooperación Regional para la Educación de Adultos en América Latina y el Caribe, 2006.

———. *Ética de La Liberación En La Edad de La Globalización Y de La Exclusión*. 7th ed. Madrid: Trota, 2011.

———. *Filosofía de la liberación*. México: Fondo de Cultura Económica, 2011.

———. *Método para una Filosofía de La Liberación. Superación analéctica de la dialéctica hegeliana*. Salamanca: Ediciones Sigueme, 1974.

———. *Para una ética de la liberación latinoamericana. Tomo I*. México: Siglo veintiuno editores, 2014.

Gutiérrez-Otero, Patricia. "Qué Es La Constituyente Popular," February 14, 2015, sec. Cultura en México. Accessed March 25, 2015. www.siempre.com.mx/2015/02/que-es-la-constituyente-ciudadana-popular/.

Hardt, Michael, and Antonio Negri. *Multitude*. New York: The Penguin Press, 2004.

Holloway, John. *Cómo cambiar el mundo sin tomar el poder*. Buenos Aires: Herramienta, 2002.

Laclau, Ernesto. *La Razón Populista*. México: Fondo de Cultura Económica, 2005.

Levinas, Emmanuel. *Totalité et Infini*. Paris: Le livre de poche. Biblio essaís, 1987.

Modonesi, Massimo. "De la generación zapatista al # Yo Soy 132. Identidades y culturas políticas juveniles En México." In *Observatorio Social de América Latina*, edited by P. Gentili, 119–42. Buenos Aires: Consejo Latinoamericano de Ciencias Sociales., 2102.

Muñoz Ramírez, Gloria. *# Yo Soy 132 voces del movimiento*. México, D.F.: Ediciones Bola de Cristal, 2011.

Pineda, Cesar Enrique. Entrevista. Interview by Luis Rubén Díaz Cepeda, March 24, 2015.

Ramírez Gallo, Arturo. "Obispo Raúl Vera propone creación de nueva Constitución." *Milenio. Jalisco*, enero 2015, sec. Región. www.milenio.com/region/Obispo-Raul-Vera-creacion-constitucion_0_448155374.html.

Staudt, Kathleen, and Zulma Mendez. *Courage, Resistance and Women in Ciudad Juárez: Challenges to Militarization in Ciudad Juárez*. The University of Texas Press, 2015.

Tarrow, Sidney. *Power in Movement. Social Movements and Contentious Politics*. 3rd ed. The United States of America: Cambridge University Press, 2011.

Tilly, Charles. *From Mobilization to Revolution*. New York: McGraw-Hill, New York, 1978.

Index

About the Contributors

Robert Aman is lecturer in inclusive education based at the School of Education, University of Glasgow. Aman primary conducts research on the relationship between education, the geopolitics of knowledge, and various forms of exclusion and marginalization, drawing on decolonial theories. He is a former visiting fellow with the Program in Literature, Duke University; at the faculty of English Language and Literature, University of Oxford; and, most recently, at the Centre d'Etudes et de Recherches Internationales, Sciences Po Paris. He is the author of *Impossible Interculturality? Education and the Colonial Difference in a Multicultural World* (2014). Aman cofounder and editor of the interdisciplinary peer-reviewed journal *Confero: Essays on Education, Philosophy & Politics* as well as having guest edited, together with Timothy Ireland, a special issue of *International Journal of Lifelong Education* (*IJLE*) on "Education and other modes of thinking" in the context of Latin America.

Anders Burman is associate senior lecturer in the Department of Human Geography and the Human Ecology Division at Lund University in Sweden. He completed his PhD in social anthropology for the University of Gothenberg in 2009. His research is in areas of indigenous activism, ritual practice, decolonization, perceptions of landscape and space, and Bolivian state politics. He was a postdoctoral scholar at the Department of Ethnic Studies at the University of California at Berkeley from 2009–2011. Some of his publication include, "Places to Think with, Books to Think About: Words, Experience and the Decolonization of Knowledge in the Bolivian Andes," *Human Architecture: Journal of the Sociology of Self-Knowledge* 10 (2013): 101–119; "Chachawarmi: Silence and Rival Voices on Decolonization and Gender," *Journal of Latin American Studies* 43 (2011): 65–91; and "The Strange and the Native: Ritual and Activism in the Aymara Quest for Decolonization" *The Journal of Latin American and Caribbean Anthropology* 15 (2010): 457–475.

Luis Rubén Díaz Cepeda is a PhD candidate supervised by Enrique Dussel at the Universidad Autónoma Metropolitana–Iztapalapa in Mexico City, Mexico. He holds master's degrees in philosophy and sociology from the University of Texas at El Paso, where he occasionally serves as a visiting scholar and lecturer in the Philosophy Department. His research focuses on ethics, borders, social movements and critical theory, philoso-

phy of liberation, and philosophy of the city. Luis has organized interna-
tional conferences in El Paso, Ciudad Juarez, and Mexico City. Published
in Mexico, Argentina, and the United States, recent works include "#Yo
Soy 132: A Networked Social Movement of Mexican Youth," in *Waves of
Social Movement Mobilizations in the Twenty-First Century: Challenges to the
Neo-Liberal World Order and Democracy* (2015), and he is an editor and
contributor to the anthology, *Philosophy and Neoliberal Policy: Reflecting on
Twenty Years of NAFTA* (forthcoming). He is currently working on a manuscript titled, *From Juarez to Ayotzinapa: Understanding Social Mobilization
in Mexico*.

Ramón Grosfoguel is associate professor of ethnic studies at the University of California, Berkley, and a senior research associate of the Maison
des Sciences de l'Homme in Paris. He has published many articles and
books on the political economy of the world-system and on Caribbean
migrations to Western Europe and the United States. He is the author of
Colonial Subjects: Puerto Ricans in a Global Perspective (2003). He also coed-
ited with José David Saldívar and Nelson Maldonado-Torres, *Latin@s in
the World System: Decolonization Struggles in the 21st Century US Empire*
(2005).

Roberto Hernández is assistant professor of Chicana/o Studies at San
Diego State University. He received a PhD in the Department of Ethnic
Studies at the University of California, Berkeley. For the past six years, he
has coordinated the *Decolonizing Knowledge and Power* Summer Institute
in Barcelona, Spain. He completed a two-year term as an At-Large Representative on the board of the National Association for Chicana and Chicano Studies during the height of the legal battle over the legality of Mexican American Studies courses in Arizona high schools and served as one
of the coauthors of an amicus brief in said case.

Nelson Maldonado-Torres is associate professor of the Department of
Latino and Hispanic Caribbean Studies and the Program in Comparative
Literature at Rutgers University. He specializes on decolonial and critical
theorizing, comparative ethnic studies, and ethical and political thought.
He is the author of *Against War: Views from the Underside of Modernity*
(2008), and is currently working on a project that seeks to spell out fundamental elements in the epistemology of interdisciplinary and emancipatory fields. The current essay is based on a presentation in a colloquium
entitled "The Humanities and the Crisis of the Public University" at the
University of California, Berkeley, on October 15, 2010.

Kwame Nimako (MA, sociology; PhD, economics, University of Amsterdam) teaches international relations at the Graduate School of Social Sciences of the University of Amsterdam. He has authored, with Glenn

Willemsen, *The Dutch Atlantic: Slavery, Abolition and Emancipation* (2011). His recent publications include "Designs and (Co)-incidents: Cultures of Scholarship and Public Policy on Immigrants/Minorities in the Netherlands" (with Philomena Essed), *International Journal of Comparative Sociology* (Vol. 47, 2006). He has a book chapter: "Theorizing Black Europe and African Diaspora: Implications for Citizenship, Nativism and Xenophobia" (with Stephen Small) in *Black Europe and the African Diaspora* edited by Darlene Clark Hine, Trica Danielle Keaton, and Stephen Small (2009). Nimako is working with Stephen Small on a book entitled *Public History, Museums and African Diasporic Memory in England and the Netherlands.*

Nassim Noroozi is an Iranian doctoral candidate and lecturer at the Department of Integrated Studies in Education at McGill University. She is trained in philosophy of education. Her research interests are informed by decolonial philosophies. More specifically her work examines the potentials of wonderment as a decolonial epistemology in education and pedagogy. Nassim's works have appeared in the Philosophy of Education Society journal.

Camilo Pérez-Bustillo is executive director at the Human Rights Center and research professor of human rights and law at the University of Dayton. He is also research associate at FLACSO–Guatemala and fellow of Comparative Research Program on Poverty (CROP, University of Bergen, Norway). He is the coordinator, secretariat of the International Tribunal of Conscience of Peoples in Movement/Tribunal Internacional de Conciencia de los Pueblos en Movimiento. He is coauthor with Karla Hernández Mares of *Human Rights, Hegemony and Utopia in Latin America: Poverty, Forced Migration and Resistance in Mexico and Colombia* (2016). He is the former coordinator of the Border Human Rights Documentation Project based at New Mexico State University, Las Cruces, August 2013 to May 2016.

Andrea J. Pitts is assistant professor of philosophy at University of North Carolina, Charlotte. Their research interests include social epistemology, philosophy of race and gender, Latin American and US Latina/o philosophy, and philosophy of medicine. Their publications appear in *Hypatia, Radical Philosophy Review,* and *Inter-American Journal of Philosophy.* Andrea is also currently coediting two forthcoming volumes: one on the reception of the work of Henri Bergson in decolonial thought, feminism, and critical race studies, and a volume on contemporary scholarship in US Latina and Latin American feminist philosophy.

Amy Reed-Sandoval is assistant professor of philosophy at University of Texas, El Paso. Her primary areas of research are political philosophy (particularly the political philosophy of immigration), Latin American and Latina/o philosophy, and philosophy for children. She is the founding director of two active children programs: the Oaxaca Philosophy for Children Initiative and the Philosophy for Children in the Borderlands Program in UTEP.

Ernesto Rosen Velásquez is assistant professor of philosophy at the University of Dayton. His areas of research are Latina/o philosophy, political philosophy, and critical race theory. Some of his publications include: "Critically Theorizing Folk Uses of Ethnoracial Terms: 'Wiggas,' 'White Chocolate' and Afro-Latinicity" in *APA Newsletter on Hispanic/Latino Issues in Philosophy,* (Spring 2013): 23–27; and "States of Violence and the Right to Exclude" in *Journal of Poverty* published online June 15, 2016, see www.tandfonline.com/doi/abs/10.1080/10875549.2016.1186777? journalCode=wpov20.

Tendayi Sithole is associate professor in the Department of Political Sciences at University of South Africa. He is affiliated with the Africa Decolonial Research Network. His forthcoming book, *Steve Biko: Decolonial Meditations*, will be published by Lexington Books. He recently completed a manuscript provisionally titled "Meditations in Black: Essays from the Limits of Being."

Boaventura de Sousa Santos is professor of sociology at the School of Economics, University of Coimbra (Portugal), Distinguished Legal Scholar at the University of Wisconsin–Madison Law School, and Global Legal Scholar at the University of Warwick. He is director of the Center for Social Studies of the University of Coimbra and scientific coordinator of the Permanent Observatory for Portuguese Justice. He has published widely on globalization, sociology of law and the state, epistemology, democracy, and human rights in Portuguese, Spanish, English, Italian, French, and German. His most recent project—ALICE: Leading Europe to a New Way of Sharing the World Experiences—is funded by an Advanced Grant of the European Research Council. The project was initiated in 2011 and will continue for the next five years.